MUTINY AND INSURGENCY IN INDIA 1857–1858

*In memory of my mother
who died while this work was in progress.
The daughter, daughter-in-law,
wife,
sister, sister-in-law,
aunt,
mother,
and grandmother
of British service personnel.*

MUTINY AND INSURGENCY IN INDIA 1857–1858

The British Army in a Bloody Civil War

T.A. Heathcote

With a Foreword by
Richard Holmes

Pen & Sword
MILITARY

First published in Great Britain in 2007 by
PEN & SWORD MILITARY
an imprint of
Pen & Sword Books Ltd
47 Church Street
Barnsley
South Yorkshire
S70 2AS

Copyright T.A. Heathcote, 2007
ISBN 978-1-84415-593

A CIP catalogue record for this book is
available from the British Library

Typeset in 11/13 Sabon by Concept, Huddersfield, West Yorkshire
Printed and bound in England by CPI UK

Pen & Sword Books Ltd incorporates the Imprints of
Pen & Sword Aviation, Pen & Sword Maritime, Pen & Sword Military,
Wharncliffe Local History, Pen & Sword Select,
Pen & Sword Military Classics and Leo Cooper

For a complete list of Pen & Sword titles please contact
PEN & SWORD BOOKS LIMITED
47 Church Street, Barnsley, South Yorkshire, S70 2AS, England
E-mail: enquiries@pen-and-sword.co.uk
Website: www.pen-and-sword.co.uk

CONTENTS

These, in the days when heaven was falling,
The hour when earth's foundations fled,
Followed their mercenary calling
And took their wages and are dead.

Their shoulders held the sky suspended;
They stood and earth's foundations stay;
What God abandoned, these defended,
And saved the sum of things for pay.

A.E. *Housman* Epitaph on an Army of Mercenaries

FOREWORD

by Professor E.R. Holmes, Cranfield University,
Colonel, The Princess of Wales's Royal Regiment
(Queen's and Royal Hampshire)

I seem to have reached that stage of my career when requests to write forewords come thick and fast. I always make it a rule never to take on a book that I do not admire (which reduces the pile substantially), and not to say anything that I do not mean. However, there are occasionally moments when I find myself balancing long friendship against academic objectivity with more than a little difficulty. Happily, that was never going to be the case here. Tony Heathcote is an old friend from my time teaching at Sandhurst. Over the past thirty years I have become familiar with his writings, not least during my research for *Sahib,* my book on the British soldier in India, when I was indebted to his own work on the Indian Army, and was struck, once again, by admiration for the sheer quality of his prose.

His strengths begin with his training at the School of Oriental and African Studies at the University of London, which, I am sure, accounts for his deep cultural understanding, and has always encouraged him to put his subject in an oriental rather than simply an imperial context. His command of language gives him an advantage not enjoyed by so many of the military historians who, like myself, find themselves wrestling with the relative merits of Punjab, Panjab or even Punjaub, and sometimes forgetting that although *pultan* may have been inspired by the French word *peloton* which gives us platoon (about thirty men commanded by an officer), it actually means regiment, a bigger beast altogether. Reading the early pages of the first chapter we can already begin to sense the cultural gulf that was beginning to yawn between Indian soldiers and their British officers, and the overriding importance for sepoys of 'the tight embrace of regimental comradeship, family and caste'.

Although few historians have written about the Mutiny with a better understanding of the cultural tensions which did so much to provoke it, Tony Heathcote's chief concern is with the British officers and soldiers who fought against what he is right to call 'a mutiny that within days turned into an insurgency'. Here his aim is unerring. British victory owed much to the personal qualities of regimental officers who provided leadership of which their enemies, by the very act of mutiny, had deprived themselves. If there was a bright side to the British combat motivation, with 'the spirit of comradeship and a shared pride in the achievement of their regiments', there was a darker side too. A deep-seated notion of racial superiority was often linked to a desire to protect or avenge the wives and children of European military or civilians, and those resolute, sun-tanned and occasionally sentimental men in grubby red or white coats could indeed be roused to 'a pitiless rage' at the mistreatment of women and children who had often become their own surrogate families.

The cartridge-grease question, once widely regarded as the proximate cause of the Mutiny but then downplayed by many historians, is put in its correct perspective here. The military authorities had indeed taken steps to ensure that newly-issued Enfield cartridges were not greased with fat from pigs (unclean to Moslems) or cows (sacred to Hindus), but rumour outran fact, and the incident that provoked the mutiny at Meerut in May 1857 was, at the very least, worsened by an inept regimental commander. The explosion at Meerut, followed immediately by the fall of Delhi, 'struck British India with much the same impact as the Japanese attack on Pearl Harbor or the Islamist attacks on the Pentagon and the World Trade Center on 11 September 2001'. The ethnic cleansing which flared out across northern India inspired a British policy of frightfulness, although, as Dr Heathcote observes, it is impossible to be sure that the attack on the surrendered garrison of Kanpur was deliberate, and some soldiers, inflamed by lurid but false reports that Englishwomen had been the victims of sexual assault, behaved appallingly at the first opportunity.

Tony Heathcote dismisses the conspiracy theories that grew up around the Mutiny. It was inspired by neither Russia nor Iran, and, more pertinently, was not a cohesive proto-nationalist conspiracy: after all, the British could scarcely have won without very substantial Indian support. Rather, the events of 1857 were 'a series of military revolts by soldiers fearful for their futures, in this world or the next, and the exploitation of these by civil or religious leaders who wished to do away with the changes brought by British rule'. Dr Heathcote believes that the British did not come close to losing India in 1857. Once they had recovered from their original disorganization and had corrected the distortion to their strategy caused by the need to relieve Lucknow, the superior economic and political resources that had given the British their Indian Empire would ensure that they would retain it.

I share the author's affection for India and its history, and there is much in 1857–8 that redounds little to the credit of either the insurgents or their opponents. Indeed, as I read these pages I can see precisely why I once described the Mutiny as a livid scar across the face of British India. That does not mean, however, that the subject should be submerged beneath post-colonial breast-beating, or that our ability to see both sides of this terrible story should prevent us from recognizing the achievements of the men who have played such a large part in my own books over the past decade, British soldiers and their regimental officers. One veteran raja who saw British infantry storm the battery at Badli-ki-Serai, just outside Delhi, assured a brother ruler that 'the nation that could produce such men were sure to succeed in the end, whatever the odds might be', and he was absolutely right. One of the many strengths of this admirable book is that it puts these tough and determined (though often, for that matter, no less harsh and opinionated) men in the centre of the conflict's stage, where they deserve to be.

Richard Holmes

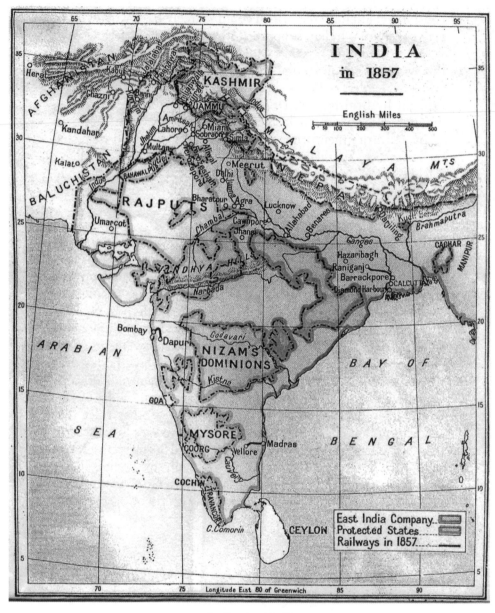

India in 1857

Map of northern India

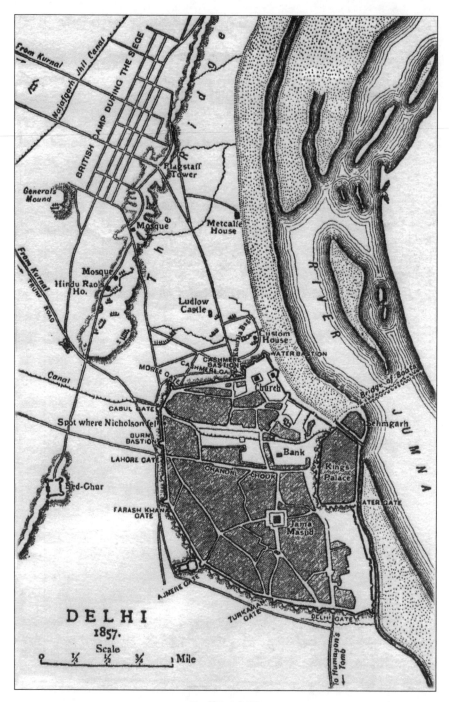

Delhi 1857

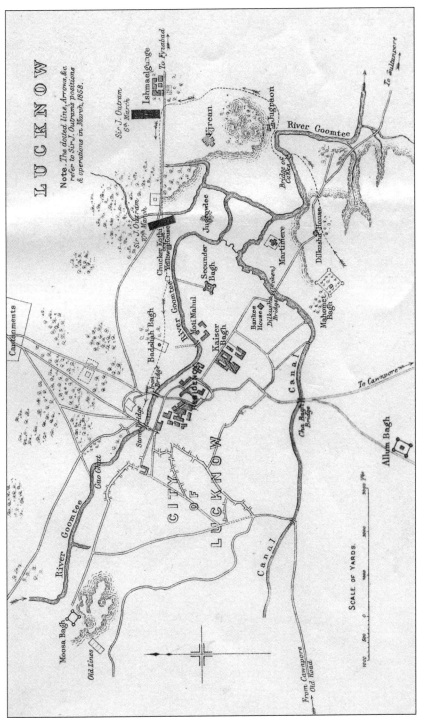

Lucknow

xiii

INTRODUCTION AND ACKNOWLEDGEMENTS

This book is about a war that, with its impact on the British Army and British society dwarfed by the two world wars of the twentieth century, has largely disappeared from British popular consciousness. It was still remembered while the British ruled India, when the well at Kanpur was a place of pilgrimage for every British soldier and the ruined Residency at Lucknow was the only station in the British Empire where the flag was never lowered by night or day. With the British Empire, in India as elsewhere, having become one with Nineveh and Tyre, as its poet Rudyard Kipling warned it would, Indian historians, even Indian politicians, no longer speak of 'the first war of Indian independence'. This may have been a useful phrase when independence was an issue (especially when the British banned a book with a similar title) but, with its actual achievement, is acknowledged to be a fallacy and is now used mostly by those in search of political correctness.

In 1857 the war began with a mutiny that within days turned into an insurgency, as the sword with which the British had conquered India broke in their hands. It was a civil war in that the fighting was between an existing government and its own subjects, who sought to replace it with another. Like civil wars, too, it was one in which men took up arms to defend their religion or way of life against what they perceived to be a tyrannical government, just as they had done in the English Civil War over two centuries earlier, and as they would in the American Civil War four years later. In all three cases economic and class factors also had their part to play. As in every civil war,

1

professional soldiers chose their side according to the circumstances in which they found themselves, and fought against those who had once been friends and comrades.

The insurgency of 1857 was demonstrably not a national rising, as the fighting was confined to northern and central India. Away from the main towns, few Indians had even seen English people, though they might not have heard much good of them. In the war, at least as many Indians served with the British as against them, sometimes with brothers, fathers and sons fighting on opposite sides, as is the way in civil wars. The divide stretched through all classes. Some Indian princes, with their own dynastic interests to consider, readily placed their men and purses at the disposal of the British. Others, for the same reasons, took up arms against them. Muslim clerics in Delhi preached against British rule. Western-educated professors in Calcutta passed resolutions condemning the mutinies. Ordinary labourers variously aided or attacked British refugees and worked for either side indiscriminately. Indeed, without Indian manpower, civil and military, the British would not have been able to fight the war at all. It was not a war for national independence, if only because South Asia at the time was no more of a single nation than was Western Europe, or indeed than are either of these sub-continents today. In both cases there was, and is, a common culture and heritage, but different religions, languages and ethnic groups. At most, it was a series of local wars for liberation, where dispossessed elites combined with mutinous sepoys in the hope of regaining their former power. It only came to an end when the insurgents were treated, in Queen Victoria's words, as the losing side in a bloody civil war.

Though their Indian auxiliaries and allies played an essential part in the struggle, it was the officers and men of the British Army who shouldered the burden of the war and kept the British Raj in place. Though their regiments have been renamed, amalgamated and reduced with increasing frequency since that time, the successors of those who fought then are, at the time of writing, once more engaged with insurgencies in eastern theatres. British soldiers, and indeed British marines and seamen, have done it all before. Those who doubt this have only to look about them at the many memorials still to be found in public areas and places of worship all over the United Kingdom.

After the Reformation, the cult of saints was replaced in English churches by the cult of the country gentleman. Virtually every historic parish church or cathedral has memorials to the local nobility and gentry where there were once side-chapels and images. Because younger sons commonly made their living with their swords, such memorials often refer to military service, and because almost half the British Army served in India during the Mutiny (eight regiments of cavalry and sixty-eight battalions of infantry, as well as units of the Royal Artillery, Royal Engineers and Military Train), many relate to that war. Not every unit took part in combat operations, but between them their dead numbered 195 officers and 10,826 men, of whom 86 officers and 1,948 men were killed or died of wounds and 109 officers and 8,878 men died of disease, heat or exhaustion. Added to these must be the European personnel of the East India Company's services. Even the most remote country church may contain some memorial to an officer born or settled in the neighbourhood who served in the Indian Mutiny. Ireland, with the martial traditions of the Anglo-Irish squirearchy, has its share and the cathedral at Lisburn houses a fulsome memorial to John Nicholson, a hero of the Punjab, put there by his mother. Not all were actual parishioners of the places where they are memorialized. St Paul's Cathedral, for instance, has a tablet in honour of Colonel John Finnis of the 11th Bengal Native Infantry, the first senior officer killed in the war, placed in the cathedral by his brother who was Lord Mayor of London at the time.

Just as country gentlemen took the place of saints, regiments of the British Army found a niche left by the departure of religious guilds. Thus Exeter cathedral contains an impressive monument to the services of the 9th Royal Lancers during the Mutiny campaign, containing the names of 3 officers and 44 soldiers who fell to enemy action, and 2 officers and 67 soldiers who died from the effects of climate. Nearby is a memorial to the 32nd Foot's dead, 15 officers and 448 soldiers, together with the 4 officers' ladies, 43 soldiers' wives and 56 children of that regiment who perished at Kanpur. A memorial in St Giles's Cathedral, Edinburgh, contains the Mutiny memorial of the 72nd Duke of Albany's Highlanders, Lichfield Cathedral that of the 64th Foot, and York Minster that of the 33rd. Such monuments are not confined to places of worship alone. Edinburgh Castle Esplanade has a Runic Cross with the names of eight officers and 248 other ranks of the 78th Highlanders who died in the campaign. That to the naval brigade of HMS *Shannon*, made from the bronze of a gun captured at Lucknow, overlooks the front at Southsea.

The Indian Mutiny, more accurately called the Indian Revolt or Rising of 1857, has been studied by British, Indian and other historians for nearly 150 years, and has been the setting of many works of fiction and several feature films. Because this book concentrates on the British Army's part in the war, I have left the broader field to the many recent works by other writers. If only for reasons of space, the parts played by the Indian services, including their British members, and the stories of non-combatants caught up in genocides, have been mentioned only in passing, and only as much general historical background is given as is necessary to set the scene. In transliterating Indian words and proper nouns I have used the Hunterian system adopted by the Government of India in the British period, but without the diacritic marks that non-specialists find superfluous and publishers expensive. For the same two reasons, as this is a book for the general reader rather than the researcher, sources are not given in detail as footnotes, but in general as the bibliography. Place names are given in the form used by the current edition of the *Times Atlas of the World*, on the principle that even though these may include inconsistencies, they are the forms currently in use, and will enable students to find quickly the places mentioned in the text. The maps used in this book are taken from older publications and thus retain the spellings used in former times.

I take this opportunity of expressing my gratitude to all those who have helped in the preparation of this book, and especially Andrew Orgill and his staff in the library of the Royal Military Academy Sandhurst, together with staff of the India Office Collections in the British Library, and the School of Oriental and African Studies in the University of London. My thanks are due also to Elizabeth Gant, of the SOAS Bulletin; to Surgeon Commander Dennis Freshwater RN, for advice on gastro-enteric illnesses; to Katie Beale-Preston for her Cambridge University dissertation on the effect of the Mutiny on the British perception of themselves; to Dr Peter Thwaite, Curator of the RMAS Collection; to the archivists of the 52nd Light Infantry at Oxford; to Dr Ann Saunders for advice on London's monuments; and to my wife Mary, herself a School of Oriental and African

Studies graduate in the history of South Asia, who in addition to performing her usual roles of research assistant and proofreader, photographed the several memorials used as illustrations.

T.A. Heathcote
Camberley

Chapter 1

THE DRESS REHEARSAL.
VELLORE, 1806

Enter RUMOUR, painted full of tongues.
'Open your ears; for which of you will stop
The vent of hearing when loud Rumour speaks?'

Henry IV Pt II, *Induction*

In 1805 the East India Company's Madras Army could look
forward to resuming normal peacetime soldiering. The long wars
against Mysore had ended in 1799 with the defeat and death of
Tipu Sultan. His territories had been divided between the British
and their allies. His surviving sons, granted handsome pensions
and accompanied by a large retinue, had been exiled to a palace
within the great fortress of Vellore, some 75 miles inland of Fort
St George, Madras (the modern Chennai). During 1803 and
1804 the armies of the great Maratha princes Sindhia of Gwalior,
Holkar of Indore and the Raja of Berar were defeated and, at the
insistence of their British allies, the armies of the Peshwa (head of
the Maratha Confederacy) and the Nizam of Hyderabad were
significantly reduced. As Tipu had been, and the Nizam was, a
Muslim prince, and as the Marathas were Hindus, both of India's
major religions were equally affected by the triumph of a
notionally Christian power. With their other victories elsewhere
in India, the Feringhi (*Faring* or Franks, though the word had
come to mean any kind of European) seemed to be taking over
the country.

As was the case with the Company's other two armies (those of
Bengal and Bombay respectively), that of Madras was made up
of a small number of units from the British Army serving in India
for a limited period, an even smaller number of European units
raised by the Company for permanent service there, and a much
larger number of Indian units under British officers with Indian
officers as their assistants. The official term for an Indian regular

6

soldier was 'sepoy', from the Persian *sipah*. *Spahis*, the Arab cavalry troops of French North Africa, took their name from the same word. In India a mounted trooper was a 'sowar' (from the Persian *sawar*, a rider). A gunner was a 'golandaz' or ball-thrower, from *gul*, a ball (an Urdu word that, through the medium of the barrack room, later entered vulgar English usage). An ordinary soldier was a 'jawan', which, like the Latin *juvens*, means 'youth' or any man of military age, and corresponds to 'our boys' in modern journalese.

In all armies, the return to peace is usually followed by the adoption of new uniforms, partly to take account of practical lessons learned during the recent campaigns, partly to restore standards of smartness relaxed under the pressures of service in the field, and partly to follow the latest dictates of military fashion. In 1805 Lieutenant General Sir John Cradock, a 43-year-old veteran of the British Army's campaigns against the French in the West Indies and Egypt, and the Irish Rising of 1798, became C-in-C, Madras, and approved a new pattern of headdress, adorned with leather cockades, for his sepoys.

At much the same time leather stocks, such as were worn by the Europeans and which were thought to increase smartness by making the wearer keep his head up, were introduced for the necks of the sepoys' coatees. New regulations were issued forbidding sepoys to wear caste marks on their face when in uniform, and ordering them to shave their beards and trim their moustaches to a standard pattern. A special commission composed of military officers and senior civil servants subsequently declared 'nothing would appear to be more trivial to the public interest than the length of hair on the upper lip of a sepoy, yet to the individual himself, the shape and fashion of the whisker is a badge of his caste, and an article of his religion.'

Castes (*Jati*) – groups whose members normally follow the same occupations, eat only with each other and marry only within their group – form a distinctive feature of Indian culture and were vital to an individual's place in the world. A man expelled from his caste was cut off from his family and ostracized by his peers, at least until he could find a priest willing to perform lengthy and expensive purification ceremonies. The caste system was so important in Indian society that it entered even those groups that had originally rejected it. Hindu reformers forbade caste among their followers, but in time these followings became castes themselves and even subdivided into new castes. Sikhs, despite the egalitarian teachings of their founding gurus, never broke free of caste prejudices. Indian Muslims, notwithstanding their belief in the equality before God of all believers, formed caste groups, and so did many Indian Christians converted by Portuguese missionaries during the sixteenth century. The Portuguese called such groups 'families' (*casta*) and it was from this that the English word 'caste' is derived.

Hindus were additionally divided into the four great classes (*varna*) of Brahman, Ksatriya, Vaisya, and Sudra, equating to priests and law-givers, rulers and warriors, merchants and businessmen, and peasants or workers. The first three were 'Twice-born', invested with the sacred thread of initiation to Hindu society on reaching manhood. As not all men were in a position to restrict themselves to the occupations prescribed for their class, they were allowed by the sacred Hindu texts to take up other professions that had a similar status. Among these was that of a regular soldier in the ranks (which in India, unlike in England, was a respectable occupation). Brahmans and Ksatryas alike clung to their class and thought its display by appropriate marks a matter of importance. In the same way, Muslims felt the need to distinguish themselves by outward appearance from the idolatrous Hindus and thereby to remind others that all India had once been under Muslim rule. Caste and religion in India, where for centuries most of the population had lived under rulers of alien origin, were the focus of loyalties that elsewhere men tended to give to their country or city. In the words of the modern European Declaration of Human Rights, the sepoys claimed the right to 'manifest their religion or belief'.

Both Hindus and Muslim soldiers wore beards, as much for outward evidence of their virility as from fashion. Strict Muslims, then as later, considered that to shave the chin was contrary to the fundamental tenets of their faith. Men of neither religion wished to appear like the clean-shaven Christian soldiers, people who ate the flesh of cows (sacred to Hindus) and pigs (unclean to Muslims) indiscriminately, drank alcohol (forbidden to Muslims and avoided by respectable Hindus) intemperately, and failed to perform the frequent ablutions that both Islam and Hinduism prescribed. For Australians to say 'Here comes a Pom, hide your wallet under the soap' may be regarded as a jest. For the sepoys, cleanliness was not merely next to godliness but essential to it. That the new headdress would make them look more like British soldiers was emphatically not a recommendation in their eyes. Even worse, it made them look like the regimental drummers, who were recruited from the Eurasian Christian community.

This objection was strengthened by rumours that the leather cockade of the new headdress was made of cowhide or pigskin, the touch of which would bring ritual pollution to Hindus or Muslims respectively. Although sophisticated townsmen in India, as in many societies, might have been lax in their religious observances, the ordinary sepoy came from respectable peasant communities. Indeed, since English is one of the few languages in which to call a man a peasant is to insult him, the social status of such men is better indicated by referring to them as 'yeomen'. The anxieties of the Madras sepoys in 1806 were not so different from those of British Protestants scarcely a century earlier, who had deposed a king to preserve their religion.

Thus it was that at Vellore, early in May 1806, Lieutenant Colonel Darley, commanding the 2nd Battalion, 4th Madras Native Infantry, learned that most of his elite grenadier company had refused to accept the new headdress. This was reported to the C-in-C, Madras, who consulted his staff and was assured that there was no good reason for the objection. He therefore decided to treat the matter as one of insubordination and ordered the leaders of the protest (ten Muslims and eleven Hindus) to be punished. Despite delaying tactics on the part of their officers, who obviously had some sympathy with the men and foresaw trouble if their complaints were ignored, all the NCOs of the grenadier company, except two who had accepted the new headdress, were to be reduced to the ranks, and the Indian officers of the battalion were to begin wearing it at once, on pain of dismissal.

Courts martial in the Company's armies followed the same principles as those in the British Army, with a group of officers (Indian officers, when sepoys were the accused) in place of a jury, who also decided the sentence. A British officer acted as judge advocate, ensuring that the trial was conducted in accordance with the law and in this respect corresponding to a judge in ordinary criminal courts. British officers acted as prosecutors and the accused were allowed to defend themselves or ask another British officer to speak for them. The weakness of the system was that Indian officers were commonly believed to bring in the verdict that they thought the judge advocate expected of them. Such beliefs, indeed, are not unknown in military justice elsewhere. This court martial found all the accused guilty and sentenced one Muslim and one Hindu to flogging and dismissal. The remaining nineteen were sentenced to 500 lashes each, but punishment was remitted when they admitted their error and gave assurances of future good conduct.

Cradock made a tour of inspection, in the course of which he received an official letter from Lieutenant Colonel James Brunton, Military Auditor General, Madras, reporting that the new headdress caused great discontent, and strongly recommending its withdrawal. This matched what Cradock had discovered for himself, and on 29 June he sent Brunton's letter to the Governor of Madras, saying that the objections were 'almost universal, and that it was commonly believed that the next attempt would be to force the sepoys to become Christians'. If the question concerned British soldiers, he said, he would know what to do, but because it required knowledge of Indian soldiers, he sought advice from the Madras government.

The government there was headed by the 31-year-old Lord William Cavendish-Bentinck, second son of the former Prime Minister, the 3rd Duke of Portland. Lord William had seen active service on the staff of the Duke of York in Flanders, with the Russians in northern Italy and with the Austrians at Marengo. In 1803, through his father's influence, but against the wishes of the Company's Court of Directors, he had been appointed Governor of Madras. Brunton's warning was disregarded on the grounds that he had long been in bad health, that his nerves were gone, and that he suffered from 'great despondency'. Nevertheless, the Madras government produced a draft General Order, with the intention of reassuring the sepoys, but Cradock decided that, as opposition seemed to be fading, he would let sleeping dogs lie.

At Vellore, however, the dogs were not sleeping at all. The 2nd Battalion, 4th Madras Native Infantry, had been replaced by the 2nd Battalion, 23rd Madras NI, from Walajapet (Wallajabad), a dozen miles away, but the new arrivals were equally determined to defend their religion. Clandestine meetings were held in the lines of the 23rd and its companion sepoy unit, the 1st Battalion, 1st Madras NI. Most of the Indian officers attended, together with courtiers from Tipu Sultan's family in the nearby palace, and all swore to resist the new regulations. Determined not to share the fate of the 4th's grenadiers, they decided that they would seize their weapons, which were stored in Vellore fort with the sepoys themselves being quartered outside. To do so, however, they would have to deal with a wing of the 69th Foot, totalling eleven officers and 372 men, whose barracks were inside the fort.

On 17 June, Sepoy Mustafa Beg of the 1st Madras NI reported to his commanding officer, Lieutenant Colonel Forbes, that there was a plan to rise and attack the British. Forbes asked his Indian officers to investigate. They, unsurprisingly, reported that Mustafa Beg was insane and persuaded the Colonel to throw him in the cells as a troublemaker. About the same time, a European woman, Mrs Burke, went to see the station commander, Colonel Fancourt about her late husband's prize money and, while there, told him of what was rumoured in the bazaar. According to her later evidence, 'on his asking her if she was a married woman, and her replying that she was a widow, he said he took her to be a bad woman and bade her go away.' Whatever the merits of Fancourt's suspicions about Mrs Burke's profession, he had made a disastrously wrong assessment of the intelligence that she provided.

On the night of 9 July the men of the 23rd Madras NI were given permission to sleep inside the fort in order to be ready for an early parade the next morning. The orderly officer, Captain Miller of the 23rd, decided not to bother with his evening rounds and delegated this duty to the orderly subadar (Indian captain). This officer delegated it to the orderly jemadar (Indian lieutenant), Jemadar Shaikh Kasim, who was one of the leaders of the plot. At moonrise, about 2.30 a.m., sepoys of the 23rd suddenly turned on the British soldiers with whom they were sharing guard duties, and began firing into the 69th's lines. Five of the 69th's officers assembled at the adjutant's quarters, disarmed the four sepoy sentries posted there, and began an exchange of fire with their attackers. At first light Sergeant Brady of the 69th went out to discover what was happening and returned an hour later to give a good clear report that all the British sentries and several European officers, including Colonel Fancourt, had been killed, the 69th's barracks were under fire from musketry and artillery, and Mysorean colours had been hoisted over the flagstaff bastion.

At about 7.00 a.m., it being by this time fully light, the adjutant, Lieutenant Thomas Mitchell, made a dash for the barracks. The remaining officers moved into the house of the battalion medical officer, Surgeon Jones, before making their way under fire to the barracks. There they found Mitchell and their men trying to take cover from the two 6-pdrs in sepoy hands, whose shot repeatedly passed down the length of the barrack rooms. With many men already killed or wounded and ammunition running low (they had begun with only six rounds per man in their pouches), Captain Archibald Maclachlan, the senior officer present, decided to lead the two hundred or so still standing in a sally through the barrack windows, to dislodge the sepoys from the nearby ramparts.

This was done, though Maclachlan was badly wounded in the process, and command passed to Captain C.J. Barrow. They then fought their way along the walls and captured the gateway, despite heavy fire from the nearby palace. Leaving a party there, the rest went on to the main magazine, almost opposite the barracks from which they had started, but found just a few barrels of blank cartridges and a quantity of loose gunpowder. The British sentry was later discovered dead at his post, with one round left in his pouch and the bodies of nine sepoys around him. The 69th's only ammunition by this time consisted of what had been taken from the pouches of the dead of either side. This was augmented by a large number of rupees, found loose in the paymaster's office and now fired with the blank cartridges.

Using their bayonets, the British retreated to the gateway and its neighbouring bastions, but suffered more casualties from musketry fire. Barrow himself fell wounded and the only two officers left in action were Surgeon Jones and Assistant Surgeon Dean. Under their command, the wounded were placed in a cavalier (a raised work within a bastion) with such of the women and children as had escaped from the Regiment's married quarters. The fighting men, by now reduced to about sixty, manned the walls. Out of ammunition, they watched helplessly while fifteen of their sick comrades were dragged from the hospital and killed. Outside, Major Coates of the 69th, unable to join his men in the fort, sent an urgent message to Lieutenant Colonel Rollo Gillespie, 19th Light Dragoons, the forty-year-old commandant of the cavalry post 16 miles away at Arcot.

Gillespie, an Ulsterman of the Anglo-Irish Protestant Ascendancy, had a reputation for boldness and daring that more than compensated for his small stature. At the age of twenty he had caused a scandal by eloping with the nineteen-year-old sister of a Dublin squire in whose house he had been a guest. A year later, challenged to a duel by a noted marksman, he levelled the odds by stipulating that the participants would hold a corner of the same handkerchief in one hand and a pistol in the other. His opponent was killed and Gillespie was indicted for murder. Acquitted by an Anglo-Irish jury, he left the court with no other stain on his character.

On the evening of 9 July he had been engaged to dine at Vellore with Fancourt (an old friend with whom he had served in the West Indies), but a sudden duty had kept him at Arcot. Coates's message reached him at about 7.00 a.m. just after he had begun to ride to Vellore with his apologies. He immediately returned to barracks, turned out the duty troop of the 19th and a troop of the 5th Madras Light Cavalry, and led them at full speed to the rescue. Lieutenant Colonel Kennedy of the 19th was ordered to follow as fast as possible with the rest of the Regiment, their close support 'galloper guns' and every other man, British or Indian, who could ride, leaving only a small garrison behind.

At about 8.30 the watchers on Vellore's ramparts saw horsemen approaching, with a single figure far in advance of it. Sergeant Brady, still in action, recognized him and knew his reputation. 'If Colonel Gillespie be alive,' he shouted, 'that is he, and God Almighty has sent him from the West Indies to save our lives in the East.' Reaching the fort, Gillespie found the drawbridge down, two outer gates open, and the two inner ones closed. The scene, he later wrote, 'was heart-rending, the white people over the gateway shrieking for assistance, which it was impracticable to afford them from the height of the walls and the strength of the gate which was shut'. A party of the 69th buckled their belts together and climbed down to open the third gate from the inside. Led by Gillespie, they forced open a wicket door and tried to open the fourth gate, but were driven back by intense musketry fire.

Gillespie then found a rope hanging down from the gateway and climbed up to join the men there and put new heart into them. 'I found a pair of colours [not belonging to the 69th], which I seized, gave a loud shriek and at their head, under a tremendous fire, took possession of a cavalier of three guns.' Despite having nothing to fire from them, he ordered the guns to be traversed round towards the palace, where a mass of mutineers had assembled. He then decided to make a bayonet attack on the grand arsenal, but was forestalled by the arrival at about 10.00 a.m. of the main force from Arcot. 'It was,' he wrote, in a masterpiece of understatement, 'a fortunate circumstance that I was not reduced to this expedient, which however necessary for the purpose of obtaining ammunition, would undoubtedly have been attended with considerable loss.'

On Gillespie's shouted orders, the horse gunners used their standard tactic of galloping up to the gateway and opening fire from close range. The gates of South Asian fortresses were always remarkably unprotected by European standards, and the first salvo blew the innermost gate wide open. Gillespie led a charge down from the ramparts to clear a space for the cavalry to deploy. Trapped inside the fort, about 350 mutineers were killed, with no quarter given. One group held out inside a barrack block, but was wiped out in a dismounted assault by British troopers of the 19th and Indian sowars of the Governor of Madras's Bodyguard. The rest escaped through a sally port, but the light dragoons and the 7th Madras Light Cavalry cut many down in the surrounding roads and fields. Within fifteen minutes Vellore was once more under British control but the discovery of the mutilated bodies of the sick from the hospital roused the dragoons to fury. Some were seen hunting for mutineers in the magazine, oblivious to the fact that at any time a spark from their spurs or steel scabbards could have ignited the loose powder, the most dangerous kind of explosive then in existence. A large number of mutineers found hiding in the palace were lined up and killed by repeated salvos of canister from the guns.

Vellore, however, was not the only station where discontent was openly expressed. Sepoys at Hyderabad shared the belief that there was a government plan to abolish all caste distinction and convert them to Christianity. Moreover, an oracle had stated that there was a well full of treasure in the European barracks whose guardian spirit required human heads as an offering and that the European troops on that account were about to murder their Indian comrades. With only one British unit, the 33rd Foot, in the garrison, the local authorities decided to cancel the new dress regulations in order to preserve discipline.

At Vellore on 12 July Gillespie heard rumours of widespread disturbances elsewhere in Madras and received warnings from several local sources that a general rising was planned for the same evening. He issued a proclamation denying the rumours and warned that, if these continued to be spread, he would turn his guns on the sepoy lines outside the fort and unleash the much-feared 19th Light Dragoons. Pending the arrival of three companies of the 59th Foot, who were expected the following day, he doubled the guard on the Mysorean princes and reported that he would 'not permit a single black soldier to remain within the walls this night'.

The light dragoons had lost one man killed and three wounded. Gillespie escaped with a badly bruised arm, having been accidentally ridden down during the final melee. The 69th, however, had lost heavily. Out of 11 officers and 372 men, 2 subalterns and 115 men were killed or died of wounds, and another 3 officers and 76 men were badly wounded. Among the victors, Gillespie was the hero of the hour and was awarded Rs 24,500. Sergeant Brady was awarded Rs 2,800 and offered a commission, but instead accepted the warrant of a Conductor in the Ordnance Department. Sergeant Angus McManus and Private Philip Bottom of the 69th, who had risked their lives to pull down the Mysore flag, received cash awards. The 400 Madras cavalrymen were given a permanent increase in their pay and the British dragoons each received a month's extra wages. Mustafa Beg, found in the cells, was awarded the retirement pension of a subadar.

The subsequent commission of enquiry found that the prime cause of the mutiny was fear that the new regulations would cause the sepoys to lose their caste. 'In this country the prejudices of the conquered have always triumphed over the arms of the conqueror ... Any innovation, therefore, in that respect must be calculated to call forth their feelings, and the more trivial the object to be sacrificed, the stronger, in our opinion, would be the reluctance to make it.' Caste marks, said their report, added to the esteem of an individual within his society and created a sense of personal honour that did more to maintain discipline than fear of punishment. What distinguished the Vellore mutiny from its several predecessors, in their view, was that for the first time the sepoys turned on their officers, and the only new factor was the presence of the dispossessed princes of Mysore, who had stirred up the religious feelings of the sepoys in the hope of restoring Muslim power.

Six months later, when the reports of these proceedings reached London, the Company's Court of Directors took firm action. In practice, the Directors no longer had the power to appoint governors and commanders-in-chief, as the British government of the day had a veto over their nominations, but they retained the right to recall them. Both Bentinck and Cradock were ordered home. Bentinck (against whom the Directors had several other complaints) was blamed for not enquiring more closely into the sentiments of the sepoys before supporting Cradock. Cradock was told he must accept responsibility for enforcing the 'injudicious regulations' even though it was on the advice of his staff, and for 'the remarkable degree in which he was unacquainted with the state of his own army just at the eve of an insurrection, when he thought all was calm'. The question was, said the Directors, not whether there was any real justification for the sepoys' alarm, but whether that alarm existed at all. If the men really believed that obedience to the new regulations meant that their fellow caste members would no longer associate with them, 'no compliance was to be expected from them, whatever might be the sacrifice'. Bentinck, however, pre-empted this by ordering all stocks of the new headdress to be destroyed and giving permission for moustaches and caste marks of any pattern.

Previous mutinies had been relatively minor affairs, mostly springing from financial grievances, and had at separate times involved officers as much as men and Europeans as much as Indians. In the Indian military labour market, such activities could be regarded merely as collective attempts to renegotiate unsatisfactory terms of employment. They would, indeed, long continue to appear from time to time among the same groups. In 1806, however, the new feature was that attacks were made not on British officers alone, but on Christians of all kinds, including sick, women and children, in a frenzy of ethnic cleansing. Nor indeed, were only sepoys involved. The murderers included menials from the sepoy lines, using drill carbines as clubs. Some sepoys, on the other hand, attacked only officers or fighting men. Lieutenant Eley of the 69th was bayoneted with his baby in his

16

arms and his wife by his side, yet both Mrs Eley and the child were left unharmed. Mrs Fancourt's Indian servants helped her children to escape. Non-combatant Europeans living outside the fort were not attacked.

The Vellore Mutiny in many ways pre-figured the much greater one that would convulse the Bengal Army half a century later. It did not matter to the Madras sepoys in 1806 that the new headdress was not so very different from one that had been worn in the recent campaigns, nor that in many units caste marks were worn in uniform only discreetly or not at all. It did not really matter to the Bengal sepoys in 1857 that the new Enfield rifle had a cartridge that required lubrication. What mattered in both cases was that the times were out of joint and men wanted a return to the good old days. The British had taken control of Muslim and Hindu states alike, in a tide of conquest that was as rapid as it was extensive. British reforms of the land revenue caused severe hardship to many in the rural communities from which the sepoys came. The princes of Mysore and their devoted courtiers were not the only people to have been dispossessed and humiliated. As would be the case in northern India fifty years later, along with the nobility and gentry went the livelihoods of all who had depended upon them, and for whom the new British officials had no requirement. Men whose nation was their religion expressed their discontent as religious issues and were ready, even determined, to be offended on religious grounds. If leather cockades or greasy cartridges had not emerged as the catalyst, some other new procedure or drill could have served equally well.

The prophecies were spread of the end of British rule either fifty or a hundred years after Plassey, though it was not clear whether these years were to be calculated according to the Christian, Muslim or Hindu systems of measuring time, nor to which part of India they referred. As Francis Bacon shrewdly observed of prophecies 'men mark when they hit, but not when they miss.' A further paranormal occurrence thought to be of great significance, though none could say what it was, was the distribution of chapatis, a food now so well known in Indian restaurants throughout the United Kingdom as no longer to need a translation. Like an Internet warning or chain letter, each recipient (in this case, village headmen or other minor officials) was called on to make several copies and send them on to others.

Such chains had appeared before 1806 and would do so again thereafter, but the mysterious nature of their origin always had an unsettling effect. Any noteworthy event occurring soon after their appearance was easily attributed to them. Just such a chain spread in the period before the mutiny of 1857.

It was from this turmoil of political change and uncertainty that there arose both in 1806 and 1857 the fear among sepoys that their British employers were using military reforms as a means of making them lose caste and turn Christian. The nature of conspiracy theories in all societies is such that rational counter-argument can make no headway against them. Anything put forward to disprove such theories is immediately met with objections that seem to have some validity. When Indian officers and clerics declared that the new headdress items were accept-able, it was said that no career-minded officer would contradict his superiors, and that, as there were many ways to interpret the holy laws, the government could always find an amenable cleric of some kind to support its case. Such arguments, indeed, have some credibility in any Army at any time.

Any intelligence report including the phrase 'it is rumoured in the bazaar' is one to be ignored at the analyst's peril. Sepoys had no life outside the tight embrace of regimental comradeship, family and caste. Any one group, and still more a mutually reinforcing combination of all three, produced an element of the homogeneity that in any army is a valuable source of unit cohesion and a powerful incitement to valour. Against this, any social group that is in some way a peculiar people, isolated or introspective, is vulnerable to the spread of rumours. Suspicions are passed on from one individual to another within the group, then repeated to others and confirmed in a process of circular reporting so as to become 'group-think', accepted as self-evident by all.

The military seem especially prone to such influences, and officers seeking to reassure their anxious men that rumours are false can seem ignorant of what higher authority is planning. When rumours are justified by subsequent events, even the best-respected officer seems either a liar or a dupe. What the sepoys of a regiment thought was, by virtue of their narrow recruitment base, the same as what their kinship and caste groups thought as well, and there was no external influence to moderate the mutually reinforcing fears that arose in all of them at the same time.

The East India Company was always aware that its Indian subjects would fear a British attempt to convert them to Christianity. Many Muslim conquerors had made converts at the point of the sword and so had the Portuguese in the days of their Indian empire. If anything, the Christian Portuguese had been the more zealous, for they had even persecuted other Christians, notably those whose church originated with St Thomas, the apostle of India, and denied the supremacy of Rome. Some of the great Mughal emperors had adopted a policy of tolerance towards non-Muslims, but others, more puritanical in their views, had waged war on Sikhs, Hindu Rajputs and Marathas, and Shi'a Muslims alike. Tipu, who by 1806 had come to be regarded as a Muslim martyr, had made many conversions, often forcibly, and had polluted Brahmans by compelling them to slaughter cows. It was not unreasonable for anyone in India to think that the English, having become the new conquerors, would act in the same way, nor to disbelieve their repeated denials of such a plan.

It was in an attempt to prevent such thoughts that the Company for generations kept Christian missionaries out of its dominions and denied them passage on its ships. Most British officials in 1806 believed that missionary activity unsettled Indian minds and some even objected to missionaries (or at least to the Nonconformists) on the grounds of their humble origins. Charles Marsh, an eminent barrister in Madras, railed against 'these low and base-born mechanics . . . these apostates from the loom and anvil'. (One later authority noted that it was surprising he omitted the carpenter's bench.) Vellore only confirmed official reservations on the subject. In 1811 the Governor-General, Lord Minto, ordered that Baptist publications produced in the Danish enclave at Serhampur, near the capital of British India at Calcutta, should be censored to stop them advocating the abolition of caste. 'A proposal to efface a mark of caste from the foreheads of soldiers on parade,' he noted, 'has had its share in a massacre of Christians.'

The Vellore mutiny prefigured the Bengal mutiny in its military as well as its religious and political aspects. In 1857 increasing numbers on the British side had the new Enfield rifle, the introduction of which brought the same fear of pollution to the Bengal sepoys that the new headdress had brought to the Madras sepoys, but the standard weapon was still the smooth-bore musket. Enfields were in short supply in 1857 and were at first issued only to picked men and used much as were light machine guns in later wars. In both mutinies, the sepoys preferred fighting from a distance with their muskets rather than at close quarters with their bayonets. It was rare in set-piece battles of the time for infantry to cross bayonets in a melee. More usually, one side or the other gave way before the opposing lines made contact. To advance against an enemy in position, or to stand firm against an approaching attack, required an iron discipline which mutiny, by its very nature, tends to weaken. Even more, it required leadership by well-trained and determined officers, of which those who mutinied had by that very act deprived themselves. By concentrating on the fire-fight, they minimized this tactical weakness but without officers they were always at a disadvantage in close action.

In hand-to-hand fighting, moreover, the British soldiers generally had advantages of weight and height, stemming partly from genetic factors and partly from the largely vegetarian diet of their opponents. In the microcosm of Vellore it is noticeable that the sepoys, with a tradition of marksmanship dating from Mughal times, relied on their musketry, but were driven from the walls by the bayonets of numerically inferior British infantrymen. In the same way, during the campaigns of 1857–8, shock action by British troops often overcame missile action by their enemies. Any advantage the sepoys might have derived from good shooting was lost when British rifles outranged sepoy muskets by several hundred yards.

Gillespie, the hero of Vellore, gained further laurels but his luck finally ran out during the Nepal War of 1814, when he fell as a major general, leading a rush on the Gurkha fortress of Kalunga. By an irony of fate he, who had suppressed the mutiny of 1806, was buried near Meerut, where the mutiny of 1857 was destined to begin.

Chapter 2

THE THEATRE OF OPERATIONS, MAY 1857 – THE STAGE, THE SETTING AND THE PLAYERS

For Solon said well to Croesus (when in ostentation he showed him his gold) 'Sir, if any other come that hath better iron than you, he will be master of all this gold.'

Francis Bacon, Essays. Of the True Greatness of Kingdoms

At the beginning of 1857 the British controlled a South Asian empire greater in extent than that held by any ruler in Indian history. Not Chandragupta Maurya, who drove out the Indo-Bactrian garrisons that succeeded Alexander the Great, nor the noble Asoka, nor Samudra Gupta, the Napoleon of India, had made such extensive conquests. Even the last of the great Mughals, the puritanical Aurangzeb, under whom their empire reached its greatest extent, never conquered as far south as Cape Comorin, where the peninsula points like a great fingertip into the Indian Ocean. Indeed, on his death in 1707, still in the field in an unfinished campaign that had lasted twenty years, the empire was crumbling behind him under the revolts that his extremism had stirred up. A century and a half later, British influence stretched from Cape Comorin to the Himalayas, and from the eastern borders of Iran to the western borders of Thailand, distances comparable to those between northern Scotland and southern Italy, or between New York and San Francisco.

The sub-continent's northern plains can be cool in winter but unbearably hot in summer. Their great rivers are constantly fed by melt-water from the Himalayan snows but may become shallow in places during the spring drought. This affects navigation and had a significant impact on the military events of 1857. The most important feature of the Indian climate is the monsoon. Between October and May rainfall is rare. By early June, in the northern plains, the thermometer may rise to over 110 degrees F and winds are hotter than the ambient temperature. Trees and vegetation are parched, agriculture depends on irrigation and, in the uncultivated forest (*jangal*) areas, animals die for lack of food or water. Then torrential storms arrive, followed by floods and plagues. The average annual rainfall around Delhi is some 25 inches, about the same as in London, but most of it comes in cloudbursts during the few months of the rainy season. In the days before metalled roads, travelling during the monsoon was not to be thought of, least of all by armies. Alexander the Great's operations in the Punjab were hampered by heavy rain. The great Central Asian conqueror Timur, whose descendants founded the Mughal Empire, lost many of his horses in the same area to the same cause. Just as European armies went into winter quarters, Indian armies ceased operations at the onset of the monsoon and did not resume them until the Dasara (Dushera) festival in mid-October. In 1857–8, political imperatives forced the British to fight on during the monsoon for the first time since Clive.

The legitimacy of British power in this sub-continent derived from two sources. On the one hand the East India Company, the vehicle through which the British governed India, existed by virtue of parliamentary charters, generally granted for a period of twenty years at a time. In 1857, it was not a 'multinational corporation' but rather a 'quango' or nationalized industry, with the government kept at a distance from day-to-day management, but implementing national policies at the strategic level. On the other hand, it held its possessions in India by virtue of *sanads* or treaties with local Indian princes, who were, or once had been, subjects of the Mughal Empire. It mattered little to the jurists that the actual relationship of these princes to their overlord in Delhi was mostly one of defiance, if not of actual rebellion. The Mughal Emperor was still considered to be the ultimate fount of titles and honours and Indian princes struggled for the custody of his person until 1805, when the British rescued the poverty-stricken Shah Alam II from the Marathas. He was given the title of King of Delhi, with his city administered by a British resident, and until 1835 the East India Company's coins still bore his superscription.

In 1849 the then king, Bahadur Shah Zafar II, reluctantly agreed that his successor would give up the royal title and vacate the Red Fort and palace from which his ancestors had once ruled. Meanwhile, protected by the Company's troops and supported by its subsidies (which Mughal courtiers chose to regard as tribute), Delhi once more became a centre where Urdu poets, Muslim theologians and Indian scholars and craftsmen of all kinds flourished. Despite pressure from their officials in India, the British government in London thought it not worth alienating Indian, and especially Muslim, public opinion by hastening the end of an anachronism.

By 1857 the Company had become just as much an anachronism as the Mughals. In 1784 Parliament, alarmed at British subjects in India maintaining their own armies and conducting their own foreign policy, set up a Board of Control for the affairs of India, whose President sat in cabinet as a secretary of state. As appointments to public office in the late eighteenth century were corrupt even by the standards of the early twenty-first, it was feared that any government controlling 'the patronage of India' (the right to nominate young men to appointments there) would be able to procure so much support in Parliament as to maintain itself in office indefinitely.

The Company was therefore left in existence as the vehicle through which the British governed their possessions in India, and its Court of Directors continued to appoint its own nominees, rather than those of government ministers, to the Indian military, medical and covenanted civil services. 'Covenanted' was the term for the senior or first division of the civil service, deriving from the time when they were required to sign a covenant that they would not take bribes, a temptation that had effectively been removed by the device of paying them so well that they could afford to stay honest. The junior or uncovenanted service was recruited locally, from Eurasians and Indians. Eurasians were not enlisted in the army, except as drummers and musicians, but the sons of marriages between Company officers and Eurasian or Indian ladies were eligible for nominations as cadets. In 1857 at least two of the five Bengal Army generals commanding divisions had Eurasian sons serving as their ADCs.

In 1813 the Company lost its monopoly of trade with India and was ordered to separate its political from its trading activities. In 1833 it was forbidden from commercial activities anywhere. The mid-Victorian concept of filling official posts by open competitive examination eased the patronage question and the 1853 Charter Act renewed the Company not for the usual twenty years, but only for as long as Parliament should think necessary, which most people supposed would not be for very long. Its only trading activities left were in opium and salt, which had long been government monopolies, and on which much of its revenue depended. Its dividends, unlike those of a multinational, were fixed by Parliament, and holders of East India stock were, in effect, merely investors in government bonds. It was generally recognized as a British government agency, so when in 1856 Queen Victoria addressed her Prime Minister, Lord Palmerston, on the subject (referring to herself in the third person) she wrote: 'She takes a deep and natural interest in her Indian Empire and must consider the selection of the fittest person for the post of Governor-General as of paramount importance.'

Within India, British rule was conducted under a Governor-General, based at Calcutta. He, like the governors of the two junior presidencies, Madras and Bombay, was usually a minor British politician, and often one whose family fortunes stood in need of the handsome salary that compensated for five years' exile in an unpleasant climate. At this time he governed with a council of four, who conducted business jointly though each department had it own specialist permanent secretary. British rule in southern and western India was conducted by the governments of Madras and Bombay respectively. Each had their own C-in-C, military and other services, all with their own hierarchies and seniority lists separate from each other and from those of Bengal, which came directly under the Governor-General of India and C-in-C, India, respectively.

The two oldest British provinces of northern India were Bengal, including Bihar, and the North-West Provinces, so-called because they lay to the north-west of the Company's original territories in Bengal (not to be confused with the North-West Frontier Province, later formed from the trans-Indus districts of the Punjab). Each of these was headed by a lieutenant governor from the Company's permanent service. The newer provinces were Awadh (Oudh or Oude), annexed in 1856, and the Punjab, annexed in 1849, each of which was headed by a chief commissioner. Sind (Sindh), annexed in 1843, had its own commissioner, known as the Commissioner in Sind, and came under the Government of Bombay. Alongside and between the British provinces were the states of Indian princes under British protection. Except for the conduct of foreign affairs, they retained their autonomy and kept up their own governments, courts of

24

justice, revenue systems and armies. British influence was exerted through officers of the local political (the Indian term for diplomatic) service based at their courts. Residents (equating to ambassadors) were stationed at the major ones and various grades of agent at the remainder.

All governments, British or Indian, saw their main purpose as the collection of revenue. Indeed, in the older or 'regulation' provinces, the district commissioner's official title was Collector. In practice, revenue meant the land revenue or the government share of the crop. The system varied greatly from one area to another, but generally the government's share was collected in the form of cash and it was frequently necessary to use troops to enforce payment and escort it to the district treasuries. A proportion was passed on to central government and the rest used for local official expenditure. In Mughal times this procedure operated like a sponge, with local rulers soaking up what they could and then being squeezed by their overlords in their turn. Many a Mughal official worked on the principle *Dihli dur ast* (Delhi is far), hoping that the tax demand, or indeed orders for any other unwelcome course of action, would never come. Much the same attitude applied in the contemporary Spanish Empire, where the phrase was *Mi venga la muerte de Spagna*, let my death come from Spain (for then it would be long in coming).

The system of collecting revenue in cash resulted in large deposits of ready money in every government station. At all times these were a temptation to robbers and needed significant numbers of troops to guard them. When the Bengal Army mutinied in 1857 they were obvious targets for the units that should have been defending them. British commanders, already concerned for the safety of the European communities around them, had the additional worry of protecting very large sums of government money, and their operational decisions were frequently affected by this factor. In almost every case, one of the first acts of the mutineers was to plunder the treasury.

Out of the revenues thus collected the East India Company garrisoned its great empire with an army that, at the beginning of 1857, amounted to 266,175 professional soldiers, plus various paramilitaries, armed police, etc. The Bengal Army was made up of 3 battalions of the Company's Europeans, 28 regiments of Indian cavalry and 91 battalions of regular Indian infantry. Also under its command were 2 regiments of cavalry and 13 battalions of infantry from the British Army. The Punjab Irregular Force consisted of 5 regiments of cavalry and 11 battalions of infantry, the Oudh Irregular Force had 3 regiments of cavalry and 10 battalions of infantry, and the Gwalior Contingent had 2 regiments of cavalry and 7 battalions of infantry. Smaller contingents, mostly about the size of modern battle groups, were maintained in minor states, and a dozen or so local units existed for the protection of border areas or internal security in wild and unsettled districts.

Contingent forces were not part of the armies of the states whose names they bore, nor were they the subjects of their rulers. They were recruited from the same sources as the rest of the Bengal Army, mostly the peasantry of the North-West Provinces and Awadh, the 'nursery of sepoys', with a long tradition of military service. Trained and equipped in the same way, and commanded by Bengal officers, they were practically indistinguishable from the regular regiments of the Bengal Army. The constitutional difference was that the cost of maintaining them fell upon the states that they in theory defended (in practice, occupied), usually by the assignment to the British of the revenues (in practice, the government) of specified districts.

All the contingents, like eighteen of the cavalry regiments and most of the various local forces, were styled Irregulars, a title that gives a false impression to those unfamiliar with the terminology of the day. They were not irregulars in the sense of being partisans or guerrillas, but were full-time soldiers in a standing army, and as such regulars in all but name. The difference in India was that regular regiments had a full establishment of twenty-seven British officers, whereas irregular regiments had no British officers of their own. They were therefore much cheaper to keep up, as half the cost of an Indian unit was the pay of its officers. The four British officers needed by an irregular regiment (commandant, second-in-command, adjutant and surgeon) were found by detaching them from the regulars.

British infantry was organized into regiments, each consisting of one or more battalions, combatant units commanded by lieutenant colonels. In 1857 only the three regiments of Foot Guards and the two elite Rifle Corps (the 60th Foot or King's Royal Rifle Corps, usually referred to as the 60th Rifles, and the Rifle Brigade) had more than one battalion and in practice the terms regiment and battalion were interchangeable. Each battalion, notionally about a thousand strong, but much weaker when actually on operations, was divided into ten companies commanded by captains. There were two majors, each of whom could command a wing of up to four companies. Every battalion had a sergeant major and every company a colour sergeant. The two 'flank companies', the grenadier and light companies, were made up of picked men, specially trained as assault troops and skirmishers respectively. Light Infantry regiments maintained their traditions as elite troops, though in practice they were, by this time, employed in much the same way as the rest of the Line. The same applied in the case of Fusilier regiments, whose dress distinctions showed them to be the British Army's equivalent of grenadier regiments in continental armies.

The same organization was followed by the Company's nine regiments of European infantry (three in each army) and by the regular native infantry, where sergeants and corporals were replaced by havildars and naiks, though a number of European sergeants also served with each unit. Native regiments had an additional hierarchy of Indian officers, with subadars and jemadars in each company, shadowing the British captains and subalterns. British cavalry regiments consisted of ten troops, each with its captain, two subalterns and troop sergeant major, though for operational purposes ad hoc squadrons were formed of two or more troops. Cavalry did not have a battalion system and extra units could only be formed by raising completely new corps. Units were commonly divided into two wings, each under a major, for administrative or operational purposes. In Indian and colonial campaigns, this was a means of eking out scarce European manpower, so that when a regiment was listed as present with a particular force, it was generally only a wing, with the remaining companies and troops detached to other tasks.

Prior to the crisis of 1857 the Royal Artillery did not serve in India. Each local Army had its own regiment, organized into brigades for the horse artillery, and battalions for the foot artillery. These were not tactical but administrative groups and were themselves divided into troops and companies respectively, each under a captain as in the case of the other arms. The Bengal Army had 9 European- and 4 Indian-manned troops of horse artillery, each equipped with five 6-pdr guns and a 12-pdr howitzer, and 24 European and 18 Indian companies of foot artillery. Twenty-one of these were formed as field batteries, with five 9-pdr guns and one 24-pdr howitzer in the light batteries and five 18-pdr guns and an 8-in mortar in the heavies. Garrison companies manned fortress or siege artillery. Guns in India were still fired by means of priming-pouches and portfires, long obsolete in European armies.

At the higher level, the Bengal Army was organized into divisions and brigades, but despite their titles, these were administrative groupings, not field forces. The latter had no permanent existence and were formed at the beginning of each campaign with units taken from the peacetime divisions. Of the seven major generals commanding Bengal divisional areas in May 1857, five were officers of the East India Company's service, and two from the British Army. At the highest level was Army Headquarters, under the C-in-C in the East Indies, usually referred to as C-in-C, India. Though selected from the British rather than the Company's service, he was not subordinate to the British War Office nor to the C-in-C of the British Army, whose sole connection with India was to provide the British troops that the Cabinet thought necessary to station there.

In 1857 the C-in-C, India, was the 59-year-old General the Honourable George Anson, who had served with the Foot Guards at Waterloo. His subsequent career had included spells as a courtier and with the Board of Ordnance in political posts, aided by his position as an MP for South Staffordshire, a seat owned by his brother, the Earl of Lichfield. He was a noted patron of the Turf and the card table, and it is quite possible that financial imperatives led him (after rising through seniority to the rank of major general) to obtain appointment as a divisional commander in Bengal in 1853. In 1854 he was appointed C-in-C, Madras and, in 1856, C-in-C, India. Both posts were in the gift of the British government of the day, where the Whig ministry included Lord Lichfield among its parliamentary supporters. Anson's sensibilities as a Guards officer were pained by the sepoys' standards of personal smartness, and he once told the Governor-General's Council that he never saw an Indian sentry without turning away in disgust at his unsoldierlike appearance. He also made a point of selecting his ADCs from the British rather than the Company's service. Nevertheless, in the way of Guards officers, he was gracious and courteous, and the Governor-General, Viscount Canning, wrote that, despite their occasional differences, 'It would be very difficult to quarrel with anyone so imperturbably good-tempered, and so thoroughly a gentleman.'

Outside Bengal, the senior ranking officer was Major General Sir Patrick Grant, the 53-year-old C-in-C, Madras. An officer of the Bengal Army, he had served both in the large-scale conventional warfare of the Sikh Wars and in low-intensity operations on the North-West Frontier. He was a brave and efficient officer, though spiteful rivals claimed that his advancement owed much to his having married the daughter of General Lord Gough, who was C-in-C, India during the Sikh Wars and on whose staff he served.

Charles Canning, 2nd Viscount Canning, born in 1812, was the third son of the distinguished statesman and former Prime Minister George Canning. He shared his father's political views and sat on the Whig benches first as an MP and then in the Lords. He had held various minor political offices (declining that of Foreign Secretary) and joined Palmerston's first Cabinet as Postmaster-General in February 1855. In the Cabinet reshuffle of July 1855 he was, to general surprise, nominated as Governor-General of India and took over from Lord Dalhousie in India on 28 February 1856. At the official banquet given by the East India Company's Court of Directors before he left London, he said that he hoped for a peaceful time in office, but 'We must not forget that in the sky of India, serene as it is, a cloud may arise, at first no bigger than a man's hand, but which growing bigger and bigger, may at last threaten us with ruin. What has happened once may happen again.'

To the Bengal sepoys of early 1857 it seemed the cloud was already there. By their courage and discipline they had conquered for the East India Company the whole of India from Calcutta to the Afghan border. Indeed, in 1839 they had occupied Afghanistan as well, until the vagaries of British domestic politics and the penury of the Government of India had led to their recall. What, however, had been the sepoys' reward? Their basic pay remained unchanged and their *batta*, the campaign allowance payable for foreign or campaign duty, was stopped as soon as the lands they conquered were annexed. With Treasury logic, this was justified by the financiers on the grounds that these lands then lay within the Company's dominions and had ceased to be foreign, but they were still as distant as previously and still as expensive to live in. Most of the Bengal sepoys were Brahmans or Ksatriyas from the plains of Hindustan, especially the eastern (*purabi*) areas of Awadh and the North-West Provinces. To the Purbiyas or 'Poorbeahs' there seemed nowhere left for them to be sent on active service except outside India.

Sea travel at this time was regarded by most respectable Hindus as something to be avoided as much for spiritual as practical reasons. Hindu religious teachers had increasingly stressed the importance of performing every detail of prescribed ritual, especially with regard to daily ablutions and the preparation of food. This did not much affect the lower classes from which most sailors or fishermen came, but it was of concern to those who made up the majority of the Bengal Army. Sailing ships were at the mercy of wind and tide. Fresh water for drinking, far less for washing, was always scarce, especially in troopships carrying hundreds of men. If a ship was becalmed or driven off course, it became scarcer still. In such cases, supplies of the food that men normally ate were also likely to be exhausted, and they might be forced to eat meat which had been prepared and put into casks by hands that were religiously as well as physically impure.

Muslim sepoys no less than their Hindu comrades had cause to dislike sea voyages, though in their case it was the fear that survival might depend on eating salt pork rather than salt beef. Aware of these scruples, the Bengal Army normally offered bounties to those who volunteered to embark, irrespective of whether the recipients actually needed to spend them on purification. In the Madras and Bombay Armies, where religious observances no longer affected military discipline, no bounties were paid, though formal consent was obtained from units ordered to embark.

Twice Bengal sepoys had been ordered to proceed to Burma (Myanmar) by sea and twice this had caused problems. In 1824, indeed, when the 47th Bengal Infantry at Barrackpur, near Calcutta, declared it would not march to any embarkation port, it had been paraded in the presence of two British battalions and then, on refusing to ground arms, had been blown away by European-manned guns of the Bengal Artillery. In 1852 the 38th Bengal Native Infantry had likewise refused to embark, though in this instance the authorities did not force the issue. In 1857 men remembered the first rather than the second incident and were chary of parading under British muskets and guns.

In February 1856 the Government of India decided to end the inconvenience and costs of Bengal sepoys being disinclined to go overseas, by introducing the General Service Enlistment Act. Although men already serving were not directly affected, all recruits would in future be engaged only on condition that they would go wherever required, by sea if necessary. This ended the bounty system at once for new entrants and would soon do so for the remainder. For those whom no amount of money would induce to cross the sea, the Act meant that the career of a soldier, pursued in their families for generations, with its financial and other benefits, would be denied to their sons. For themselves, they feared that pressure would be placed upon them to embark with their comrades, especially when in due course they found themselves in a minority. Some said it was a plot to trick men to sea, where they would be so polluted that they could never be accepted back into their own communities and therefore would be forced to turn Christian.

Religious anxieties were interwoven with economic ones. Communities that had long relied upon military service as a means of respectable employment were becoming ever more dependent on military pay and pensions. There was increasing pressure for land and decreasing returns from it. As if to compensate for their declining economic position and to avoid being reduced to the status of an ordinary cultivator, men clung even more to the distinctions of their caste. As soldiers, they refused to do menial duties regarded as more appropriate to lower castes, such as striking the gong that signalled the time to change sentries. Those who enlisted in the Bombay Army, where there was no tradition of such restrictions, were rather pitied as men who had come down in the world. A reduction in the prospects of a military career, at the very time that it was of increasing economic and social importance, only added to the feeling of injustice.

The withdrawal from Afghanistan in 1842 had suggested to some that the Company's *Iqbal* or Luck (which had emerged as a minor deity) might be losing its powers. Subsequently, however, the Hindu Maharaja Sindhia of Gwalior had been defeated in a lightning campaign in 1843, the Shi'a Muslim Amirs of Sind had been conquered in 1844, and the Sikh-ruled kingdom of Lahore, defeated in two major wars, had become the British province of the Punjab in 1849. With the largest modern army in Asia, the Company was able to annex, without resistance, any other Indian state to which it felt it had a claim. Satara was taken in 1848, Jaitpur and Sambalpur in 1849, Baghat in 1850, Udaipur in 1852, Jhansi in 1853, Nagpur in 1854 and Awadh in 1856.

Awadh, by far the largest of these, had for generations been under British influence but its king had always fulfilled his obligations to the Company. His government was said to be corrupt, but that corruption was regarded as a benefit by those sepoys, some 40,000 of them, whose homes were in his kingdom and who had therefore been his subjects, not those of the Company. In any dispute between a sepoy's relations and their neighbours, or indeed with the Awadh authorities, it was widely supposed that the question would be resolved in favour of the former, by virtue of their British connections. After annexation, the sepoy could no longer ask a British Resident to intervene on his behalf. The Resident, a diplomatic functionary, had been replaced by a Chief Commissioner, an executive one, and all were now equal under a British legal system regarded as little more than a lottery.

Everywhere, regime change meant that Indian rulers and senior government officials were replaced by British equivalents. The previously ruling elite, the natural leaders and opinion-formers of their community, became redundant. So did many of those who had depended on them for their living – poets, historians, silversmiths, jewellers, entertainers and the like – for whom the new rulers had little use. Land-holders were called upon to produce documentary titles to their estates, often impossible in a society that relied on custom and precedent. In cases where no evidence of lawful holdings could be produced, it was often supposed by British officials that they had been obtained improperly during periods of weak government, and such lands were thereupon resumed by the new rulers. Those who kept their holdings were assessed by officials who had little local knowledge but who gained promotion by increasing the land revenue. Tax defaulters were sold up and their lands transferred to carpet-baggers. The ordinary cultivators had no affection for these new men, and though they might have been exploited by the old land-holders, they saw no benefits from regime change. At least the old squires knew them and their ways, and they were bound together by old ties of blood and kinship. Although the British insisted that, in civil matters, litigants would continue to be judged according to the laws of their own religions and communities, in criminal matters it was the laws of British India that were enforced.

In the nineteenth century, Christianity, long quiescent after Christian had slaughtered Christian in the religious wars of the seventeenth century, was a confident and growing force. In response to intense lobbying, the 1813 Charter Act ended the Company's ban on missionary activity and, from then on, the spread of British power was accompanied by the arrival of British missionaries. India was not unused to the presence of Christian priests, but the new Protestant ministers seemed different from the old Catholic *padris*. Most British people at this time were as convinced of the superiority of their kind of religion as of their kind of everything else and readily attributed the latter to the former. When in 1850 the Religious Disabilities Act gave converts the right to inherit ancestral property, in theory it ensured that no one was disadvantaged by following the dictates of his conscience, but in practice it only benefited those who turned Christian. Most respectable Indians regarded converts as low-class individuals who had rejected the faith of their fathers for financial or political gain. The idea of becoming a Christian, involving as it did the loss of caste, kinship and of one's whole place in society, and indeed any hope (for Muslims) of entering a Paradise filled with beautiful virgins, or (for Hindus) of rebirth other than in some loathsome form, such as a snake or worm, was a matter for horror.

Ordinary British soldiers, in India or elsewhere, had no pretensions to respectability. Most of their compatriots regarded them as the lowest of the low. The Duke of Wellington had called them the scum of the earth, who mostly enlisted for drink. In fact they were usually very poor men for whom military service offered employment in a time of economic hardship, with the promise (often broken) of a warm coat, regular pay and meals, and the added prospect of adventure as an alternative to life as an industrial or rural wage-slave. Enlisting for ten or twelve years at a time, they entered communities that were a uniformed version of those they left behind, with the regiment as their village, the colonel as squire and magistrate, his officers as local proprietors (indeed, most bought their commissions just as their civilian counterparts bought their estates), the chaplain as parish priest, the surgeon as the local doctor, and the sergeants, men whose position gave them respectability, as overseers and stewards. The village blacksmith was represented by the armourers, the village musicians by the band, the constables by the regimental police, the innkeeper by the regimental sutler, and so on.

Not all of them were the worthless gaolbirds of popular myth – indeed, some had skills that they brought with them from civil life. Private Adwick of the Rifle Brigade, for example, had been an engine-maker and was constantly called below to help repair the engines of the troopship *Adventure* taking his unit to India. In the defence of Lucknow, Cornish tin-miners and Derbyshire colliers from the 32nd Foot dug counter-mines. All of them, however, were mercenaries, just as the German Kaiser would describe their successors in August 1914. They were not conscripts or militiamen or citizen soldiers fighting in defence of their hearths and homes. Indeed, they had no homes outside their regiments. They were professional soldiers who fought in return for their pay. If no one liked them, they did not care.

Even the hardest case could be redeemed by the spirit of comradeship and a shared pride in the achievements of their regiments. Indeed, it was generally agreed that the British Army was not an army at all but merely a collection of regiments. The battle honours embroidered on their guidons and colours, which were as arks of the covenant to those who followed them, and the stories of victories won and hardships endured that formed the home-spun sagas of unlettered men, all gave the British soldier a belief in his own worth. His predecessors had beaten Napoleon and the greatest generals of France. Only recently, in the Crimea he had won victories over the toughest soldiers in Europe, and in Iran he had defeated yet another army of Muslims. Among the truths he held self-evident were that his regiment was superior to any other in the British Army, that the British Army was superior to any in the world, and that the white man was superior to all.

Sir Colin Campbell, writing as C-in-C, India, summed up the essence of regimental pride in writing to the Duke of Cambridge, C-in-C of the British Army, about an unmerited slight on the conduct of 64th Foot. 'Such a reflection is most galling to a regiment of British soldiers – indeed almost intolerable; and the fact is remembered against it by all the other corps in Her

Majesty's service. Soldiers feel such things keenly.' In the same letter he complained that young ADCs and staff officers were leading troops forward in the hope of being noticed and given the Victoria Cross. 'We know that the private soldier expects to be led by his regimental officers, whom he knows and recognises as the leaders to whom he is bound to look in the moments of greatest trial and danger, and that he is utterly regardless of the accidental presence of an aide-de-camp or other staff officer, who is an absolute stranger to him.'

The officers were drawn from an altogether superior class. Apart from the artillery and engineers, who had attended the Royal Military Academy at Woolwich as gentlemen cadets, few had any formal military education. Those who had been gentlemen cadets at the Royal Military College, Sandhurst, were generally looked down on as having been too poor to obtain their commissions by purchase. Foreign observers supposed that the British Army had to draw its officers from a social class much higher than that of its soldiers to make up for this lack of training, as otherwise the men would not respect them. Rich or poor, however, all considered themselves gentlemen, with a code of honour that impelled them to lead men into danger and risk their own lives for the sake of glory, promotion and awards. Though their men might flag and their generals fail, the regimental officers, sustained by their personal code of honour and sense of professional duty, invariably accepted disproportionate losses among their own number. It was the price they paid for the position they held in their society, something as important to them as was caste to the Indian sepoys. The possibility of death and the certainty of hardship were regarded by them, as by their men, as natural parts of a soldier's life. It went with the pretty girls and the prize-money.

Officers of the East India Company's armies, though of more modest means, and promoted through seniority not purchase, came from the same social level and shared the same code, demanding the same kind of personal courage and leadership that were essential in close-quarter fighting. Having deprived themselves of such leaders by the very act of mutiny, the sepoys depended on the Indian officers whose hierarchy paralleled that of the British. The weakness of this dependence was that Indian officers lacked the military education that most of the Company's officers had received at its Military Seminary in Addiscombe.

They were competent as company or troop officers, but not as field or staff officers. Indian officers were not socially superior to their men, but were promoted from the ranks through seniority, to prevent favouritism. This meant that they could claim leadership neither by training nor place in society and, by the time they received their commissions, most were no longer fit for the intense physical activity demanded of junior officers on the battlefield. Though personally just as brave as any other men, and often admired for their personal courage by their British opponents, they were under no moral compulsion to go recklessly in harm's way. Indeed, as experienced soldiers, they were well able to judge when an attack was worth pressing home and when it was better to fall back. Like their men, they were victims of their own training, and knew how to deploy into line and advance better than how to fight as guerrillas.

While the sepoys found their self-worth in their religion and caste, the British found theirs in their race. In the mid-nineteenth century, and indeed for a century afterwards, most people of European origin round the world took it for granted that they were not merely different from but superior to the rest of humanity. Scientific and technological progress had given them immense economic and military strength, and the losers had mostly been people of darker pigmentation and non-Christian beliefs. Anything that challenged this assumption of superiority was as offensive to them as a threat to his caste was to the Indian. Even the humblest soldier, subjected to years of harsh usage and brutal punishment in his own society, would not endure it. Indians of any social status were regarded as inferior. Such Urdu (Hindustani) words as the soldiers chose to learn often ended in 'o' (the imperative form), and always included 'soor' (*sur*) or swine, an offensive term in any language and particularly so to Muslims. Officers and men alike applied the word 'nigger' to Indians as unthinkingly as their contemporaries in the United States did to African-Americans. Indian officers had no powers of command over any European soldiers, even those on the strength of their own regiments.

The final element of the regimental village was its women and children. Many men were married, despite official discouragement. When a regiment went overseas, only 12 per cent of its soldiers' wives were allowed to accompany it. Officers were more fortunate and could take dependants at their own expense. In the

36

natural affections of most ordinary soldiers, the families of their comrades and of their officers took the place of those they had left behind or never possessed. Attacks on British women and children, whether from military or civilian families, not only challenged British racial superiority but insulted the self-esteem of British soldiers who had not been there to protect them. The effect was to rouse men to a pitiless rage.

Chapter 3

THE AFFAIR OF THE GREASY CARTRIDGES

Na Iran kiaya, na Shah Rus ne,
Angrez ko taba' kiya kartus ne

(Attrib. Muhammad Bahadur Shah, King of Delhi)

When not by Shah nor Tsar had they been smitten,
The English were brought low by cartridge bitten

(free tr., T.A.H.)

It all began with a conspiracy theory. Until 1857 the standard firearm of the East India Company's armies was the time-honoured 'Brown Bess', a smooth-bore, muzzle-loading musket. In 1840 the flintlock firing mechanism was replaced by the more efficient percussion system in which, instead of gunpowder in the pan, a copper cap containing fulminate of mercury served as the primer. The cartridge, a paper tube containing the musket-ball and its black powder propellant, remained unchanged. When loading, the soldier took a cartridge from his pouch with his right hand and opened it with his teeth, while his left hand held the weapon. He then poured the powder down the barrel and rammed the ball and paper after it.

The Crimean War of 1854–56 demonstrated the superiority in range and accuracy of the new Enfield rifle over the old smooth-bore and the Company decided to modernize the armament of its own troops. A novel feature of the new rifle was that its bullet, an elongated form of the ball previously used expanded with the heat of firing so as to fit into the rifling (the spiral grooves cut in to the bore to impart rotation to the projectile). However, to prevent the products of combustion and the hot lead of the bullets from fouling these grooves, the cartridge paper had to include some kind of lubricant. The first consignments of the new rifles arrived in India during 1856, but there were not

38

enough to rearm a quarter of a million men all at once. Even among the twenty-two British battalions then on the Indian establishment only one, the 60th Rifles, at Meerut, 40 miles south-west of Delhi, was completely equipped with the new weapon. While stocks were built up, the usual Army practice was followed of small numbers of picked men being called into training centres to learn the new drills, so that they could then return to their units and instruct their comrades. For training purposes, it was not necessary to wait for the arrival of the new rifles, but only to use the new cartridges, which would fit the exiting smooth-bores.

On 21 January 1857, Captain J.A. Wright, commanding the Rifle Instruction School in the Musketry Depot at Dum Dum, near Calcutta, learned that trainees on the course then in progress were concerned about the lubrication in the new cartridge. A tale had spread of how a low-caste kalasi or arsenal technician had asked a Brahman sepoy of the 2nd Bengal Grenadiers for a drink from his water container. When the request was refused on the grounds that the vessel would be polluted by a low-caste touch, the labourer replied that all caste would soon be extinguished as the new cartridges were lubricated with cow and pig fat, so that Hindus and Muslims alike would be defiled and obliged to turn Christian. Wright, an experienced officer with no illusions about the importance of spiritual matters in Indian society, talked to his men about their worries and they told him that the story had spread throughout India, and that when they went home their friends would refuse to eat with them.

The next day, 22 January 1857, Wright reported this to Major J. Bontein, the Musketry Depot commander, saying:

> I assured them (believing this to be the case) that the grease used is composed of mutton fat and wax; to which they replied 'It may be so, but our friends will not believe it; let us obtain the ingredients from the bazaar and make it up ourselves; we shall then know what is used, and be able to assure our fellow-soldiers and others that there is nothing in it prohibited by our caste' ... I most respectfully beg to represent that by adopting the measure suggested by the men, the possibility of any misunderstanding regarding the religious prejudices of the natives in general will be prevented.

Bontein supported the suggestion, and within six days the Military Department ordered cartridges to be issued free from grease, and sepoys to be allowed to apply their own lubricant. The same procedure was followed in the Madras and Bombay Armies and no objection was raised by any of the sepoys serving in them.

In the more sensitive Bengal Army, however, this was not quick enough to outrun rumour. Various protests were followed by a court of enquiry at which a havildar-major was asked if 'in your opinion, there was no grease in the paper, would you object to bite off the end of the cartridge?' His answer summarized the whole problem of the power of public opinion. 'I could not do it, as the other men would object.' It was clear that it was now the cartridge paper rather than the actual lubricant that was the problem. On 8 February the divisional commander, Major General Hearsey, commanding the Bengal Presidency Division at Barrackpur, outside Calcutta, reported that it 'would be both idle and unwise' to attempt to persuade the troops that the new paper did not contain cow or pig fat, and recommended that the old type of paper be used for the new cartridges in order to meet their objections.

At Dum Dum, Bontein suggested that the whole issue could be avoided by simply changing the drill, which, he said, was really a relic of the days when muskets were fired by flintlocks, which required priming with a small amount of powder from the cartridge before the rest was rammed down the barrel. Since the adoption of the percussion system, several regiments had unofficially followed the practice of raising the cartridge to the lips with the right hand, as required by the drill, but not biting it. Instead, when the cartridge was then brought down to the muzzle of the musket (held in the soldier's left hand) prior to loading, the men opened the cartridge by tearing it with the finger and thumb of the left hand holding the musket. Bontein proposed that this procedure be authorized for the whole army and this was subsequently done.

Nevertheless, at Berhampur, a hundred miles to the north, the 19th Bengal Native Infantry refused to prepare for musketry training. Their commanding officer went to their lines, pointed out that the cartridges with which they were to be issued had been made up more than a year previously, and said that anyone who disobeyed his orders would be severely punished. In a subsequent

40

petition, the Indian officers and NCOs of the regiment declared, 'He gave this order so angrily that we were convinced the cartridges were greased, otherwise he would not have spoken so.' After further incidents, the Government of India determined to make an example of the regiment by disbanding it and ordered the 84th Foot from Rangoon to Barrackpur to ensure that no resistance took place.

Meanwhile, at the court martial of Jemadar Salik Ram Singh for stating that he would not bite the new cartridges, Colonel A. Abbott, Inspector-General of Ordnance, said that the tallow used to lubricate the new cartridges was supplied by contractors and might have come from cows or other animals. As soon as he realized this, he said, he had stopped their issue, but news of this sensational evidence rapidly spread throughout the Army, where every soldier knew that defence contractors were greedy profiteers who invariably supplied the cheapest materials they could find. Salik Ram, experienced in military litigation, sought to show that the majority of the witnesses against him were actuated by personal spite, but was found guilty and sentenced to dismissal. Anson regarded the verdict as too lenient and at first refused to confirm it, but the Indian officers forming the court martial for once resisted pressure from above.

By this stage, however, there was nothing that anyone could say that would dispel the rumours. The 84th Foot reached Calcutta on 20 March and, together with a wing of the 53rd Foot, two batteries of artillery, and the Governor-General's Bodyguard, was hurried up the Ganges to Chinsura, about 8 miles away from Barrackpore. In the late afternoon of 29 March, a sepoy of the 34th ran to Hearsey's house to say that the entire brigade was turning out in confusion. Hearsey then discovered Sepoy Mangal Pande of the 34th pacing up and down outside the regimental guardroom, abusing his comrades for failing to join him in defending their religion against the newly arrived European troops. Jemadar Iswari Pande, the guard commander, had made no effort to arrest Mangal, who was armed both with a musket and an Indian sword, and had wounded both his adjutant and his sergeant major when they came to investigate. A group of British officers had gathered to watch these proceedings and one shouted to Hearsey that the sepoy had a loaded musket.

The General arrested Mangal Pande, who tried to commit suicide with his own musket but succeeded only in wounding himself and setting fire to his clothes. Hearsey rode among the men of the 34th, telling them that they had failed in their duty by not arresting Mangal Pande. Some answered that the man was mad from excessive use of *bhang* (hemp or cannabis) to which he replied, 'Could you not have seized him, and if he resisted have shot him or maimed him. Would you not have done so to a mad elephant or to a mad dog, and what difference was there in the dangerous madness of a man and the same in an elephant or a dog?' Not disputing their general's attitude to the treatment of mental ill-health, they said, 'He had loaded his musket', provoking the scornful reply, 'What, are you afraid of a loaded musket?' With the example of their own officers before them, they clearly were, but no one argued with him and Hearsey dismissed them to their lines.

A week later, on Monday, 6 April 1857, a court martial found Sepoy Mangal Pande guilty of mutiny and violence against his senior officers, and sentenced him to death by hanging. Two days later Jemadar Iswari Pande was sentenced to death for refusing direct orders from his commanding officer to lead the guard against him, and for actively discouraging those members of the guard who wanted to do their duty. The 84th, who had gone back to Chinsura, were recalled to Barrackpur for the execution parade. They arrived late at night in pouring rain and found their tents a foot deep in water, and the next day, as the execution warrant had not arrived, some of the officers went to see the prisoner, held in the guard tent of the 53rd Foot. 'On our entering he got up, salaamed, and seemed very civil,' wrote Lieutenant George Blake of the 84th. The next day the warrant came and the sentence was carried out. Pande was a common name among the purbiyas, and as it was that of these two mutineers, the British subsequently referred to all sepoys in arms against them as 'Pandies'.

Writing privately to his friend Lord Granville in England Canning said that he had been anxious about the Barrackpur mutiny but 'I am rather pleased with the way in which it has been dealt with. Do not whisper it, but to say the truth, I have been rather glad to have the Commander-in-Chief up in the far North-West. He has plenty of pluck and plenty of coolness; but I doubt his judgement as to when and what to yield.' In the meanwhile, Anson and his staff were moving towards Shimla, in the Himalayan foothills, where Army Headquarters was normally located during the summer heat. On the way they passed through Ambala, in the Punjab, where one of the musketry training depots was located. In response to an appeal from one of the officers there, whose men had been denounced by their comrades for handling the new cartridges, Anson went down to the musketry school and for the first time (rather late in the day for a C-in-C whose army was in disarray over this very subject) saw them for himself. Writing to Canning on 23 March, he said: 'I am not so much surprised at their objections to the cartridges, having seen them. I had no idea they contained, or rather are smeared with, such a quantity of grease, which looks exactly like fat. After ramming down the ball, the muzzle of the musket is covered with it.'

He went on to say that he was inclined to postpone any further training with the new rifle for a year to allow the excitement to die down while a full enquiry into the whole cartridge question was held. Canning's reply, on 4 April, was that although in the matter of the grease the government had been in the wrong, by not taking sufficient care to exclude objectionable ingredients, the authorities could not give way, especially after disbanding the 19th Bengal NI, officially for seizing their arms, but really for refusing the cartridges. Anson addressed the course students in person and assured them, as one soldier speaking to others, that there was no reason for them to fear the new cartridges. He asked how his words had been received and was told that the men knew that the rumours were false, but also knew that for every Indian who disbelieved the tale, ten thousand believed it, and it was believed not only in their regiments but also in their villages and homes. He was, however, equally concerned by continuing outbreaks of arson in the sepoys' lines, similar to those that had recently occurred at Berhampur. Back in Calcutta, it was decided that, with 400 of its men having stood by while their adjutant and sergeant major were cut down, the 34th should be disbanded on 4 May. The 84th Foot again moved to Barrackpur and this time the sepoys dispersed in a bad humour. Canning himself thought that the crisis was over.

Some 800 miles up the Ganges valley from Calcutta lay the military station of Meerut, a divisional headquarters housing the 6th Dragoon Guards (Carabiniers), the 1st Battalion of the 60th Rifles, the 3rd Bengal Light Cavalry and the 11th and 20th Bengal NI. It also contained a troop of Bengal Horse Artillery and a company of Bengal Artillery, both manned by Europeans, and the artillery regimental depot, with both European and Indian recruits. A number of Indian recruits who refused to handle carbine cartridges had recently been sent home without disciplinary action, as they had not actually been attested. The commanding officer of the 3rd Light Cavalry, Brevet Colonel G.M. Carmichael Smyth, decided that his regiment would be the first to practise the new loading drill. On 23 April he ordered that the fifteen men in each troop who were armed with carbines, so as to operate as skirmishers, should parade the next morning for the new drill. This caused a great stir and Havildar Hira Singh went to his troop commander, Captain Henry Craigie, to ask for a postponement, explaining that the skirmishers feared the consequences of being the first Indian troops in the station to handle the new cartridges.

Craigie tried to persuade him that the fears were groundless, but discovered there was no way of overcoming the rumours. He therefore sent a note (later described as 'objectionable' by Army Headquarters) to his adjutant, saying:

> Go at once to Smyth and tell him that the men of my troop have requested in a body that the skirmishing tomorrow may be countermanded as there is a commotion throughout the native troops about cartridges ... I understand that in all six troops a report of the same kind is being made ... *This is a most serious matter and we shall have the whole regiment in mutiny in half an hour if this is not attended to.*

He ended by saying that there were no new cartridges for issue, but the men believed that firing any kind of cartridge would be just as bad.

Craigie's opinion was ignored and the parade took place as ordered. The havildar major, Shaykh Baksh Ali, demonstrated the new drill and fired his carbine. Smyth then ordered each of the ninety skirmishers to be issued with three blank cartridges, but only five men accepted them. He then ordered each man individually to accept the cartridges, but they refused, saying that they did not wish to be the first to use them and would only do so if the rest of the regiment did. A court of enquiry into the incident, conducted by Indian officers under British guidance in the usual way, assembled on 27 April and found that there was no adequate cause for the disobedience. It accepted that there was a vague rumour about the purity of the cartridges but declared there was no evidence of anything objectionable in them, and that they could be freely used as they had been previously, without any offence to the religious scruples of either Hindus or Muslims.

Army Headquarters was becoming increasingly concerned at such incidents and on 29 April Anson ordered an immediate court martial for the eighty-five recusants. Colonel Keith Young, his Judge Advocate General, wrote home to a friend that he hoped to hear within a week that all were at work on the roads, or that some had been hanged. 'Severe methods are the only ones left to us if we wish to quell the mutinous spirit now so prevalent.' The court, made up of six Muslim and nine Hindu officers from seven different regiments, sat from 6 to 8 May. The accused made a joint statement that, on being warned for firing parade:

> a number of us said to each other: if we use the greased cartridges we shall lose our caste, and shall never again be able to return to our homes. We then consulted as to what was to be done, and came to the conclusion that we ought to report the circumstances to the captains of our troops, so that something might be done to save our caste.

Their statement continued that the next morning, not knowing what their troop commanders might have said or done, they had turned out as ordered and their colonel had told them, 'Listen to what I am about to say. If you will fire off these cartridges, the Commander-in-Chief will be much pleased, and you will have a great name, and I shall likewise get great praise, and I will have the whole affair published in the papers.' They had refused and been dismissed from parade, but before dispersing begged to say that 'if the other regiments will fire one cartridge, we will fire ten.' By a majority of fourteen to one, the court found them all guilty and sentenced them to ten years' hard labour, though asking for leniency in view of their previous good characters and because they had been misled by rumours. The divisional commander, Major General William Hewitt, an old Bengal officer, thought that their previous good character only made the offence worse and that their attempts to avert the crisis only showed that their disobedience on parade was preplanned. He confirmed the sentence, with a remission of five years in the case of the eleven youngest men.

On 9 May the whole Meerut garrison was paraded under the guns of European artillery, cavalry and riflemen to witness the prisoners being put in irons. The dismal affair lasted for more than two hours, after which the convicted men shuffled off to the town gaol, about 2 miles away, escorted by a company of the 60th Rifles. The junior subaltern of the 3rd Light Cavalry, Lieutenant McNabb, wrote to his mother on 10 May that the men had actually been firing the new cartridges in the riding school and would have fired them on parade for almost any other officer than Smyth (whom, he said, they hated).

McNabb's view is supported by a letter from Craigie's wife, published in the London *Daily News* on 29 July: 'Henry feels convinced that he could have got the men to fire or the parade might have been turned into an explanation of the new cartridge, without any firing being proposed.' She also said that Hewitt was extremely angry with Smyth for having needlessly provoked a crisis. The low opinion of their commanding officer in the Craigie household is suggested by the wording of Craigie's note to the regimental adjutant, in which he referred to him with scant courtesy as 'Smyth' rather than 'the Colonel' and it seems that Smyth was equally unpopular with his other officers, as careerists usually are. Certainly a regimental commanding officer, with his adjutant in attendance, would not normally have conducted a drill parade and it seems likely that he hoped to achieve some kind of a personal triumph.

The unprecedented severity of the sentence shocked everyone except the authorities at Simla, who had made it clear they expected it, though even Anson officially expressed regret that men had been put in irons. Such offences in the case of the 19th and 34th Bengal NI had been dealt with by dismissal rather than imprisonment, and in that no violence had been threatened against their officers, the case of the 3rd Light Cavalry was less serious than that of the infantry. Junior officers who witnessed the degradation of their troopers on the punishment parade wrote home expressing their sorrow at the fate of men who had served so well for so long. One officer, of another regiment, when asked later if he would order sepoys to handle the cartridges, said, 'No, no more than I would order a European soldier to do something that was disgusting to him.'

The Indian troops felt even more strongly about their comrades, men goaded into mutiny by orders they could not obey without losing their very place in the world. Who next would be ordered to take the cartridges? When they disobeyed, as they surely must, they could only expect the same refusal to listen to their case, the same injustice and the same punishment, until every sepoy was in chains. Canning, Anson, Hewitt, Young, Smyth and those who thought like them had intended to smash resistance into a pulp. Instead, they had hammered it into steel. The sepoys had seen their fellow soldiers put in irons, and the iron had entered into their soul.

Chapter 4

THE CHALLENGE.
MEERUT AND DELHI, MAY 1857

For they have sown the wind, and they shall reap the whirlwind.

Hosea *viii.* 7

The mutinies at Meerut and Delhi on 10 and 11 May 1857 struck British India with much the same impact as the Japanese attack on Pearl Harbor on 7 December 1941, or the Islamist attacks on the Pentagon and the World Trade Center on 11 September 2001 later had on the USA. In each case a great imperial power was taken off guard and suffered dreadful losses in blood, treasure and prestige. In each case, there had been warnings and indicators that a threat existed and these, if recognized and acted upon in time, would have been enough to counter it. The problem, as always in the assessment of intelligence, was in grading the reliability of the source and the accuracy of what was being reported.

Such warnings had been discounted in the Bengal Army on a variety of grounds. The criticism seemed to come mostly from British Army officers who only served in India for a few years and were unfamiliar with Indian ways, or from Bombay Army officers such as Colonel John Jacob, who gave offence to Lord Dalhousie by comparing the peacekeeping successes of his own Sind Frontier Force with the disturbed border of Dalhousie's show province, held by the much-vaunted, and much larger, Punjab Irregular Force. Sir Charles Napier, the conqueror of Sind, had published a book entitled *The Defects, Civil and Military, of the Government of India,* but he had his own grudge against that government because Dalhousie had publicly rebuked him for having (as C-in-C, India) cancelled its orders reducing his soldiers' field allowance.

Critics of the Bengal Army said that any officer able to do so left his regiment in order to obtain a better paid post with

48

the new irregular units or in civil employ, leaving the old units with too few officers. Yet the Army Lists of 1857 show that on average, only ten out of the twenty-five officers on the establishment of each regiment were permanently detached or on long furlough. It was also said that the British officers could not communicate with their men and relied on the regimental interpreter (a post held by one of the regimental officers with extra allowances). Nevertheless official reports and private letters describing incidents in 1857 show officers of every rank from lieutenant to major general speaking to their soldiers in fluent Urdu, the lingua franca of northern India.

Originating as the language of the camp or horde (*ordu*), Urdu is an Indo-Germanic language and most English-speakers can acquire its basics without too much difficulty. The greatest hurdle is probably its Persi-Arabic script, designed not for an Indo-Germanic but a Semitic tongue, but for most military purposes it was speech, not writing, that was needed. No one could deny that mutinies had from time to time occurred, but these had generally been confined to single units and speedily suppressed or settled by their own officers. An army as indisciplined and prone to mutiny as its critics made out could scarcely have won so many victories as it had.

Nevertheless, even some Bengal officers were becoming worried. Hearsey at Barrackpur had told his superiors in February 1857 that he was sitting on a mine and several other officers reported similar anxieties. The Government of India therefore knew that many of its sepoys were unsettled, and had taken action to deal with the problem by a mixture of concessions and severity. It had not, however, appreciated the possibility of a combination between discontented soldiers and disaffected civilians.

At Meerut, after the punishment parade, intelligence was equally difficult to assess. Officers of the 3rd Light Cavalry who went to the gaol to pay off their former soldiers found them resigned to their fate and anxious only for the cash to go to their families. Three officers of the regiment planned to set up a subscription for the relief of wives and children left destitute. Some of the troopers consulted lawyers with a view to an appeal. None of this suggested that a rising was imminent, though Harvey Greathed, the local civil commissioner, had thought there might be trouble brewing and returned home a day early.

On the evening of Saturday, 9 May, with his wife Elisa, he dined with Colonel William Custance, commanding the Carabiniers. Mrs Greathed afterwards recalled that another lady in the dinner party mentioned placards in the city calling on all Muslims to rise up and kill the English. 'The threat was greeted by us all with indignant disbelief.'

Others, however, had heard similar rumours. Barely a mile away from the chaste ears of ladies at the Custance table, sex workers (allegedly led by the widow of a European sergeant) were denying their favours to sepoys who had stood and watched their comrades put in irons. Lieutenant Hugh Gough of the Light Cavalry was told by one of his Indian officers that a rising was planned for the following day. He reported this to his CO, but Smyth told him not to listen to such idle words. Gough who, like his fellow subaltern McNabb had been greatly moved by the fate of the unfortunate skirmishers, was nevertheless so concerned that, in breach of military etiquette, he told his tale to the brigade commander, Brigadier Archdale Wilson of the Artillery. Wilson had just returned from sick leave, and despite his cautious nature, thought the warning could be disregarded.

In the late afternoon of the next day, Sunday, 10 May, a cry was raised in the main bazaar that the Europeans were coming with artillery and infantry to seize the regimental arms. Accompanied by a crowd of townsmen, off-duty sepoys ran back to their lines to warn their comrades. British officers heard the noise and hurried to their regiments, where several were shot by their men. As military discipline collapsed, a group of cavalry-men rode down to the gaol and released their former comrades. Hundreds of ordinary convicts escaped with the soldiers. At this time the troopers were more concerned to help their friends than to attack Europeans. One saved the lives of a group of European gunners in the bazaar by riding up and warning them to flee. Another rode to Lieutenant Gough's bungalow to warn him of the mutiny. Shopkeepers hurriedly closed their premises and secured their goods, while a mob made up of the type of individual that can be found in any great city, at any period, and in any country, joined the escaped convicts and began a rampage of robbery, arson and slaughter.

Outside the city lived members of the Gujar community, a predominantly pastoral people who populated much of the hill country of the North-West Provinces. As is common among cowboys in any society, many saw little wrong with cattle-rustling or indeed the theft of any other kind of easily movable property and, though they often took paid employment as security men of various kinds, this was really only a long-established form of protection racket. Now, as law and order dissolved in Meerut, they sent word to their homes in the surrounding villages that the city was unprotected.

Captain Craigie's wife and the unmarried sister of their neighbour, Lieutenant Mackenzie, on their way to the evening church service, had been warned by their mess servants to return home, as the infantry had mutinied and there was fighting in the bazaar. Their driver turned the carriage and hurried back to Craigie's house, stopping en route to rescue a British trooper of the Carabiniers as he fled from a mob. Craigie left them in the house with his servants while he headed for his regiment, meeting Mackenzie on the way. Unable to maintain his original aim of reaching the gaol, Craigie picked four volunteers to protect his wife while he went to the artillery lines, where the civil and military officers of the station and their families were beginning to assemble. They were joined by Gough, who had been escorted there by one of his Indian officers and two sowars. Gough urged the officer to stay, but he answered 'whether it was for life or death, they must return to the regiment.' Craigie, finding neither his wife nor Miss Mackenzie among the refugees, obtained permission to go back and look for them.

Meanwhile the two women discovered how to load Craigie's double-barrelled shotguns, though without help from the rescued dragoon, who seems to have been in a state of trauma following his narrow escape. He may also, given the military and social structure of the time, have been overawed by two feisty officers' ladies, who ordered him to change out of his uniform into a set of Craigie's plain clothes, in case it was only soldiers that the mob was after. They were soon disabused of this belief when they saw their neighbour, Charlotte Chambers, aged twenty-three and only recently arrived in India, on her veranda, as rioters set fire to her bungalow. Her husband, the adjutant of the 11th, had gone to his regiment at the first alarm and she, with a baby almost due, had no one to take care of her. Mrs Craigie sent her own servants across to bring her out, but it was all too late and she was slaughtered by a butcher from the bazaar. The rioters then turned on the Craigie house, but the servants repeatedly shouted that it belonged to Captain Craigie, a friend of the people, and it should not be burned.

Mackenzie arrived and was greatly relieved to find his sister safe, as only two bungalows in the whole street were not alight. Craigie joined him and, partly for concealment, partly to minimize the risk of fire, they wrapped dark horse blankets around the light muslin dresses in which the ladies had set out for church a few hours earlier, and got them into a small brick-built shrine in the garden. Word spread among the survivors of Craigie's troop that he was in danger, and about thirty rallied to him. Craigie then decided to take his party to the artillery lines. His men assured him that the ladies would be safe where they were, but he insisted they must move as soon as they could bundle together some clothes and their jewellery. At the idea of going with them into the European cantonment, the gallant thirty, as he reported, 'looked very blank', fearing that they would be taken prisoner. Craigie, whose leadership was one of the bright stars in the dark night of this entire episode, and whose troop was the only body of sepoys to keep together under British command, once more persuaded them to stay with him, and the whole party then rode off to the European lines.

Several hours earlier, one of the chaplains, the Reverend J.E.W. Rotton, heard a woman servant say to his wife, 'O madam, don't go to church this afternoon.' As their carriage was already at the door and the service was due to start in fifteen minutes, Rotton asked, 'Why should not madam go to church?' and was answered, 'Because there will be a fight.' 'Who will fight?' he said, and was told, 'The sepoys.' Reluctant to believe this, and to waste the afternoon's labour he had put into his sermon, he decided to go to church, but to allay his wife's fears, took their two children with them and armed himself with a walking stick. As they left, he saw the smoke of burning buildings, and then heard the sound of musketry and the bugles of the 60th Rifles sounding the urgent notes of the Alarm, a call to which generations of British soldiers had put the words: 'There's a nigger on the wall, there's a nigger on the wall, there's a nigger on the wall.' He placed his family in the regimental quarter guard and went on to find out what was happening to his congregation.

One of them was Mrs Dunbar Muter, wife of the captain of A Company of the 60th. She had driven herself to church, where she waited for the sound of the regimental band bringing up the troops. She was then told that they had been called to deal with a disturbance and, on turning her *bagghi* (buggy) round to drive home, saw the whole horizon in flames. On reaching home, narrowly escaping a mob that was stoning two European artillerymen, she was told by her house steward to hide herself, a proposal she met with some indignation. 'To conceal myself in my own house, in the lines of a regiment that had reckoned up a century of renown!'

The 60th Rifles, like their fellows in the Rifle Brigade, were the elite of the whole British infantry, trained to act as individual marksmen and skirmishers, and on that account wore green rather the red coats of ordinary line regiments, and she clearly shared the pride of all those connected with these corps. Nevertheless, she allowed herself to be escorted to the regimental quarter guard by a sergeant her husband had sent to collect her, and there found all the ladies in a state of panic, as 'fearful rumours were rapidly circulated, and as rapidly followed by others still more dreadful, a favourite being that the silver ornaments on the pouch-belt worn by officers of the 60th formed an excellent mark and that as soon as the officers had been killed the battalion would become disorganised and helpless.'

Most of 60th Rifles had gathered in their lines, waiting for the bugle to sound the Assembly ('Fall in A, fall in B, fall in all the com-pan-ee') prior to church parade. The adjutant, Lieutenant Cromer-Ashburnham, was then astonished by a rifleman running up to him and being unable to gasp out what he wanted to say. While waiting for the man to get his breath, he saw the rest of the troops running into their barrack rooms and reappearing with their rifles and swords (the term used by riflemen for their bayonets). The commanding officer, Lieutenant Colonel John Jones, later dubbed 'Jones the Avenger', then arrived, by which time Cromer-Ashburnham had discovered what was happening, and the regiment, including all those who had been excused church parade, was forming up by companies.

Cromer-Ashburnham reminded his commanding officer that the men, for financial reasons, had only been issued with ten rounds of ammunition in their pouches. Jones then ordered the magazine to be opened and another fifty rounds per man served out. On his own initiative Muter sent half of his own company (the first ready to move) under Lieutenant Austin to replace the sepoy guard on the Treasury, a mile and a half away. At the time, the extent of the outbreak was still unclear, and Austin's orders were on no account to fire on sepoys. Rifleman Brownlow, seeing a group of Europeans fleeing from a hostile crowd, opened fired on the pursuers and was promptly put under arrest, only to be released moments later. Subsequently two sections were sent from the Treasury to investigate disturbances in a nearby bungalow, and opened volley fire on the pillagers. Austin demanded to know why his orders not to fire had been disobeyed, but the two sergeants commanding the sections assured him that it was in self-defence.

With the rest of the 60th assembled, Brigadier Wilson ordered one company to remain and protect their barracks and led the remainder (less the Treasury guard) towards the native infantry lines, meeting the Carabiniers en route. The Carabiniers, summoned by Wilson at the first alarm, had been delayed while their CO held a roll-call. Several men were unaccounted for, one of them still being with Mrs Craigie. In the meantime, the two artillery units, having hurriedly harnessed or yoked their respective horse and bullock gun-teams, reached the 60th's lines in company with the divisional commander.

The Carabiniers had only recently reached India from the United Kingdom. On disembarking, they had been ordered to draw half of their horses from the remount depot and the rest from other cavalry regiments, whose riding masters, in the usual Army way, had selected only those they could most easily spare. With half its troop-horses virtually unbroken, and the other half either sluggish or vicious, the regiment was not at its peak of efficiency, especially as a good number of its troopers were recruits who scarcely knew how to mount a horse. These last were left behind with some 200 artillery recruits, who had mastered neither carbine nor gun drill. They were, however, judged fit to stand guard over the European lines, including their own artillery school, a large brick-built gun shed which was the only building in the entire cantonment with walls strong enough to provide protection against attack.

When Wilson and his men reached the native infantry lines they found the mutineers long gone. It was by this time fully dark, with the only light coming from buildings burning in the civil lines. A few sowars were spotted returning to their own lines from the direction of the city and the 60th exchanged a desultory fire with them before the troopers made off in the direction of a small copse. The horse artillery unlimbered and fired a few salvoes after them, making a comforting noise as far as the troops were concerned, but with no other effect. Wilson judged the ground to be too broken for the guns to advance further in the dark and thought that the sepoys and city mob were heading for the weakly held European lines. The best course open was to march back and protect them.

In the lines, the duty subaltern, Ensign Alfred Heathcote, who had joined the Army after an adventurous career in civilian life, went out at about 8.00 p.m. on his pony to make his rounds of the sentries. He suddenly found himself having to cut his way through a crowd of sepoys and returned to the quarter guard with his sword covered in blood, where he was surrounded by distressed women begging for news of their husbands. He was sent out again with a party to take over the station magazine from its sepoy guards. The moon, rising just before 9.00 p.m., now gave ample light and after an hour or so, Hewitt returned with his whole force, leaving strong bridge guards along the watercourse that separated the European from the native lines. Mrs Muter and her companions in the quarter guard had heard the distant gunfire with some unease, but were reassured by the tramp of British infantry approaching. It was later said that Captain Rosser of the Carabiniers wanted to take his men after the mutineers. Unlike Gillespie, he was not a commandant but merely the captain of a troop and his proposal, if it ever reached the ears of his superiors, was disregarded.

Dawn revealed the usual scenes that follow an urban riot. The civil and native military lines were smoking ruins. The rioters, satisfied with their loot and fearing the consequences, had dispersed to their homes. The mutineers had mostly kept together and bivouacked about 6 miles south-west of the city, still undecided what to do next. Respectable members of the Indian community, several of whom had saved Christian lives at the risk of their own, examined the damage to their own properties. Subsequently Rotton and the other chaplains buried a total of 41 European soldiers and civilians, including 8 women, 8 children and 25 men. Eight officers of the mutinied regiments were killed, among them Lieutenant McNabb, murdered as he made his way back from dining with friends in the artillery. Mrs Muter remembered bodies being found in streets and ditches and that 'with horror the officers saw the mangled remains, scarcely to be distinguished, of ladies they knew well, lying naked on the ground, hacked with sabres. The soldiers picked up their comrades. The men spoke little. There was no outburst of feeling, though in their hearts was seared the memory of the scene.'

On Monday, 11 May Hewitt sent a situation report to Shimla, summarizing the events of the previous evening and listing his casualties. 'Efficient measures are being taken to secure the treasury, ammunition and barracks, and to place the females and European inhabitants in the greatest security available ... The electric wire having been destroyed, it was impossible to communicate the state of things except by express, which was done to Delhi and Umballa.' The express message reached Ambala the following day, but was never received at Delhi. Indeed, Lieutenant Moller later stated that he had offered to ride to warn Delhi himself, but was prevented by Hewitt and Wilson, who failed to realize that the normal mail system had collapsed.

The first official report from Meerut to Agra, the capital of the North-West Provinces, reached the authorities there on Tuesday, 12 May. A private telegram, sent by the sister of the Meerut postmaster, warning her aunt not to travel there as planned, actually reached Agra on the previous Sunday evening. Its opening words – 'The cavalry have risen setting fire to their own houses and several officers' houses besides having killed all European officers and soldiers they could find' – suggests that the sender knew only what was happening in the city, not in the cantonments. As is often the case, it was journalists who were first with the intelligence, when the telegram appeared in the Monday morning newspapers. The Lieutenant Governor telegraphed the news to the Government of India at Calcutta, from where the Military Secretary vainly tried to contact Hewitt.

Hewitt made no effort to follow the mutineers, but contented himself with supporting Greathed's efforts to re-establish authority in the city. Captain Moller found Mrs Chambers's murderer and had him hanged. Otherwise, 1,500 well-armed European soldiers did no more than strengthen their defences, guard the refugees and wait for reinforcements, when they were desperately needed elsewhere. Rotton, who had retrieved his family from the 60th's quarter guard and kept them in his bungalow until the following morning, wrote in his memoirs:

56

'In truth, our military authorities were paralysed. No one knew what best to do, and nothing was accordingly done.'

On 2 June the Government of India, referring to 'the apparent want of energy and prompt action, owing to which the escape of a very large body of mutineers appeared to be alone attributable', relieved Hewitt of his command and ordered Major General Sir Hugh Wheeler, commanding the Cawnpore Division, to send Major General Nicholas Penny (twenty-seven places junior to Hewitt in the Army List) to take over from him. With the mails disrupted by the spread of hostilities, the message failed to arrive and it was not until 24 June (by which time Wheeler and his staff were all dead) that the Military Department enquired what action had been taken.

Hewitt appealed against his removal and blamed Wilson, as the brigade commander, for not having taken more action. Wilson, quite correctly, pointed out that responsibility lay with Hewitt, the divisional commander, who was present beside him at the critical time. Nevertheless, he readily accepted that he had suggested returning to the European lines and remaining there.

> I may or I may not have been wrong in offering the opinion I did to the Major-General. I acted to the best of my judgement at the time, and under the circumstances I still believe I was right. Had the brigade blindly followed in the hope of finding the fugitives, and the remaining portion of the cantonment been thereby sacrificed, with all our sick, women, children, and valuable stores, the outcry against those in command at Meerut would have been still greater than it has been.

The sight of murdered Europeans lying in the streets may well have influenced his decision not to risk the same fate befalling the rest of the Meerut community. Captain and Mrs Muter were among those who always believed he was right. Writing to his wife on 12 May, Wilson asked: 'What can we do? The mutineers will most probably go on to Agra or they may return here. It is impossible to say.' The British could not follow them in any case, he said, as the only transport animals available were fifteen elephants and a few bullocks.

Not everyone sympathized with this view. Sir Patrick Grant, a veteran of the Sikh Wars and Anson's temporary replacement as C-in-C, India, observed that Hewitt's own account 'fully proves that he is quite unequal to dealing with an emergency where decision, promptitude, and action are of the greatest consequence'. Certainly, there was little justification for Hewitt's remaining inactive on the day after the outbreak. It was true that many of the Carabiniers were recruits, but others were veterans of the Crimea. When the Meerut postmaster asked for troops to bring in a party of nuns from an orphanage at Sirhana, three hours distant, he was told that not a single British soldier could be spared. He armed some of his own staff and went to rescue them himself, though the nuns, with characteristic determination, refused to be rescued without their charges, so the postmaster had to return the next day with a larger party of civilian volunteers, who escorted them into Meerut.

Hewitt sent for four companies of Bengal Sappers and Miners from their depot at Rurki, 50 miles north of Meerut, to strengthen and repair his station. They arrived on 15 May and began work in the cantonment, but the next day, when their armouries were being emptied, half of them mutinied, killed their commandant and havildar major, and set out for Delhi. By this time the British commanders had recovered their nerve, and Wilson pursued them with two guns and two troops of Carabiniers. After 6 miles he came up with a group about fifty strong who attempted to make a stand, but were all killed in a dismounted attack with only one British life lost. The rest, about 280 in all, escaped to Delhi with their weapons. The other two companies not implicated in the rising volunteered to serve on as unarmed pioneers, but the defection of the sappers, mostly low-class men thought unlikely to sympathize with the higher classes predominating in the other arms, suggested that disaffection was widespread.

The Meerut mutineers, unmolested by the British garrison, were initially undecided what to do next. Some were simply for dispersing to their homes, since at this point few on either side could imagine that the mutiny of a single brigade would threaten British authority throughout northern India. Others argued that it would be better to head for Delhi, 30 miles away to the south-west. There were no British units there and thus the mutineers would be safe from British vengeance, at least in the short term. Moreover, Delhi contained another brigade of Bengal sepoys who might well join them rather than be treated in the same way as the skirmishers of the 3rd Light Cavalry. Indeed, it seems likely that some at least of the Meerut ringleaders had already been in communication with their fellows in Delhi.

Finally, though it is doubtful whether those advocating this course thought of it for the first time in the middle of the night after several hours of arson and killing, Delhi was the seat of the old Mughal Empire. Although it had been over a century since the Mughals had exercised any real authority, the dynasty still appealed to Indian sentiment and, for those who rejected British rule, might seem a possible alternative to it. Delhi's proximity to Meerut made it almost inevitable that the mutineers would head there. Without Delhi, their mutiny might never have been more than the largest of the many in the history of the Bengal Army. The civilian rioters of Meerut never again rose as freedom fighters, even when many in the neighbouring provinces took up arms. As events were to prove, there were other former capital cities and other dynasties around which insurgents could gather, but none could be compared to Delhi. The political significance of its gain or loss was immediately understood by British and Indians alike.

The first bands of mutineers crossed Delhi's bridge of boats over the Yamuna (Jumna), and entered the city early in the morning of 11 May, shouting that they had come to fight for their religion and calling on the King to lead them. The King, Bahadur Shah Zafar II, then aged eighty-two, and a better poet than he was a statesman, at first refused to deal with them. Joined by anti-British elements among the population, with cries of *Din, Din* (the Faith, the Faith) and *Maro Farang* (Kill the Franks), they stormed through the streets, murdering every European, Eurasian and Indian Christian they could find. Teachers, missionaries, bankers, newspapermen, businessmen and public employees of all kinds were slaughtered indiscriminately along with their wives and children. The first casualty was an Indian convert, Sub-Assistant Surgeon Chaman Lal, cut down outside his own dispensary. The insurgents then entered the palace where they killed the British captain of the King's guard, and the two senior British civil officials in the city, together with the Reverend Midgeley Jennings (a prominent missionary), his 21-year-old daughter Anne and her friend, the 24-year-old Mary Clifford, the sister of a young Bengal civil servant.

The military cantonment, 2 miles away from the city, housed an Indian troop of the Bengal Horse Artillery and three regiments of Native Infantry, the 38th, 54th and 74th. They had been paraded at daybreak, when it was still cool, to have read out to them details of the court martial and execution of Jemadar Iswari Pande, a proceeding that the C-in-C, India, had intended to impress his army with the consequences of defying authority. It was ill received and when, a few hours later, the 54th was turned out in response to reports of disturbances in the city, its discipline seemed unsteady. By the end of the day, together with the rest of the Delhi brigade, it had joined the mutineers from Meerut. Some men shot their officers without compunction and thereby dragged the rest of the regiments into the revolt. Others joined only reluctantly, and helped their officers escape. The disorder was not a single incident but a series of episodes spread over several hours. If help had come from Meerut, there might still have been a chance to restore discipline.

As the day wore on, most of the military officers and their families gathered outside the city walls at the Flagstaff Tower. The two Eurasian clerks manning the telegraph office (located halfway between the city and the cantonments) signalled to Ambala, the next station on the line, that mutineers had come from Meerut, that several Europeans had been killed, including their supervisor, Charles Todd (who had gone out to investigate the break in communications) and that they were closing down. Then, taking a reluctant Mrs Todd with them, they made for the Flagstaff Tower, reaching there about an hour later.

Inside the city, after a valiant defence, the Ordnance officers blew up the magazine. The survivors escaped through a sally port, but for all their courage, they had denied the insurgents only a few thousand musket balls and fifty barrels of gunpowder. Large quantities of tools, small arms, bayonets and swords remained in the burnt-out sheds and, with all the artillery pieces, were later salvaged by the mutineers. Worse still for the British was the loss of 3,000 barrels of powder in the New Magazine, 3 miles outside the city.

From the Flagstaff Tower, Brigadier Henry Graves, the brigade commander, persuaded the two telegraphers to return to their station and send another message to Ambala. This, sent at about 4.00 p.m., read:

Cantonment in a state of siege. Mutineers from Meerut, 3rd light cavalry, numbers not known, cut off communication with Meerut;

taken possession of the bridge of boats; 54th N.I. sent against them but would not act. Several officers killed and wounded. City in a state of considerable excitement. Troops sent down, but nothing certain yet. Information will be forwarded.

As an intelligence report, this left much to be desired. Nothing was said about the location of two infantry regiments from Meerut, while 'considerable excitement', a vague term at best, gave no idea that so many had been killed.

The Europeans were much hampered by the need to protect their women and children. As in other episodes of this war, many of these dependants were ill-prepared for the hardships in which they suddenly found themselves. The younger married women were mostly either pregnant or accompanied by small children. The older ones were often grossly overweight, the result of living for years in a country where both the climate and the plethora of domestic servants discouraged physical activity. For those of any age, the dictates of mid-Victorian fashion, with its full skirts and petticoats, and tightly cut bodices, produced a costume that was ill-adapted for life anywhere in the summer heat of northern India, still less in a battle zone. Graves decided that his position was untenable and ordered a general evacuation, using the carriages and horses with which the refugees had arrived at the Flagstaff Tower. Some of the ladies protested and wished to wait for their husbands or brothers to join them. None had the heart to tell them that the missing officers were already dead. Every vehicle was dangerously overloaded, but one group reached Meerut safely at about 8.00 p.m. the next day, while Graves and his remaining staff, with several more refugees, travelled through the night and reached Karnal. There he assumed command and sent word to the divisional headquarters at Ambala, 50 miles away to the north, asking for European troops. In the rush to leave the Flagstaff Tower there was no set order of march and many families became separated. Local robbers held them up and stole their valuables, wedding rings and so on, but none were killed. Many were aided by neighbouring land-holders and villagers as they fled.

Among those who sent help was Narindar Singh, the 35-year-old Maharaja of Patiala, one of the three Cis-Satlej or Phulkian Sikh states that had sought British protection against the Sikh-dominated kingdom of Lahore. Messengers from Delhi later appeared at his court, calling on him to join the rising and he knew that many of his people (including his own brother, who stood to gain the throne) were disposed to heed the call. Nevertheless he declared for the British and made an immediate loan of five lakhs of rupees with the offer to double it if need be. After warning the British that his troops would need evidence that they would be on the winning side, he sent some to Karnal (including a detachment to escort the refugees) and arrived in person at Ambala, wearing a suit of mail armour and grey Berlin gloves, and riding his own elephant. Of the other two Phulkian states, Nabha, ruled by its young Raja, Bharpur Singh (Narindar Singh's cousin), and Jind, under their older kinsman, the white-bearded Raja Sarup Singh, also came out for the British. When the Delhi messengers reached Jind, Sarup Singh, who was at the time reviewing his own army, immediately had them cut down.

One group of refugees sent a message to Meerut, but Hewitt, in a decision as discreditable as any of his others in this crisis, ruled against attempting to rescue anyone so close to Delhi. Gough and Mackenzie of the 3rd Light Cavalry then volunteered to go, and with their loyal men rode 40 miles in a day to bring them back on 18 May. Room was found for them in the artillery school, which had been partitioned by matting screens into emergency quarters. Their condition was that of fugitives from wars and genocides in any country, with their homes destroyed and their personal belongings lost or stolen. Most had only the clothing they had been wearing when they fled, and some had even lost much of this.

Nevertheless, Greathed at Meerut could report:

All the Delhi fugitives have to tell of some kind acts and rough hospitality: and yesterday a fakir came in with a European child he had picked up on the Jumna ... he refused any present, but expressed a hope that a well might be made in his name ... I promised to attend to his wishes; and Himam Bhartee, of Dunoura, will, I hope, long live in the memory of man.

At Delhi, while the British fled, two subadars waited upon Bahadur Shah to place their regiments at his service. His adviser and physician, Hakim Ahsanullah Khan, told them there was no money for the regular pay they had been used to receiving from the British, but they insisted they had come to fight for their religion and their king and said they would bring him the revenues of the whole empire. Lacking the mental or physical strength to resist either the demands of the soldiers or the urging of his sons, who saw a heaven-sent opportunity to restore the fallen fortunes of their dynasty, Bahadur Shah allowed himself to be carried along by the tide of events. At midnight a salute of twenty-one guns announced the restoration of the Mughal Raj.

During the days that followed, the King and his advisors, none of whom had any experience of administration, attempted to restore order in the city, where hypothetical patriots continued to disrupt business and break into the houses of rich men on the pretext of searching for Christians. The Treasury had been looted and there was neither food nor money for the troops. Having burnt down their cantonments, the soldiers billeted themselves in the palace gardens and preyed on the local inhabitants. The King's heir, Mirza Mughal, was made Commander-in-Chief and the six mutinied regiments were each given Mughal princes as their colonels, though real command remained with the regular Indian officers. The King went through the streets on an elephant and called on the merchants to reopen their shops and on all other citizens to resume their normal occupations, but terror still haunted the city.

On 16 May the mutineers accused the King's advisers of attempting to communicate with the British at Meerut, through the fifty or so Christians who had been given refuge in the palace. Mu'in al-Din Hasan Khan, a police superintendent who was never convinced that the insurgents would succeed, had earlier persuaded the King to protect the refugees on the grounds that, if the British returned, it would stand him in good stead, and even if they did not, such an act of mercy could only bring him credit. Now, however, fearing for their own lives, his courtiers handed them over to the insurgents and Mu'in al-Din could do nothing to save them. Despite the King's feeble protests that killing helpless men, women and children went against religious teachings, they were tied together on a long rope and led out to their deaths. An Indian eyewitness later deposed that 'The people looked on in dismay, and feared for Delhi.'

So they might well have, given the folk-memory of Nadir Shah, the Iranian conquerer who in 1739 had ordered a general massacre after some of his soldiers were killed in the Delhi bazaar. A Mughal historian, using the graceful Persian idiom of comparisons, had recorded that 'The streets were strewn with corpses like a garden with dead leaves, and the city looked like a burnt plain.' Even illiterates knew that *nadirshahi* was a synonym for Holocaust.

Chapter 5

THE RESPONSE.
THE PUNJAB AND THE NORTH-
WEST PROVINCES, MAY–JUNE 1857

Think, in this battered Caravanserai
Whose portals are alternate night and day,
How Sultan after Sultan with his Pomp
Abode his destin'd Hour and went his way.

Fitzgerald, Rubaiyat of Omar Khayyam, *ed. 4, xvii*

Ambala, 120 miles north of Delhi, was the headquarters of the
Sirhind Division, under a British Army veteran, Major General
Sir Henry Barnard. The first telegram reporting disturbances at
Delhi was rushed into him and he at once appreciated that the
city housed a large magazine and was held only by Indian troops.
He had also received reports of disorders at Phillur, another large
magazine held only by Indian troops, and thought it possible
there might be some kind of combination. He therefore sent
his son and ADC with a despatch to Simla and a copy of the
telegram, assessing that the message might be exaggerated, but
that it was credible, in view of the general mood of crisis then
existing, and reliable, as having come from officials of the telegraph service. He had therefore, he said, sent private despatches
to officers commanding in other hill stations 'to hold their men
ready (quietly) to move at the shortest notice', and had told the
commandant at Phillur to telegraph to Jalandhar for aid if he
thought it necessary. Captain Barnard reached Simla the next
day, and delivered his message. This was promptly passed to the
C-in-C, who was dining with guests and put the note under his
plate to read later.

Having read it, Anson sent his own ADC first to Kasali, a hill
station with a significant European community 40 miles from
Simla, with orders for the 75th Foot (already warned by Barnard
as he passed) to march from there for Ambala at once, and then

on to Dagshai and Sabathu with orders for the 1st and 2nd Bengal European Fusiliers to prepare to move. Messages were sent to all officers on leave to report back to their stations. The Judge Advocate General, Colonel Young, noted that at first his chief seemed inclined to play the crisis down. Mrs Young, as a senior Army wife, knew what was going on, and wrote to her sister: 'he ought to have started off at once' when Anson decided to wait for the arrival of written despatches. 'What is the use of the electric telegraph,' she asked crossly, 'if the news it brings is not at once to be attended to?'

When the post rider arrived from Meerut on Thursday, 13 May, Anson ordered the two Fusilier regiments to march to Ambala, the 61st Foot at Firozpur to take over the arsenal there, the 81st Foot at Mian Mir to send a detachment to secure Fort Govindgarh at Amritsar, and two companies of the 8th Foot to go from Jalandhar to Phillur. An artillery officer was sent to Phillur to assemble a light siege train to go to Ambala, and the Nasiri Gurkha Rifle Battalion, then at Jutogh (7 miles from Simla), was ordered to escort it. The Sirmoor Gurkha Rifle Battalion at Dehra Dun and the Sappers and Miners at Rurki were ordered to Meerut. In the event, the Sirmoor Gurkhas marched into Meerut on the evening of 16 May, the same day that two companies of Sappers and Miners already there mutinied and fled to Delhi. The sappers from Rurki mutinied on the way down and also headed for Delhi. Anson left Simla on Friday, 14 May, after issuing a proclamation that the British government had never sought to threaten the religious beliefs of its Indian soldiers. This was taken as further evidence of British duplicity, just as was a similar proclamation from the Governor-General of India, issued on 16 May.

After Meerut, Ambala was the nearest station to Delhi. Its garrison consisted of two European troops of Bengal Horse Artillery, 9th Royal Lancers, 4th Bengal Light Cavalry and 5th and 60th Bengal NI, totalling 2,290 Europeans and 2,819 sepoys. In the week before the outbreak at Meerut, the European elements had been constantly called out at night to deal with arson in the lines, contributing to the atmosphere of crisis referred to in Barnard's message to Shimla. On the day of the Meerut mutiny, but several hours before the disturbances began there, the 60th Bengal NI had assembled under arms without orders and seemed to threaten their officers. The European troops turned out and the crisis passed, only to be repeated about noon when the Europeans were again called out, this time to face down the 5th NI. One officer of the 9th Lancers wrote that his men, blaming the sepoys for the loss of so many nights' sleep, would have made short work of the infantry had it come to a fight. The situation was improved on Wednesday, 13 May, a mere three days after the mutiny at Meerut, by the arrival of three companies of the 75th, after a march during which they covered 48 miles in twenty-six hours with the temperature in the low 90s F (low 30s C).

This regiment got off to a bad start when its commanding officer came on parade to abuse his adjutant, Captain Richard Barter, because its bullock carts had not been properly lined up. 'This being a new manoeuvre to me I was rather taken by surprise,' he remembered, 'and I stared at him thinking he must be in jest, but I soon found he was perfectly in earnest and perceiving in a minute or two there was something the matter I sent for the Doctor, who pronounced the Colonel as mad as a march hare.' The Colonel was sent on to Ambala, where a medical board found him unfit for service, and his wife's maid came and took him back to Kasali. Meanwhile, his men lived on the rations they had brought with them in their haversacks, and the married officers shared with their bachelor brothers-in-arms the food that their careful wives had provided.

Anson and his staff reached Ambala on 15 and 16 May, and completed the concentration of his forces there with the arrival of the 2nd Bengal Fusiliers on 17 May. His initial intention had been to press on to recapture Delhi without delay, but at his first conference he discovered that his army was in no condition to take the field. Ammunition of all natures was in short supply: the 75th had arrived with only thirty rounds per man; the 1st Bengal Fusiliers, who reached Ambala on elephants and in carts, had seventy rounds per man, but in a battle this would last less than an hour; in their haste, the troops had come without tents and camp equipment. Even the horse artillery already stationed at Ambala would not be fully mobilized until it received its wagons from the arsenal at Phillur. There seemed to be neither sufficient combat supplies nor transport to carry them even if there were. The senior commissariat and medical officers reported that it would take between fifteen and twenty days before the army could be ready to move. This was because three years earlier the Government of India in the Army Department, to achieve economies, had sold the government's own transport animals, on the grounds that they and their drivers were too expensive to maintain in peacetime, and that when the need arose contractors could be used instead.

Defence contracts are a source of greed and peculation in all armies and India had never been an exception. Like most so-called efficiency savings, this decision proved a false economy because the transport contractors, as businessmen, had no animals or men standing idle, and needed time while they found them and fixed on the prices the government had to accept. Canning, writing privately to the President of the Board of Control in London, observed that reliance on contractors had seemed financially prudent, 'but I shall be surprised if General Anson was not impeded by it. Could it have been foreseen that our next operations would have been against our own regiments and subjects, no sane man would have recommended it.' The medical service was equally unready for a campaign. There were no dhoolies (*doli* or litters) to carry the sick or wounded, no medical chests and no tentage for field hospitals. Moreover, there was a general shortage of the civil labour on which all armed forces rely for support, and without which Indian armies of the time could not operate. For a time it seemed that even the normal civil contracts to supply food for men and animals would fail, because the bazaars emptied on rumours of war, and merchants hesitated to deal with a government that suddenly seemed a bad risk. The 75th, to keep their own baggage camels safe, bivouacked with them inside their lines, despite the unpleasant smells and noises associated with these animals.

At Ambala, Anson was under great pressure from John Lawrence, Chief Commissioner of the Punjab, to march on Delhi without delay. With such supplies and transport as his logisticians managed to scrape together, he sent a squadron of the 9th Lancers, a wing of the 1st Bengal Fusiliers and two horse artillery guns towards Karnal on the night of 17 May. The 9th Lancers was an experienced regiment, having been in India since 1842 and served in the Sikh Wars, but the steady turnover of men killed, dying of disease (they had lost twenty men to cholera before leaving Ambala) or time-expired, meant that every year up to eighty men were replaced by recruits from home. Their strength at this time was 16 officers and 493 men present

68

with the unit and 95 on detachment in the hills, while many officers were absent on leave and no one knew when they would rejoin. They were glad to leave Ambala, however, where they had been obliged to hand over their regimental schoolroom to accommodate refugee families, 'who turned it into a bear-garden' as one officer complained. Along with the other British troops, they were inflamed by lurid newspaper reports of the fate of Europeans at Delhi and determined to have their revenge.

Lawrence could not believe that Anson's difficulties were as great as his staff reported, and told him that two or three days should be sufficient to collect all that the army needed to take with it. There had been a good harvest that year, he said (in fact there had been three in a row), grain could be brought in along the way and the troops in his province were moving easily, even through areas that were practically desert. He had already urged Anson, on 13 May, to accept the aid offered by Patiala, Jind and Nabha. With the small number of European troops under his command, Anson was doubtful about the practicality of retaking Delhi, a city whose 7 miles of walls had been modernized by British fortress engineers, and thought it impossible to do so without the siege train from Phillur (delayed by its intended escort being sent to deal with panics at Shimla and Kasali, when it was wrongly feared that the Nasiri Gurkha battalion had mutinied). A defeat would place the entire British position in northern India at risk and he invited Lawrence to consider this prospect. Lawrence replied that 'with good management on the part of the civil officers, Delhi would open its gates on the approach of our troops.' Despite his reservations, Anson appreciated the political necessity of advancing on Delhi and concentrated his army at Karnal by 23 May. On the way, prompted by Lawrence, he issued a general order withdrawing the new cartridges from any kind of use. It was, however, by this time almost a fortnight after the first shots at Meerut.

Although the accident of Delhi being so near to Meerut had helped the insurgents, geography also aided the British, for the neighbouring Punjab held the greatest concentration of European troops in all India. It contained one of the 4 regiments of British cavalry on the Indian establishment, and 12 (including 2 of the Company's 3 Bengal European regiments) of the 31 European infantry battalions. One reason for this preponderance was the suitability of the Punjab for European troops. There were several hill stations along its northern districts, and even in the plains the climate was less extreme than further east. Europeans were the Government of India's most valuable military assets but they were expensive to maintain (the main reason why there were so few of them and so many sepoys, who were a cheaper substitute). Military necessity required two British battalions to be stationed at Peshawar, a notoriously fever-ridden district, but even supposedly healthier stations took their toll, such as Mian Mir, where in 1856 the 81st Foot lost 119 soldiers and many women and children to cholera.

Another reason for the strength of the garrison was that the Punjab was the most recently conquered, as distinct from being peacefully annexed, province of British India. Many of the inhabitants were ex-regular soldiers who had been fighting against the British, at times quite successfully, barely eight years earlier. Along with its 13,000 British troops, the Punjab garrison included 60,000 Indian soldiers who were essential for internal security and to meet the risk of invasion from Afghanistan; some stations had no British troops at all. At the very least, a mutiny among the Bengal sepoys there, even if they simply deserted, would weaken the British hold on the Punjab. In a worse case, they might be joined in rebellion against British rule by those who saw a chance for the kingdom of Lahore to rise again. While troops intended for the defence of the Punjab fought among themselves, the frontier would lie open to tribal raiders or an invasion from Afghanistan. The British, who had conquered the Punjab with the aid of Indian manpower, were thus faced with the problem of how to hold that province without it, at the very time when all their European manpower was needed elsewhere. It was fortunate for them that 34,000 of the sepoys (thirty-two regiments) based there were Purbiyas, regarded by most of the population with contempt and hatred as foreign occupiers. The remaining 9,000 were mostly Punjabi Muslims and Sikhs in the frontier and other local forces.

News of the Delhi outbreak reached the provincial capital at Lahore on the following morning, Tuesday, 12 May. In the absence of John Lawrence, the Chief Commissioner, who was en route to the hill station at Murree, the government was in the hands of the Judicial Commissioner, Robert Montgomery. The local divisional commander was also away and in his absence Brigadier Stuart Corbett, with forty years in the Company's service to his credit, was the senior ranking officer. After a quick council meeting with his senior civil and police officers, Montgomery rode to the military lines at Mian Mir, 6 miles away from the city, and held a conference with Corbett. A Sikh policeman had intercepted correspondence from sepoys at Mian Mir indicating that there was a plan to attack the local Europeans and seize the fort at Lahore. With no time for an investigation, Corbett decided to disarm the four Bengal regiments in his brigade.

By chance, the entire garrison had been warned to parade early the next morning, Wednesday, 13 May, in accordance with the C-in-C's orders that the sentences passed on the two Pandes of the 34th should be read out to every regiment in the Army. Orders for the 81st Foot to keep ten men per company fully dressed and armed throughout the night of 12–13 May were accepted as no more than a routine precaution in view of the news of events in Meerut and Delhi. On the same night a ball was to be given by the officers of the Bengal Horse Artillery in return for the hospitality they had enjoyed from those of the 81st, which was soon to leave the station. To preserve the appearance of normality, the ball was not cancelled. Stands of arms were brought in from the old Lahore arsenal, ostensibly to decorate the mess in the usual military way (they were still there at least eighty years later) but available for use in emergency. Lieutenant Arthur Moffat Lang of the Bengal Engineers later wrote home to his mother that the ball was 'a perfect sham of smiles over tears. Half the Ladies were not present and those who were could barely disguise their anxiety.' Nevertheless they whirled the hot May night away in a scene echoing the Duchess of Richmond's ball before Waterloo. Captain Lambert Denne's partner was puzzled at his insistence that after the ball she should ignore her fatigue, to rise early, have her horse saddled and to go down to watch the parade. Outwardly, this was no more than an invitation to enjoy a colourful spectacle, but Denne, who as an artillery officer knew what was planned, thereby ensured that, if trouble occurred she, and any other ladies persuaded to change from their ball gowns into their riding habits, would be up on their horses and safe in the midst of European troops.

The European element of the garrison consisted of two troops of horse artillery, four companies of foot artillery and the 81st Foot, still much under strength from the previous year's cholera outbreak. They were paraded at 4.00 a.m. and issued with ball cartridges. According to Frederick Cooper, a local civil servant, many wondered what lay behind so unusual an order, 'but the explanation given by one of the men of the 81st was considered wholly satisfactory: "I suppose it's them niggers again."' In the event, the parade passed off quietly. A proclamation was read to the sepoys declaring that they were being disarmed to preserve their regiments' reputation, and to remove temptation from those who would lead them into ruin.

The 81st then fell back to reveal the two troops of horse artillery behind them, each with their six guns unlimbered and ready for action, while the foot artillerymen, who had been ordered to parade without their guns, remained as a reserve. Lieutenant Colonel Henry Renny, commanding the 81st, ordered his men to load and added, 'If you have to fire, men, fire with effect.' The 16th Bengal Grenadiers, who were the first to be given the order to pile arms, seemed to hesitate, but faced by gunners with portfires in their hands and British infantry with loaded weapons at the ready, obeyed orders and their example was followed by the other regiments without further incident. Their European officers, most of whom had no foreknowledge of what was planned, remained with their men, where they would have had little chance if a mutiny had occurred. Lieutenant Lang joined the foot artillery line, 'where old Boileau, revolver in belt, was beginning to look cheerful and poor Mrs Boileau and the Misses were waiting anxiously'. The field officer so disrespectfully described here by a 25-year-old subaltern of engineers was Lieutenant Colonel Francis Boileau, commandant of the artillery and, as events were to prove, Lang's future father-in-law.

Thus the British had succeeded in disarming four regiments at Lahore within forty-eight hours of the outbreak at Delhi, but the garrison remained unsettled. On 14 May, a number of sepoys fled after hearing rumours that they would be forced to bite the new cartridges. They were persuaded to return to duty, but in the meanwhile the senior civilians took refuge with their ladies in the fort while their clerks fled to the central gaol. 'The Artillery Ladies all fled in tears and fright to the Artillery hospital,' wrote Lang, complaining that 'Mrs Corbett who should have had a dinner party and fed me last night, won't come out of the Artillery hospital at any price.' This lady was the wife of Brigadier Stuart Corbett who had ordered the disarmament parade, and was almost certainly among those who knew what was planned, since Lang had previously written of 'poor Mrs Brigadier, who is nearly wild with fright'. He later found a meal with the Commissioner and Mrs Montgomery, who remained in the civil lines and refused to cancel their engagements.

Thirty miles east of Lahore, Govindgarh fort, held only by a company of European artillery, guarded Amritsar, the sacred city of the Sikhs. In a way that foreshadowed the taxis of the Marne in August 1914, a company of the 81st Foot was loaded into forty *ekka garis* (one-horse carts that were the mainstay of the *dak* or mail) and sent from Lahore on 14 May. It reached Govindgarh before first light and reinforced the fort as planned. Firozpur, just inside the North-West Provinces, 50 miles south-east of Lahore, had been an important British frontier station prior to the annexation of the Punjab. It still housed the largest arsenal in northern India after Fort William at Calcutta and had a garrison of three infantry regiments (the 61st Foot and the 45th and 57th Bengal NI) with one regiment of Bengal Light Cavalry. The 61st occupied the arsenal as ordered by Anson, but this provoked a mutiny in the two sepoy infantry regiments. The newly appointed brigade commander, Brigadier Peter Innes, was blamed for having mishandled the whole affair, but the great arsenal had been saved and thus between 13 and 14 May the British secured three major stations, each of political, religious or military importance.

In the Punjab as elsewhere, all those with anything to gain or lose had to decide where their best interests lay. They had to choose between supporting the British, joining the insurgency, or remaining aloof while settling old feuds of their own. From the beginning of the insurgency Sikhs had appeared ready to aid the British, if only because they had little reason to welcome a restoration of the Mughals, persecutors of the early gurus and their followers. Pro-British Sikh princes who had been given protection against the ambitions of the late Maharaja Ranjit Singh had no reason to seek a revival of his Kingdom of Lahore, even had any of their co-religionists in his former dominions sought it. They were, moreover, aware that if the British fell, so would those who had supported them. The Jats, Hindu farmers with a strong martial tradition, had no incentive either to join the Purbiya sepoys who had defeated them thirty years previously, or to fight for the Muslim Mughals. Punjabi Muslims had to balance dislike of the occupying Purbiyas against sympathy for fellow Muslims fighting for their faith. This was especially a factor around Peshawar and the neighbouring tribal territories, where the unsophisticated population mostly followed a fundamentalist form of Islam, and where the puritanical Wahabi sect had in recent years acquired much influence. If the Peshawar garrison mutinied, Punjabi Muslims, followed by Pathans from beyond the frontier, might join the sepoys in the march to Delhi, while Sikhs threw off British rule and set up a new raj of their own.

Peshawar, guardian city of the Khyber Pass, the historic gateway to India, was the headquarters of the greatest peacetime concentration of troops anywhere in the British Empire, totalling nearly 16,000 men, including 3,000 Europeans. News of the events at Delhi reached there on the evening of Monday, 11 May. Two days later Herbert Edwardes, the 38-year-old commissioner of Peshawar, convened a joint civil-military conference including his deputy, the 35-year-old John Nicholson. A man of impressive physical strength, personal courage and commanding presence, Nicholson had achieved a remarkable influence over Muslim hill tribesmen and Sikh villagers alike, and had become the focus of a new sect, the Nikhal Seyns. Like many British military officers, he was a scion of the Anglo-Irish Protestant Ascendancy, and shared their firm belief in the superiority of their own religion and values.

The military element at the conference consisted of Major General Thomas Reed, commanding the Punjab Division, a British Army officer who had served in the Peninsular War; the 64-year-old Brigadier Sydney Cotton, a Bengal Army officer commanding the Peshawar garrison; the 37-year-old Lieutenant Colonel Neville Chamberlain, a veteran of the Afghan and Sikh Wars, the inventor of snooker and commandant of the Punjab Irregular Force; and Second Lieutenant Frederick Sleigh Roberts, Bengal Horse Artillery, present as a junior staff officer. Both Chamberlain and Roberts survived to become field marshals. Edwardes had already received approval from John Lawrence for forming a mobile force or 'moveable column' of European and Punjab Irregular Force troops, located at Lahore, the capital of the Punjab, where it would be well placed to deal with any outbreak inside the province, and prevent any collaboration with the stations that had already mutinied (at this time only Meerut and Delhi).

The conference endorsed this plan, with the change that the Moveable Column should concentrate at Jhelum, where the Grand Trunk Road crosses the Jhelum River. Reed, as general officer commanding the Punjab Division, would leave Brigadier Cotton in command at Peshawar and join Lawrence at Rawal Pindi. The Bengal infantry at Attock, where the Grand Trunk Road crosses the Indus about halfway between Peshawar and Rawal Pindi, was to be replaced by elements of the Punjab Irregular Force and Chamberlain was nominated as commander-designate of the Moveable Column. Edwardes and Nicholson undertook to use their influence with the local Pathans to raise new levies, offering them the prospect of steady, well-paid employment as an alternative to raiding across the weakened frontier.

Reed and Chamberlain reached Rawal Pindi on 16 May, where on the same day a telegram arrived from Canning in Calcutta promising Lawrence full support, but stressing the importance of recovering Delhi. Lawrence shared Canning's view of the political importance of Delhi and had already urged Anson to move against it. When Anson considered entrenching Ambala while he gathered supplies, Lawrence sent him the message 'Clubs, not spades, are trumps', an allusion to Anson's reputation as the finest whist player in Europe. The Corps of Guides, a mixed cavalry and infantry corps, which had just reached Rawal Pindi from the frontier, marched out again the next day, heading for Delhi. On 20 May the 52nd Light Infantry from Sialkot joined the Moveable Column. Its CO, Lieutenant Colonel George Campbell, was senior to Chamberlain but, under protest, accepted Lawrence's ruling that, for political reasons, Chamberlain (one of the Chief Commissioner's favourites) must retain command.

Canning at this time was convinced that Anson, with four European regiments from the Punjab's normal garrison of twelve, and various Indian units still under command, would easily crush the six sepoy regiments at Delhi. His greater concern was for Awadh, Bihar, Bengal and the North-West Provinces, where between Meerut and Calcutta, each of which held two European regiments, there were only another three. These were the 10th Foot at Dinapur, nearly 400 miles up-country from Calcutta, guarding Patna, capital of Bihar, on whose opium crop the

Government of India relied for much of its revenue; the 32nd Foot at Lucknow, capital of the recently annexed province of Oude; and the 3rd Bengal Europeans at Agra. Along the vital military artery of the Grand Trunk Road, every important crossing of the Ganges, including Varanasi (Benares), the holy city of the Hindus, Allahabad, at the confluence of the Ganges and Yamuna, and Kanpur, a major logistics base on the Awadh border, was left to sepoy units and a few European artillerymen. The same applied in the case of the numerous minor stations, most of which were held by single regiments, though Bareilly, in Rohilkhand, the hilly northernmost region of the North-West Provinces, between the Punjab and Awadh, housed an entire brigade.

First reports of the Meerut outbreak reached Calcutta, a thousand miles to the east, via Agra, on 12 May. More information arrived during the next two days and on 14 May, realizing the extent of the emergency, Canning began to gather what European reinforcements he could. The 35th Foot, on the Bengal establishment, was summoned from Myanmar. Lord Elphinstone, Governor of Bombay, was asked to hurry two British regiments (64th Foot and 78th Highlanders) back from the Gulf, where the brief war against Iran had just ended. From the Bombay establishment, a British regiment from Karachi was to be sent by steamer up the Indus and cross from Sind into the Punjab. Lord Harris, Governor of Madras, was asked to send the 1st Madras Fusiliers and the wing of the 43rd Foot that had recently landed from South Africa, leaving him with the two remaining regiments of Madras Europeans, two regiments of Foot, and the 12th Royal Lancers. Sir Henry Ward, the Governor of Ceylon (Sri Lanka), a separate colony not under the Government of India, was asked to spare 500 Europeans.

All responded to Canning's call, and on 17 May Elphinstone offered to speed news of the outbreak to London by sending a fast steamer from Bombay to overtake the weekly mail that had left four days earlier. Unaccountably, Canning declined this offer and sent his despatch by the usual schedule from Calcutta two days later. By the same mail he asked for the restoration to the Indian establishment of the two British regiments that had been withdrawn at the time of the Crimean War, and also for authority to raise three more regiments of the Company's Europeans. Mindful of the constant demand by military

76

establishers for 'compensating reductions', he explained that these would replace the six mutinied sepoy units.

On 19 May Canning sent officially to Lord Elgin, at sea en route to China with a British expeditionary force, appealing for the temporary diversion of his troops to Bengal. Writing to him privately at the same time, he gave a clear appreciation of the British position at that time. 'Our hold of Bengal – and the Upper Provinces – depends on the turn of a word – a look.' While Delhi remained in rebel hands, he said, a single act by a foolish commanding officer might lead to a general rising in those areas where there were no British troops 'and where an army in rebellion would have everything its own way for weeks and months to come'. If any one of the regiments below Agra mutinied, 'there is not a fort, or cantonment, or station in the plains of the Ganges that would not be in their hands in a fortnight. It would be exactly the same in Oude ... the critical moments are now – and for the next ten or twelve days to come.' He still hoped things might go well, but he asked Elgin for his troops, not to deal with the immediate crisis, which he admitted they would not arrive in time to affect, but with the consequences if mutiny spread. Elgin, who had reached Singapore before the mails found him on 4 June, sent his troops to India and went on to Hong Kong, never expecting that they would be detained as long as, in the event, they were.

Despite his concerns, Canning put on a bold face and insisted that Calcutta routine should go on as normal. He declined suggestions that he should replace his Indian escort with Europeans, and Lady Canning continued to take her usual evening drive round the city escorted by sowars of the Governor-General's Bodyguard. To avoid the appearance of alarm, he ordered the annual ball held in honour of the Queen's birthday to go ahead on 25 May as planned. Many among the British community in Calcutta, however, reading blood-curdling reports in their newspapers and fearing for the safety of themselves and their families, took a different attitude. The Prussian Marshal Blücher had said some fifty years earlier, on visiting the capital of his British allies, 'What a city to loot'. Much the same, its European community felt, could be said of Calcutta, the second city of the Empire. With only two British regiments to stop them, why would not the sepoys at Barrackpur and Berhampore, a day's march away, follow the example of those at Meerut and

Delhi? Respectable citizens went about wearing side arms, and turned out at the inevitable false alarms. Some took to sleeping aboard ship. Others, including members of chambers of trade, the Freemasons, and the French and Armenian associations, offered to form themselves into volunteer corps for the defence of their hearths and homes. Canning rejected their military ambitions, which he thought would only alienate their Indian fellow-subjects and told them they could be sworn as special constables, an answer they found unsatisfactory. In a letter of 20 May to the President of the Board of Control, he spoke scornfully of officers and officials who crawled about 'with their tails between their legs frightening themselves and everybody else with their whinings' and thought that by such panicky behaviour they might bring about the very events that they feared.

Even greater alarm was being felt in Agra, 800 miles up the Ganges. The news from Meerut was received initially with mixed reaction. The special edition of Agra's *Mofussullite* newspaper published on the morning of 11 May expected that the two British regiments at Meerut would speedily restore order there, and it was only in the course of the following two days that the extent of the rising emerged. On 13 May there came a report that the mutineers were about to appear before Agra, though a moment's analysis would have shown that this meant an unlikely march of some 150 miles in less than three days. The Lieutenant Governor of the North-West Provinces, the 50-year-old John Colvin, planned to move all the Christians into the city's great Mughal palace-fortress but, in response to protests that this would mean abandoning his capital to the insurgents, decided only to place some British troops in the fort and raise European volunteers as reinforcements. Having just heard of the armistice with Iran, he telegraphed Canning to ask for the British regiments no longer required there.

Despite his initial decision to withdraw into the fort, Colvin was well aware of the need to show a bold front. He saw the rising as a Muslim rebellion and decided to play the religious card himself. Accordingly, he called on the great Hindu princes on his borders, the Maharaja Sindhia of Gwalior and the Raja of Bharatpur, to send troops to help him maintain British rule. Both rulers did so, though Sindhia warned that his men were unreliable and the Bharatpur men proved to be ill-armed peasants. Colvin reviewed his troops and urged the Europeans to regard the sepoys as comrades in arms. Speaking to the sepoys, he told them they had his confidence, but that if anyone wished to take his discharge, they had only to step forward. None did so, and on 16 May he felt able to telegraph to Canning that the worst of the storm had passed. Three days later the 9th Bengal NI at Aligarh, 50 miles north of Agra, mutinied, opened the gaol, plundered the treasury and marched for Delhi.

As the British hold on the North-West Provinces began to weaken, the position on the Punjab's north-west frontier became critical. On 21 May it was decided to disarm most of the Purbiyas there and use their equipment for new local levies. This decision proved a brilliant success, as it produced a large number of warlike individuals for the British service and at the same time removed them from where they might have posed a danger. The hill tribes had no love for the British, but the moon of Muslim solidarity paled before the dawning sun of prospective loot. Only in British uniforms could they emulate their ancestors and reach the fabulous wealth of Hindustan. Once there, the remoteness of their mountain homes would keep them loyal to their British paymasters.

In the North-West Provinces, with the insurgents at Delhi between them and the C-in-C's Punjab-based army, the only course open was to hold on until reinforcements arrived from Calcutta. At Agra, Colvin was strongly influenced by an appeal from Colonel Colin Troup, second-in-command at Bareilly, for a statement that would allay the religious fears that were the cause of the troubles, but avoid any mention of punishment for mutiny. He telegraphed Canning on 24 May, saying he was sure that many men among the rebels were only there reluctantly and many genuinely believed that the British wanted to destroy their caste. His view was that the only way of ending the revolt (still only two weeks old) before it turned into a civil war was to assure those who had not yet joined it that the government had no designs on their religion, and to give the rest a chance of returning to duty.

The next day, without waiting for a reply from Canning, he issued a proclamation on his own authority. 'A weighty reason with me has been the total dissolution of order and the loss of every means of control in many districts,' he told the Governor-General. 'My latest letter from Meerut is now seven days old and not a single letter has reached me from the Commander-in-Chief.'

Accordingly, he proclaimed that men who wished to return quietly to their homes would be allowed to do so on giving up their arms at any government post. Only those who had instigated disturbances or who were 'guilty of heinous crimes against private persons' would be punished. Anyone who subsequently bore arms against the government would be treated as an enemy.

The proclamation was supported by all Colvin's advisers at Agra, but met a quite different reception at Calcutta, where it was roundly condemned as shameful and humiliating. Writing privately to the President of the Board of Control, Canning declared: 'I was never more amazed in my life than when I saw what Colvin had done. His judgement had been so calm and sound up to that moment.' Colvin was ordered to withdraw his proclamation and issue a new one from Canning, offering amnesty to men of regiments that had simply deserted, but not of those in which officers had been murdered. None of the mutineers responded to either proclamation. Those who had been in the murderous regiments, even though as individuals they might have been innocent, still had no incentive to leave their comrades. Those who believed that the government planned to destroy their caste saw these proclamations as they had all previous ones – further proof of government deception. In any case, as the British were losing control of district after district, any offers from them were, as would be said of offers made nearly ninety years later, post-dated cheques drawn on a failing bank. For men who had placed their feet in the stirrups of rebellion and had their hands on the reins of success, this was not a time to consider abandoning what they had already gained.

Canning's disinclination to temporize owed something to the knowledge that the 1st Madras Fusiliers had arrived on 23 May, and that in anticipation of this the 84th Foot had begun to move up-country to Varanasi three days earlier. For the first 120 miles they went by rail to Raniganj, where the line ended. From there some went on by river steamer, but at this season the Ganges was at its lowest, and the boats had to weave their way slowly between shallows and sandbars, and took sixteen days on the journey. Handicapped by the same shortage of transport that had delayed Anson's departure from Amritsar, the rest of the regiment moved up the Grand Trunk Road in horse-drawn ekkas and bullock carts. The *ekka gari* could carry only two passengers, and the system took five days to deliver eighteen men (later increased to twenty-four when two extra carriages were added) from Raniganj to Varanasi. There were enough bullock carts to carry a hundred men at a time. Notionally men could go faster than bullocks, which moved at a pace of one and a half miles per hour, but Europeans could not march in the summer heat. Once the road trains were established, with fresh animals replacing tired ones at every stage to allow continuous progress, they moved their tiny loads forward in a steady stream, with 124 men arriving at their destination every day. Lady Canning thought that it was like sending reinforcements in teaspoonfuls. The first sixteen men of the 84th reached Varanasi on 25 May, having covered the 250 miles from the Raniganj railhead in five days and nights.

The Madras Fusiliers followed the 84th as soon as they disembarked. Their commanding officer, Colonel James Neill, a stern figure in the mould of Cromwell's Ironsides, was just as convinced of the righteousness of his own religion as his Muslim and Hindu foes were of theirs. With previous service in Myanmar to his credit, he had volunteered for the Crimea but arrived when the fighting was almost over. Ordered to Bengal with his regiment on the outbreak of the Mutiny, he saw the chance to do God's work zealously and hurried his men forward. The barges bringing them from their steamer to the Calcutta railway station were delayed by the low water in the river and, with their locomotive in full steam, the railway officials refused to hold up the departure of a scheduled train for them. Strong words were exchanged and Neill was told that he had no powers of command over the railway. He told the railwaymen that they were no better than traitors and placed the stationmaster, engineer and stoker under arrest while his men entrained.

In the Punjab, General Anson re-established communications between his own headquarters at Ambala and Hewitt at Meerut. The telegraph line was repaired and played a vital part in the British conduct of operations ('These were the strings that strangled us,' said one Indian officer after the war) but Anson preferred to use staff officers. The road was found clear and the two forces thereafter remained in contact. On 23 May he ordered Hewitt to march from Meerut on 1 or 2 June and rendezvous with him at Bhagpat four days later. Ambala, with most of the European families sent to hill stations for safety, would be left with two companies of fusiliers supported by those Europeans unfit for field duty. On 21 May Anson had noted that the 9th Lancers, about to leave for Karnal, had reported cases of cholera. On 27 May his Adjutant General, Colonel Charles Chester, reported to the Military Secretary at Calcutta that Anson had died from the same cause, Barnard had succeeded to the command and Reed was joining them from Lahore.

Complying with Anson's last orders, Hewitt sent out half of his troops on 27 May, under the command of Archdale Wilson. The military element of the column consisted of two squadrons of the Carabiniers, a wing of the 60th Rifles, an artillery brigade made up of a troop of horse artillery under Major Henry Tombs, a light field battery and two 18-pdrs, a detachment of sappers and some irregular cavalry, totalling less than a thousand effectives. With them went a horde of non-combatant camp followers, drivers, grooms, grass-cutters, bearers, water-carriers, sweepers (sanitary men), tent-pitchers, caterers, merchants, and all the others who made up the moving township of an Indian army on campaign. Wilson's own headquarters was joined by Greathed as commissioner in charge of civil affairs. John Rotton went along as chaplain, experiencing camp life for the first time. He afterwards wrote that 'many and strange thoughts' filled his mind, and 'While I dwelt with pleasure on happy anticipation of the future, I could not altogether divest myself of some feelings of misgiving and pain.'

Marching by night and resting by day so as to escape the summer heat, they reached the iron suspension bridge over the Hindan River at Ghazi-al-Din Nagar, 9 miles from Delhi, on the morning of 30 May. At about 4.00 p.m, while most of his men dozed, Wilson's picquets galloped in to report that an attack was imminent. They were immediately followed by heavy artillery rounds landing in the camp. While his two 18-pdrs, already in position, replied, Wilson sent two companies of Rifles, supported by Tombs's troop and a squadron of Carabiniers, over the bridge. When these parties came under fire from heavy guns, he ordered two more companies forward, with the sappers and a troop of Carabiniers in support, while the light battery came into action below the bridge. The sepoy gun line had been established beyond the bridge at the end of a 600-yard-long causeway, where in normal times a bar collected tolls from passing traffic. Counter-battery fire from the 18-pdrs and Tombs's troop silenced the enemy heavy guns, already under long-range fire from the Enfields of riflemen advancing under cover of the causeway's embankments.

The sepoys had marched from Delhi under the command of the King's grandson, Mirza Abu Bakr, with the aim of taking Meerut. The King himself encouraged this as a means of removing large numbers of unruly soldiers from the city, along with Abu Bakr himself, who had been leading their robbery of his grandfather's own subjects. With tactical command left to the regular officers, Abu Bakr, lacking military training and combat experience, could only observe the battle and send messages to his troops praising the good shooting of their artillery. When British shells exploded near him, he took himself to the rear with his escort. This disheartened his men, who began to abandon their guns and followed him from the field. The British moved round to attack a nearby village where a number of the mutineers had taken cover and killed about fifty of them there. British casualties amounted to eleven killed and nineteen wounded. Though satisfied with the performance of his men in this, the first conventional engagement of the war, Wilson knew he could not afford even these losses and sent to Hewitt for battle casualty replacements. The captured stores included carts full of sandbags and entrenching tools, and the captured artillery were all heavy guns, so it was deduced that the sepoys had been intending to fortify the bridge against the advancing British, but had been forestalled by their arrival there earlier in the day. These items, however, would have been equally useful against the defences of Meerut, had Abu Bakr's force reached there.

The next day, 31 May, the sepoys reappeared and established a line on a ridge about a mile from the bridge. After an artillery duel lasting two hours, the Rifles took a village on the left of the toll bar and, when the sepoy artillery fire slackened, the whole British line advanced to the ridge. After firing a final salvo of canister, the sepoys withdrew at speed but in good order towards Delhi. Two hours fighting in the midday heat had left the British unable to follow them. Surgeon Innes of the 60th and Ensign Phillips brought the water carriers forward, but of the twenty-four British casualties, ten were attributed to the effects of thirst and heat. An Indian chronicler, Munshi Jiwan Lal, maintaining the Persian literary idiom, wrote that 'the firing of the English had been so good that many of the rebels, covered with dust, had gone to hell; many, like birds on the wing, had fled back to the city ... these wicked men, like decapitated fowls with bloody wounds, had now themselves been tossed hither and thither.'

Wilson spent the next three days at Ghazi-al-Din Nagar, reinforced on 1 June by the arrival of the 500-strong Sirmoor Gurkhas. Not Indians but subjects of the independent kingdom of Nepal, Gurkha soldiers were then, and ever afterwards, liked and admired by their British comrades, not least for what a contemporary writer described as 'the resemblance between the two races in the point which of all others mars the efficiency of the British army' (i.e. a fondness for strong drink). Even the most bigoted British soldier made an exception for the Gurkhas. While waiting orders to move, Wilson strengthened his position by destroying a nearby village to clear a field of fire. Greathed noticed government elephants being used to push down the dwellings of harmless cultivators, but supposed that such collateral damage was an unfortunate necessity in time of war.

Greathed, supported by Hewitt (who failed to send reinforcements), thought that moving further towards Delhi would uncover Meerut to an insurgent counter-attack. Wilson, who had formed a low opinion of Hewitt's ability and personal courage, shared the opinion at Army Headquarters that Meerut was safe enough and that nothing should detract from the aim of recapturing Delhi. He marched on 4 June and reached the bridge of boats across the Yamuna at Bhagpat on 6 June, where the column slept on the river bank, 'like so many alligators' as Greathed put it. The next day he joined forces with Barnard at Alipur, 10 miles short of Delhi. Colonel Young wrote to his anxious wife: 'Brigadier Wilson's force marched in this morning. I can't tell you how well they looked ... Colonel Jones of the Rifles, as fat and rosy as ever. The Rifles in particular, though they had had a long march, came along stepping out merrily and singing in chorus.' The wing of Rifles left at Meerut was later mounted on elephants and, together with a troop of volunteer cavalry, conducted a series of minor operations to secure the surrounding area.

Barnard reached the concentration point three days ahead of Wilson and was joined there by the siege train from Phillur on 6 June. The Delhi Field Force thus assembled consisted of the 9th Lancers, 4 troops of the Carabiniers and various irregular cavalry units (including one raised by the controversial Captain

William Hodson, late commandant of the Corps of Guides and now Anson's chief of Intelligence); the 75th Foot; a wing of the 60th Rifles; the 1st and 2nd Bengal Fusiliers and the Sirmoor Gurkhas; 3 troops of horse artillery and a field battery, with 22 field guns between them; the siege train of eight 18-pdrs and 16 heavy mortars; and the sappers and miners from Meerut. The whole force amounted to some 3,500 effectives, though when Barnard marched for Delhi at midnight on 7 June, a good number were hospital patients who had returned to their units rather than be left behind and miss the coming fight.

Barnard's scouts had reported the Grand Trunk Road was blocked by a fortified position at Badli-ki-Serai, halfway along his route to Delhi. He accordingly sent Hope Grant, commanding the cavalry brigade, with the 9th Lancers and two troops of horse artillery, to outflank the left of the sepoy defences. His infantry was organized in two brigades, made up respectively of the 75th and 1st Bengal Fusiliers under Brigadier Showers, and the 60th Rifles and 2nd Bengal Fusiliers, under Brigadier Graves, the former garrison commander at Delhi, each with a horse or field battery. They deployed either side of the road and advanced, coming under a heavy artillery fire that the light British pieces were unable to suppress. Almost every unattached officer, including those from the mutinied regiments and Colonel Young, the Judge Advocate General, was with Barnard's staff. A large group, conspicuous on their chargers, they made an attractive target for the sepoy gunners and three were killed, including Chester, the Adjutant General. Losing men fast, Barnard ordered the 75th to charge forward, a move that was supported by the 1st Bengal Fusiliers in their own brigade and by Graves on the enemy right. Grant then appeared in the enemy left rear and after about an hour's fighting, the sepoys abandoned their heavy guns and fell back.

In the attack, the 75th lost one officer and 21 men killed and 11 officers (including their colonel, adjutant, paymaster and surgeon) and 45 men wounded. Raja Sarup Singh of Jind, an experienced warrior, wrote to Narindar Singh of Patiala, who was anxious to know how his British allies were performing, and said that 'he saw the rush of the white soldiers at Badli-ki-Serai. In the face of heavy fire there was no hesitation or halting or seeking cover.' He also said that he saw the men who were killed lying across their rifles, on the glacis, and judged that, although it was a difficult time for the British, 'the nation that could produce such men were sure to succeed in the end, whatever the odds might be.' After the battle Barnard rode down to thank the regiment in person and Ensign Wadeson became its first member to be awarded the recently instituted Victoria Cross for valour.

The same award was given to Lieutenant A.S. Jones of the 9th Lancers, who afterwards wrote that, before the battle, he had sometimes wondered if 'the small numbers and inexperience of the officers we had would bring us to grief'. As the sepoys retreated the Lancers pursued them and 'we rode over lots of stragglers who generally threw themselves flat on the ground ... but we were going too fast to get a lance into them.' He spotted a 9-pdr field gun leaving and soon caught up with it on his Arab charger, but 'the six drivers were very plucky little fellows, plying their whips as they looked at me over their right shoulders.' When he came within a sword's length, they crouched between their horses, but were killed by other lancers following him. Jones complained that his men used their pistols rather than lances and thereby wounded the four lead horses about their fetlocks, so he was left with only the two wheelers to drag his prize into camp. His regiment lost fourteen men killed and eleven wounded, a testament to the resistance put up by their opponents even when caught at their most vulnerable.

The effect of the 9th Lancers on sepoy morale was mentioned in the post-war narrative of Sayyad Mububarak Shah, an officer of police who was inside Delhi at the time. Although he confused the combat on the Hindan with that at Badli-ki-Serai, he refers to two parties of Lancers (who were not at the Hindan) advancing slowly towards the rebel troops, 'shaking their lances and making them glisten in the sun. The mutineers did not like the look of the Lancers, and their artillerymen losing nerve, withdrew one of the guns', while their Mughal commander was told by his regular adviser, 'Come along, your Highness – look, the English are advancing along the line and the Lancers are coming with those fearful lances.'

Determined not to allow the enemy to rally, Barnard divided his force into two columns and, despite his own men's exhaustion, maintained the attack. He went himself with Graves's brigade straight down the Grand Trunk Road while Wilson took Showers' brigade through the empty cantonments. Barnard soon came under artillery fire from the ridge overlooking Delhi and moved into the cantonments himself, so as to take advantage of their cover and turn the sepoys' flank. The sepoys hastily redeployed their guns to meet this threat, but Wilson, having fought his way through a maze of obstacles, emerged to take their position in the rear. The mutineers once more abandoned their guns and, as Barnard reported, 'We swept the whole ridge from the flag-staff to Hindu Rao's house, where I had the satisfaction of meeting Brigadier Wilson; and the object of the day having been thus effected, the force was at once placed in position before Delhi.' Barnard's casualties totalled 182, low as a percentage of his whole force, but high among the irreplaceable British infantry, with especially heavy losses among the 75th.

On 8 June 1857, within a month of the proclaimed restoration of the Mughal Empire, the first shells landed in the Imperial capital. The British were back, and this time they were angry.

Chapter 6

THE ETHNIC CLEANSING

Kill the poys and the luggage! 't is expressly against the law of arms: 't is as arrant a piece of knavery, mark you now, as can be offer't. In your conscience now, is it not?

Henry V, *Act iv, sc.7, Captain Fluellen*

Both Canning and John Lawrence had originally expected that as soon as British troops reached Delhi they would take the city and end the insurgency. During the month that followed, however, although British control was secured in the Punjab, it collapsed in most of the North-West Provinces, beginning at Bareilly. Events there followed the same pattern as at Delhi. Europeans who failed to escape in time were killed. An elderly nobleman, Khan Bahadur Khan, whose family had ruled Rohilkhand before its annexation by the British in 1801, saw the chance to restore the fortunes of his house and declared himself Nawab-Nazim or Mughal Viceroy. The mutineers released convicts from the gaol, and then joined with them and other criminal elements in looting the city, ostensibly in search of Christians. Subedar Bakht Khan, a corpulent artillery officer, took command of the Bareilly brigade and led it to Delhi, where he persuaded the King to appoint him Commander-in-Chief. He took the contents of the Bareilly treasury with him, but refused to share it with anyone at Delhi, thus enabling him to pay his men regularly and maintain their cohesion as a separate body.

Fatehgarh, a thriving commercial centre on the Ganges, 70 miles south of Bareilly, was garrisoned by the 10th Bengal NI. Despite the assurances of its commanding officer, few Europeans doubted that his men would soon follow the examples of Meerut and Delhi. The wife of Lieutenant John Monkton of the Bengal Engineers wrote home to her family in a spirit of Christian resignation to say that everyone felt death staring them in the face, but 'We are quite prepared for the worst; and feel that to depart and be with Christ is far better.' She wished her daughter was in England, 'but God can take care of her too, or He will save her from troubles to come by removing her to Himself'. Mrs Freeman, wife of one of the four American Presbyterian missionaries at Fatehgarh, expressed much the same sentiments. God might permit their bodies to be slain, she wrote, 'and if he does, we know He has wise reasons for it. I sometimes think that our deaths would do more good than we could do in all our lives.' Both sides had their martyrs. A rising did occur, and about 150 Christians died there, or while trying to escape, or in captivity at Kanpur. A local Rajput land-holder, Hardeo Baksh, sheltered others in his fort and after three months, in a mixture of bluff and daring, his men took them downstream to safety.

Similar episodes were enacted from Rajasthan in the west to Bundelkhand in the east, as regiment after regiment rose in mutiny, burnt European lines, emptied treasuries, opened gaols and plundered merchants. Sometimes the officers and their families, warned by their servants or helped by their own men, escaped or were given refuge by local chieftains. Sometimes they were betrayed and killed. One notorious incident in Bundelkhand was at Jhansi, annexed by the British in 1854. The late Maharaja, Gangadhar Rao, a minor Maratha prince who had been a good friend of the British government, had no sons of his own, but adopted on his deathbed Damodar Rao, a boy from another branch of his family. Rather like the British king Prasutagus of the Iceni, he sought to conciliate the new imperial power and in his will asked it to care for his widow, whom he nominated as regent until his adopted son came of age.

The widow, Rani Lakshmi Bai, born in 1835, was spared personal ill-treatment but became in other respects the Boudicca of India. Dalhousie refused to acknowledge the adoption as valid other than for private purposes and declared that, under the Doctrine of Lapse, Jhansi reverted to the paramount power in default of direct heirs. The Rani was granted an annual pension (which at first she refused to take) of Rs 60,000 for life and was given her own palace in Jhansi city, with exemption from British jurisdiction for herself and her retainers. She subsequently found the pension was subject to deductions on account of Gangadhar Rao's debts, which she considered to be state rather than personal matters. To pay for the expenses of Damodar Rao's sacred thread ceremony, she asked for a lakh of rupees out of the six held in trust for this prince, but the Government of India withheld the money until she produced guarantors for its repayment if he demanded the money when he came of age. Like other princes aggrieved by Dalhousie's decisions, she sent representatives to lay her case before the Court of Directors in London, but with no result except the loss of the Rs 60,000 that this mission cost her. As with regime change elsewhere, many who had depended on the state or the Court lost their livelihoods. The army was disbanded and replaced by sepoys of the Bengal Army. When these mutinied on 4 June the senior British official, Captain Alexander Skene, moved all the Europeans and Eurasians into Jhansi fort. Without food and ammunition, they were unable to stand a siege and resistance ended on 8 June. With the exception of a dark-skinned Eurasian and her son, who were mistaken for Indians, all the fifty-six Christians, including women and children, were led off to execution. The sepoys then marched to Delhi, leaving the Rani to resume the government.

At Gwalior, the Brigadier commanding the 8,000 strong Contingent disregarded all warnings, including several from the Maharaja Sindhia himself, that his sepoys would join the revolt. He insisted that the British officers and their families remain with their units as a sign of confidence in them, though Sindhia told him this would only be taken as evidence of British duplicity. After various episodes in outlying stations, the main body mutinied at Morar, the cantonment of Gwalior, on 14 June. Most of the European women and children were spared, and some sepoys helped their own officers to safety, but about twenty men, including the chaplain, were killed. Helped by Rana of Dhaulpur and the ingenuity of their own servants, the surviving ladies eventually reached Agra, though on the way they were robbed of their jewellery and rings, and were inspected by villagers assessing their sale value. They were judged not to be worth much, except for Mrs Campbell, the station beauty, who was thought likely to fetch one anna (one-sixteenth of a rupee). Her husband was at Agra and the two were reunited there.

British control over Awadh collapsed quickly. News of the outbreak at Delhi reached Lucknow, the provincial capital, on 15 May. Sir Henry Lawrence, the Chief Commissioner, whose authority already included command of the Oude Irregular Force, immediately asked Canning for powers over all troops stationed in his province. This was granted, with the rank of brigadier general (Lawrence, though in civil employ for much of his career, was a colonel in the Bengal Army). Canning wrote to Major General Sir Hugh Wheeler at Kanpur, to whose division Lawrence's regular troops had previously belonged, explaining the need for all military units in the province to be under a single commander. The troops at Lucknow consisted of three regiments of Bengal NI at Mariaon, 3 miles north of the city, and the 7th Bengal Light Cavalry nearby at Mudkipur. The garrison also included the 32nd Foot, two companies of Bengal Artillery (one European, one native) and two of Oude Irregular Artillery. Units of the Oude Irregular Force were stationed on various sides of the city.

Lawrence immediately began to prepare defences. Stores and treasure were brought into the Residency, a group of strongly constructed buildings from which, prior to annexation, British Residents had exerted their influence over the country. A second strongpoint was established at the Macchi Bhawan, an old palace with its own fortifications. Sikh soldiers were combed out of the existing units, formed into six companies and sent into the Macchi Bhawan with a company of the 32nd. Local military pensioners, Indian as well as European, were recalled to the colours. Dependants were ordered to sleep inside the Residency. A wing of the 32nd was placed in Mariaon cantonment and Lawrence himself moved his residence there, where he gave dinner parties every evening to display his confidence. By 24 May he felt secure enough to send three guns and two troops of Oude Irregular Cavalry under his military secretary, Captain Fletcher Hayes, with an understrength company of the 32nd, to strengthen Wheeler at Kanpur, where the 32nd had left its married families on relieving the 52nd Light Infantry at Lucknow the previous December.

At Lucknow, Lawrence's intelligence staff warned that there would be a rising at 9.00 p.m. on 30 May. Sunset and sunrise in Indian military stations were marked by the firing of a gun, which is why to this day, as one of the many relics of its long service in India, the British Army refers to its early morning mug of tea as 'gunfire'. Evening gunfire on 30 May went undisturbed, and Lawrence told his intelligence officer, 'Your friends are late.' A few moments later a rattle of musketry proved the intelligence correct. Lawrence went out to deal with the situation, leaving his personal sepoy escort to guard his house and warning them that he would hang them all if they allowed any harm to come to it.

Major Bruere of the 13th Bengal NI kept his men under control for a time, but then a group broke open the regimental magazine and wounded their adjutant when he tried to stop them. Bruere led his 200 remaining men with their colours to form a line alongside the 32nd Foot. Mrs Bruere, who had stayed in her bungalow in defiance of orders, was saved by loyal men of her husband's regiment, who made a hole in the wall and passed her and her children out into the night. The cavalry mostly remained under orders and patrolled the cantonments in an unsuccessful attempt to stop the burning and plundering of European residences (Lawrence's was one of the few that escaped). By mid-June 1857, however, Lucknow was the only place in Awadh still under British rule.

The great British base at Kanpur, in the North-West Provinces, 45 miles south-west of Lucknow, was a divisional headquarters commanded by Major General Sir Hugh Wheeler, aged sixty-eight, with fifty-two years in the Bengal Army to his credit. His experience with sepoys and knowledge of Indian ways (Lady Wheeler was herself of Eurasian descent) seemed to make him the ideal man to cope with the crisis and he at first hoped his station would not be affected. On 16 May he telegraphed Calcutta that all was quiet, though two days later reported 'considerable excitement' and on 19 May received a reply telling him to prepare accommodation for a large force of Europeans, and to let it be known he was doing so. The normal garrison at Kanpur was one regiment of light cavalry, three of native infantry and three companies of artillery (one European and two native). The original British element consisted of seventy invalids of the 32nd Foot, left behind with the dependants. These were joined on 22 May by a company of the 32nd sent back from Lucknow by Lawrence, together with Captain Fletcher Hayes's detachment of 240 sowars of the 2nd Oudh Cavalry and half a battery of Oudh Horse Artillery under Lieutenant Ashe. After sending a report to Lawrence about the chaotic state of Kanpur's defences, Hayes led his sowars north-westwards towards Mainpuri, where he was killed when they mutinied on 1 June.

Wheeler was reinforced by some 500 horse and foot, with two small guns, sent by a neighbouring Maratha nobleman, Raja Dondhu Pant of Bithur, better known by his title of Nana Sahib. This prince, though he had a grievance against the British government, had always been on friendly terms with the British officers at Kanpur, many of whom had enjoyed his hospitality, and he had offered, on hearing the news of Meerut, to take their ladies into his protection. Though this offer was declined, the local civil officer, Charles Hillersden, asked him to take charge of the treasury, and his troops were deployed there accordingly, while the Raja himself took up residence in the civil lines of Kanpur cantonment.

The road train pushed on up the Grand Trunk Road for six days from Varanasi, through Allahabad and Fatehpur, to deliver two companies of the 84th Foot to Kanpur. On 30 May, learning of the mutiny at Lucknow, Wheeler returned the company of the 32nd there, followed by a company of the 84th on 3 June. This left him with 59 European gunners, 60 men of the 84th, the 70 invalids of the 32nd, and 15 men of the 1st Madras Fusiliers, the latter armed with new Enfields. Anticipating that his sepoys might eventually mutiny, he had selected a place of refuge on the eastern side of his station. This was a rectangular area covering about 9 acres and containing two single-storey barrack blocks, various outbuildings and four underground magazines. The whole was surrounded by a hastily-dug shallow entrenchment, with the spoil thrown up to form a parapet about 3 feet high, sufficient to protect a rifleman standing in the trenches. It was originally intended not as a major field fortification but only as a defensive perimeter around the accommodation that Wheeler had been told to prepare for European troops.

Wheeler's appreciation was that the mutineers, as had been the case elsewhere, would march to Delhi, in the opposite direction from the entrenchments where the European and Eurasian community were told to go in an emergency. The treasury, on the far side of the cantonment, was left to the Raja's men who, as Marathas, were thought unlikely to sympathize with the Purbiya sepoys. In any case, to move the money would only increase the sepoys' suspicion that they were no longer trusted. In fact the transfer of a lakh of rupees from there to the entrenchments, to provide funds for any expenditure that would be needed if these were occupied, had this very effect. The usual conspiracy theory went round that the British, having failed to pollute their men with the cartridges, had brought in flour adulterated with bone-meal. The construction of the entrenchments and their being provisioned with a month's supplies were seen as signs of potential British treachery. Reports that more European troops were approaching decided the sepoys to act before they arrived.

Equal nervousness existed on the British side. Large parties of Gujar marauders were said to be in the area. Emma Ewart, wife of the commanding officer of the 1st Bengal NI, thought the arrival of insurgents from outside the station would lead to a mutiny and was worried for her small daughter.

> My dear little child is looking very delicate ... It is not hard to die oneself, but to see a dear child suffer and perish – that is the hard and bitter trial and the cup that I must drink should God not deem it fit that it should pass from me. My companion, Mrs Hillersdon (sic) is delightful: poor young thing, she has such a gentle spirit, so unmurmuring, so desirous to meet the trial rightly, so unselfish and sweet in every way ... She has two children, and we feel that our duty to our little ones demands that we keep up health and spirits as much as possible.

Both ladies, with their children and husbands, died in the coming conflict.

The long-expected mutiny broke out on the night on 4/5 June. The Europeans and Eurasians fled to the entrenchments, where later in the day they were joined by a few loyal Indian officers and sepoys. The mutineers started for Delhi in accordance with Wheeler's appreciation and, after opening the gaol and looting the treasury, they were joined by the Raja of Bithur's troops. At Kulyanpur, the first halting place on the road to Delhi, they decided to march back to Kanpur under the Raja's leadership.

Nana Sahib, Raja of Bithur, was the adopted heir of the last head of the Maratha Confederacy, the Peshwa Baji Rao II. The Peshwa was defeated and his dominions annexed by the British in 1817. He was exiled to Bithur, given an annual pension of eight lakhs of rupees to support himself and his family, and lived until 1852, to the chagrin of the Indian Finance Department. On his death the Government of India abolished his title of Peshwa, discontinued his pension and cancelled the extra-territorial privileges of his estate at Bithur, so that his heir was deprived both of honours and income, and subjected to British jurisdiction. Like other princes who believed the Government of India had treated them unjustly, Nana Sahib appealed to the Court of Directors and, like them, was told the decision must stand. Still convinced of the justice of his claim, he sent his personal envoy, Azimullah Khan, to plead his case in London.

Azimullah Khan, a good-looking man of Pathan descent, had been given a Western education at the Cawnpore Free School and had become fluent in English and French. In London he became a social lion, moving among the great and the good with the ease of a courtier and gaining a reputation as a lady-killer in the process. He found the hearts of the Court of Directors less easy to break, however, and went back to India empty handed, diverting from Malta to the Crimean War on his way. At Constantinople he met *The Times* correspondent, William Russell, who afterwards wrote that 'He saw the British Army in a state of some depression and he formed, as I have since heard, a very unfavourable opinion of its *morale* and *physique*.'

Nana Sahib's own account of events on 5 June offers much the same story as those put forward by the King of Delhi and the Rani of Jhansi, claiming that the sepoys – who were (at least up to that point) not his men but those whom the British should have controlled – forced him to put himself at their head. Other versions are that he had long been plotting with disaffected Indian officers, or that he readily accepted their leadership when they offered it to him, and followed them to their first halt with the intention of taking them on to Delhi. Azimullah Khan is said to have advised him that at Delhi he would be in the shadow of the Mughals (against whom Maratha princes had fought for generations) whereas at Kanpur, after driving out the British, he could become the head of his own state. Any objections that the sepoys had to this idea were overcome by lavish bonuses, and the troops then marched back to Kanpur, where they plundered the houses of wealthy citizens and killed any Christians they could find. Nana dispatched a letter to his old friend General Wheeler, saying that he would attack his entrenchments at 10 a.m. the next morning, which he did to the minute.

Though no exact returns survived, it was estimated by survivors that at this time the entrenchments contained some 900 people, including 270 European soldiers, 70 officers of the staff or the mutinied regiments, 40 Christian drummers, and 20 loyal Indian officers and sepoys. The other European or Eurasian men included about forty railway employees (many of them ex-servicemen) and sixty others capable of bearing arms, mostly civil servants and merchants. The non-combatants included 350 women and children (210 belonging to officers or soldiers) and about a hundred Indian servants. Outside the perimeter were a few dozen Indian horse artillerymen who took their discharge as soon as Wheeler offered it to them, and a larger number of sepoys from the 53rd Bengal NI, who defended an exposed position for nine days until rations began to run out and they were sent away with certificates of loyalty. The artillery amounted to eight 9-pdr field guns, a light field howitzer and an old 3-pdr post gun. These pieces were outmatched both in numbers and weight of metal by guns from the Kanpur arsenal, including three 24-pdrs and two 18-pdrs, manned by the two native companies of Bengal artillery.

The very fact that Wheeler had armed his batteries with the light field guns instead of organizing the more difficult move of these heavier equipments confirms that he had no idea of preparing for a siege. He had committed the cardinal military sin of basing his plan on the assumption that the enemy would conform to his expectations. Napoleon described this as 'making pictures', but there is no evidence that Wheeler, the archetypal sepoy general, ever studied the great captains of his age. Indeed, had he not been so convinced that the sepoys would march away, he would not have been in his entrenchments at all, but in a strongly built defensible magazine standing on the other side of the cantonments. There he could have sheltered his people and defied any mutiny that he feared such a move might provoke, using the same combat supplies that, in the event, were used against him. He did not even spike the guns left in the arsenal.

It was the artillery that decided the siege, for although the besiegers had notionally over 3,000 regular soldiers in their ranks, not counting Nana Sahib's men and various neighbourhood partisans, they never succeeded in storming Wheeler's defences. They kept up a constant bombardment though, without any trained artillery officers to control them, tending to fire as single units rather than with regular salvoes. In fact they had no need to do more, since none of the buildings within the perimeter had walls strong enough to stop artillery fire, and even if they had, there was insufficient room for everyone to shelter behind them. Nowhere was safe. Wheeler's son and ADC, already wounded, was killed by a cannonball while his mother and sister were nursing him. In the heat of the north Indian summer, water was desperately needed, but the only usable well lay open to enemy fire. On 12 June the hospital caught fire and all the medical supplies were lost. Grain supplies held up, as did those of rum and brandy, but within days the only meat obtainable was from slaughtered horses and the occasional sacred cow that came within rifle shot. One even scrambled in over the parapet, evidence of the inadequacy of this structure as a field fortification.

Throughout the siege Wheeler was able to remain in contact with Henry Lawrence at Lucknow. On 14 June (six days after Sir Harry Barnard sat down before Delhi), with no sign of the European troops that everyone at Kanpur had expected to come from the east, he appealed to Henry Lawrence for 200 men, saying that his losses had been heavy, but that with such a force he could defeat the mutineers and then aid Lucknow. But Lawrence was in no position to help. Writing on 16 June to the Commissioner of Varanasi, he said that no troops from Lucknow could reach Kanpur, as all the river crossings were in rebel hands. 'May God Almighty defend Cawnpore, for no help can we afford.' The best he could do was to urge Neill to move on from Varanasi in whatever way he could. To Wheeler, he wrote: 'Pray do not think me selfish. I would run much risk could I see a commensurate prospect of success.' In acknowledgement, Captain John Moore of the 32nd Foot, who had twice led sorties to spike enemy guns, replied on 18 June that the garrison had rations for another fortnight and ample ammunition, and were prepared to hold out to the last in the hope that this would help Lucknow. On 21 June, after the insurgents had attempted to storm the entrenchments, Major Edward Vibart, the duty field officer, signed a despatch to Lucknow saying that 'Any aid, to be effective, must be immediate. In the event of rain falling, our position would be untenable.'

A combined attack by horse and foot, made on 23 June, the hundredth anniversary of Plassey, was driven off, but the next day, in a strange mixture of situation report and personal complaint, Wheeler wrote to Lawrence:

> British spirit alone remains, but it cannot last forever ... We have been cruelly deserted and left to our fate ... The casualties have been numerous. Railway gents and merchants have swollen our ranks to what they are ... but neither they, nor I, can last forever. We have lost everything belonging to us, and I have not even a change of linen. Surely we are not to die like rats in a cage.

Lawrence replied urging him to hold on as troops from Allahabad were expected to arrive in days, and warned him against entering negotiations with Nana Sahib, who Lawrence knew to have killed the male refugees from Fatehgarh. The message never arrived, as on the morning of 25 June a letter from Nana Sahib, addressed 'To the subjects of Her Most Gracious Majesty Queen Victoria', promised that all 'soldiers and others in no way connected with the acts of Lord Dalhousie' willing to lay down their arms and give themselves up, would be spared and given safe passage to Allahabad.

The repulse of the insurgents' attack two days previously, the most determined they had made thus far, suggested that Wheeler might indeed be able to hold until relieved. If Lawrence thought the reinforcements would soon arrive, it was reasonable for Nana Sahib to think so too, and this was reinforced by disinformation from Jonah Shepherd, a Eurasian clerk in the commissariat, who escaped from the entrenchments on 24 June, disguised as an Indian cook. He was arrested and interrogated but his disguise saved his life and he was eventually sentenced to three years' hard labour and survived to tell his tale when the British recovered the city. As previously agreed with Wheeler, he assured his captors that the British were well able to fight on. The concept of a garrison being allowed to march out honourably from a fortress that could no longer be defended was a well-recognized convention in civilized warfare and Azimullah Khan, Nana Sahib's *éminence grise*, had attended, briefly, the siege of Sebastopol. Asked if he thought the British would be willing to give up the station if allowed to depart in safety, Shepherd said he thought that they might, as the ladies were anxious to leave.

Wheeler and the younger officers were minded to defy the summons and go down fighting. The older officers argued for acceptance. Moore, whose personal courage was never in doubt, pointed out further resistance was useless, not least because so many of the guns had been dismounted and there were only half a dozen artillerymen left to serve those still in action. About 250 people, including non-combatants, had been killed and the entrenchments were foul with the unburied bodies of sepoys and animals, all attracting swarms of flies and spreading disease in the unbearable heat. He urged that the soldiers had to think not of their own inclinations, but of their duty to the women and children (including many from his own regiment, his wife among them), for whom the summons offered a chance of survival. Wheeler decided to negotiate and that evening two emissaries, one of whom was Azimullah Khan, arrived to discuss the terms of evacuation.

It was finally agreed that the British should vacate the entrenchment the next morning, leaving behind their artillery and the contents of the treasury. Wheeler insisted that the British would be allowed to keep their personal weapons and the standard sixty rounds per man. It was also agreed that transport would be provided to take the women, children and wounded down to the river, and that three British officers should inspect the boats to ensure there were enough to carry more than 700 people. Three of Nana Sahib's officers spent the night inside the British lines as evidence of good faith.

On the morning of 26 June, a train of elephants and bullock carts arrived at the entrenchments. There were not enough to carry everyone and Moore, who was in charge of the move, took the first party down to the Ganges, a mile away, before returning for the remainder. The sick and wounded were carried in litters and the rest went on foot. While waiting for the transport to return, some of the sepoys went inside the abandoned defences and talked to their officers, complimenting them on having stood a twenty-one days' siege against overwhelming odds, asking after those they could not see and expressing regret on finding they had been killed. Some accounts, however, speak of attempts to rob the British of their valuables or weapons.

By 9.00 a.m. all the forty boats had been loaded. Hastily obtained from local contractors, most had thatched roofs to give protection from the sun and, during the night, work had been started on the rest. The monsoon had not yet broken and the river was so low that the boats could not lie alongside the steep banks and, for lack of gangplanks, the passengers had to wade or be carried out. As the last officer boarded, someone fired a musket and the British immediately fired back into the crowd of sepoys and spectators lining the bank. The boatmen abandoned their vessels, most of which had gone aground under the weight of their passengers and could not be moved even when men jumped overboard to push them off. The thatched roofs caught fire, either from braziers that the boatmen had stowed there or from the British muskets. Under cannon and small-arms fire, women and children hid behind what shelter they could find, or stood in the river to avoid the bullets. Cavalrymen rode into the water to cut down the British soldiers, whose cartridges had become soaked and useless. About sixty men, non-combatants among them, reached the bank only to be killed there. The surviving Indian servants were allowed to escape and the loyal sepoys were mostly spared, though placed under arrest. Wheeler perished along with the rest of his command. The valiant Captain Moore, the Hector of the defence, lay dead beside the hollow boats. The surviving 125 women and children were led away captive, like the women of Troy.

Only one boat, heavily overloaded, got away. It was constantly attacked as it travelled downriver, and of those on board only two officers and two men reached safety. On 29 June they were taken in by a Rajput land-holder, Digvijaya Singh, who kept them in his fort at Murar Mau and refused to hand them over to Nana Sahib. The only others to escape the massacre at the boats were two Eurasian girls, Wheeler's younger daughter Margaret, and Amelia Horne, the daughter of a sea officer. Both were carried off by Muslim troopers, who married them according to Sharia law. Margaret Wheeler chose never to return to British Indian society, but Amy Horne was released after ten dangerous months and published a detailed account of her experiences.

British public opinion had no doubt that Nana Sahib was responsible for a pre-planned act of treachery. More cautious commentators, contemporary British military officers among them, have suggested that the affair was not of his making. Nana Sahib himself was not present at the embarkation and sent orders to stop the killing of women and children when he heard what was happening. Indeed, one local tradition is that he had sent an orderly to ask Wheeler if everything was proceeding as agreed and wishing him a safe journey, and that this individual was standing at the salute, while Wheeler scribbled a reply, when the shooting started. Nana Sahib was acquainted with Wheeler and many other members of the British community, and had no reason to seek their lives after they had surrendered. Chivalry on his part would have brought him credit in the eyes of Indian and British alike. Nevertheless, he had already been responsible for the murder of fugitives from Fatehgarh, and Maratha princes had employed *ruses de guerre* in the past. In 1659, the great Sivaji himself had famously held a parley with a Muslim general,

Afzal Khan, stabbed him during a pretended embrace and then destroyed his army by a surprise attack.

The first musket shot might have been a deliberate signal to start the massacre. On the other hand, like 'the shot heard round the world' that began the American War of Independence, it might have been a negligent discharge by a nervous or careless individual, leading both sides, each distrustful of the other, to start shooting. Spending money and trouble on the boats and their roofs could have been evidence that Nana Sahib intended to honour his agreement. It could have been a ruse to persuade the British to leave their defences as agreed. His consent to their keeping their weapons might have been evidence of good faith, but equally might have been given in the knowledge that, once in the boats, their weapons would be of no use to them. Had he attacked them on the march, they would have fought fiercely for their lives and families, and might even have recovered their entrenchments. The boatmen might simply have been using charcoal fires for cooking, and have abandoned their boats to avoid the shooting. The cannon covering the embarkation point and emplaced further downstream might have been there to hold the river against the approach of British reinforcements. They seem, however, to have been ready for action immediately the trouble started, when the British were packed into the boats and presenting a perfect target.

As with all conspiracy theories, every argument on one side can be countered by one on the other. Nevertheless, even if the massacre of 26 June was not planned, it certainly occurred, and several hundred Europeans and Eurasians, women and small children among them, perished in an episode where the body-count exceeded the total of all the British killed in the Mutiny thus far. The slaughter of a garrison and its dependants, after it had surrendered with a promise of safe conduct, was a breach of all the rules of war. Nothing like it had happened to British troops since the surrender of Fort William Henry in New York a century earlier. The smaller tragedies already enacted, however, had been enough to inflame British anger against those who, in challenging British rule, killed defenceless non-combatants. For British soldiers, the quarrel was now personal. In response to ethnic cleansing they had adopted a policy of frightfulness.

Chapter 7

THE FALL OF THE HOUSE OF TIMUR. JUNE–SEPTEMBER 1857

He that destroyeth my flock, I shall destroy.

Major Dundee, *Reverend Dahlstrom*

At Delhi, the British force included officers of mutinied regiments who had been given staff appointments or attached to British units. One was Captain Robert Tytler of the 38th Bengal NI, who had become the army's field cashier. With him was his 28-year-old wife, Harriet, who had escaped from Delhi with their two young children. Along with other ladies who had no homes left and did not wish to be sent to the hills, she had decided to follow the army in her husband's bullock cart, India's equivalent of the American West's covered wagon.

On the way from Karnal a child's foot and shoe was found under a bridge by one of the lancers, who carried the grisly trophy through the camp on his lance point and showed it to his comrades. The troops, including some officers, then burnt several neighbouring villages, but the same evening were paraded and rebuked by Hope Grant, commanding the 9th Lancers, who pointed out that they had done more harm than good, for the villages belonged to a Rani who had helped British fugitives. Even so, nine villagers were convicted of atrocities and hanged after the parade. Rough justice of this kind followed lurid newspaper reports that Englishwomen had been the victims of sexual assault. Subsequent investigations found no evidence of this, at Delhi, Kanpur or anywhere else.

Mrs Tytler was shocked at the behaviour of the troops. After a baker was allegedly hanged by the troops for being continually late with their morning bread, she supposed that only the desperate need for European troops prevented those responsible from being indicted for murder. Colonel George Campbell of the 52nd Light Infantry later gave evidence to a separate enquiry that 'contractors will bring you morning after morning bread that is tainted' but in this case, as in many others, it is clear the wrong man was hanged. Captain Tytler subsequently intervened to rescue a camp follower from a group of European soldiers and persuaded them to hang a dog instead. The men learned that Tytler and his wife had lost all their possessions, and in the camp before Delhi some of them brought him a few clean shirts from their own scanty store, apologizing for them not being new. They could find nothing suitable for Harriet Tytler, however, and she had to wear a sheet whenever her only dress was being washed. It was not until the beginning of August that some things were found for her in a collection of civilian clothes sent by the community at Simla. The packs had been soaked by the monsoon rain, leading Colonel Young to write to his wife: 'You never saw such an exhibition as there is to the rear of our tent – every kind of female garment hung up to dry.'

Chaplain Rotton had joined the Mess of the 60th Rifles, a corps which he came to regard so highly that he later wrote: 'Whether as a parent or a Christian minister, without a moment's misgiving, I would say, if a son of mine *must* and *will* be a soldier, I hope he may have the good fortune to learn his profession, and continuously exercise it too, in no other regiment than the 60th Royal Rifles.' At first he was the only chaplain in the Delhi Field Force, and ministered impartially to Protestants and Catholics alike, before being joined after a few days by Father Bertrand, whom he described as 'a pattern Roman Catholic priest'. When the force was grouped into two divisions, they took one each, and worked irrespective of the religious beliefs of their flock until two more priests, one Anglican, one Catholic, joined them several weeks later. By then, they were visiting fourteen field hospitals between them.

The Government of India, as far as Rotton could see, judged military chaplains as a 'necessary inconvenience'. Paying tribute to his brother in Christ, at a time when Anglicans and Catholics in civil life had little good to say of each other, he mentioned that Father Bertrand had infinitely smaller allowances and infinitely fewer comforts than himself, but an equal amount of labour. 'This excellent man – and surely I may venture thus to designate him, without risk of offence to any, except the most bigoted – lived as sparingly as a hermit, while he worked as hard as an English dray-horse.'

103

The flock at Delhi included a large number of Eurasian refugees, mostly junior civil servants and customs officials with their families, who had been sheltered by local villagers and now came into the camp. Army Headquarters spared them some tents, though these were in short supply, but at first there was no food for them and, in Rotton's words, it was the ordinary British soldier who, 'with that generous and open-hearted kindness which distinguishes him at home and abroad', came to the rescue and shared his own rations with the refugees. They were traumatized by their experiences and several died in the overcrowded tents. Nothing that Rotton could say seemed to help and he was glad for their sake and his own when on 19 June they were evacuated to Meerut in a convoy with the sick and wounded.

Barnard also ordered the officers' ladies to leave. His staff found transport elephants for them, but Harriet Tytler was too far advanced in pregnancy to clamber onto the animal to which she was assigned. The matter was referred to Barnard himself, who said that an exception must be made in her case and she was left as the only lady in camp. Rotton considered her a heroine, and noted that, once allowed to remain, she could not be persuaded either 'by official eloquence or the arguments of her own husband, to desert his side'. When the monsoon broke, Tytler moved her into an empty armoury shed near his treasury cart. There she presented him with a son who, once the doctors were sure he would live, was christened Stanley Delhiforce.

The conventional procedure, when an army had driven its opponent into a fortress, was to launch an immediate attack, while the defenders were still demoralized by their defeat in the field, and before they had properly occupied their positions. The allied commanders in the Crimea had been much criticized for failing to do this three years earlier, when the Russians retreated into Sebastopol after the battle of the Alma. Six years later, General Ulysses S. Grant attacked Vicksburg immediately after defeating a Confederate army in the field, not with any anticipation of success, but because he knew that if he had not made the attempt, his men would not so readily endure a siege in the Mississippi summer heat.

Barnard therefore authorized a surprise assault, set for dawn on 13 June. The need for secrecy was carried so far as to prevent Brigadier Graves, field officer of the day, from being told why he was required to withdraw all the Europeans from the picquet line. As this meant leaving the Ridge held by Indian troops alone, he rode to Barnard for confirmation, thereby delaying any movement until daylight ended any chance of a surprise. Graves was clearly wrong in refusing to obey a verbal message. The rule, insisted on by Wellington himself, was that a message delivered by a staff officer was to be taken as if the commander were present in person. On the other hand, rigid adherence to this convention in the Crimean War had been responsible for the loss of the Light Brigade at Balaclava and might have lost the British their field force at Delhi. In neither place did the British have a cadre of trained staff officers such as those who served together for so long under Wellington.

Graves, as the former commander at Delhi, knew the city well and, when belatedly asked by Barnard for his views on the plan, said that although the British might indeed get into the city, they would not be able to keep it, because of the superior numbers inside. Barnard was happy to accept this opinion, as his decision to attempt a *coup de main* had been influenced by the same pressure from Canning and John Lawrence that had affected Anson. After initially merely postponing the assault, he decided on 16 June to wait until reinforcements arrived, to the disgust of the engineers and younger officers, who remembered that Clive had taken Arcot with far fewer than the 2,300 infantrymen in Barnard's force. Hervey Greathed, his political adviser, also urged an attack to end the insurgency before it spread further, and thought that Barnard, influenced by his experiences at Sebastopol, was too much disposed to treat the sepoys as Russians. An Indian police officer who was in Delhi at the time and survived the war later stated that if the British had attacked immediately after reaching the Ridge with the dash they had shown up to that time, they would have recovered the city, even though suffering heavy casualties in the process.

Barnard, like Anson before him, warned Canning that if his attack failed, the result would be disastrous, as he had no reserves. His only reinforcement had been the Corps of Guides (three troops of cavalry and four companies of infantry), who arrived on 9 June, after marching the 580 miles from Mardan in twenty-seven days, only a day after the main field force reached Delhi. They were just in time to counter a sortie from the city, and were in action within hours, with their commandant killed leading them. Any assault would no longer be against a garrison of panicky fugitives, but one which had had time to regroup and recover sufficient morale as to make three sallies against the 60th Rifles and Sirmoor Gurkhas holding Hindu Rao's house, a critical position on the Ridge. They were still in good heart on 23 June, when Major Charles Reid, commanding the Gurkhas, wrote: 'No men could have fought better. They charged the Rifles, the Guides and my own men again and again, and at one time I thought I must have lost the day.' By then Barnard had decided to wait for the troops that he knew were coming from the Punjab.

These, consisting of a wing of the 8th Foot, another of the 61st, the 1st Punjab Infantry and a squadron of the 1st Punjab Cavalry, with some European and Sikh artillerymen to help man the siege batteries, arrived at the end of June, together with Neville Chamberlain, previously commanding the Moveable Column, but now appointed Adjutant General in succession to Chester. Command of the Moveable Column had been given to John Nicholson, so that for the second time Colonel Campbell of the 52nd Light Infantry was, for political reasons, placed under command of a Company officer who was both junior to himself and a favourite of the Chief Commissioner of the Punjab. As a good soldier, he obeyed his orders, but sent a protest to the Duke of Cambridge, pointing out that his supercession was contrary to military protocol. Nicholson's admirers stressed the great personal influence he had over the Pathans and Sikhs with whom he served, and the enormous physical energy with which he led his new command. Indeed, he became one of the paladins of Victorian schoolbook history. Nevertheless, Campbell, a regular officer of an elite British regiment, might have been a better choice for the conventional siege warfare that was now beginning.

While Barnard waited for his reinforcements, the insurgents inside Delhi received even larger reinforcements of their own. The British had begun the siege with five infantry regiments (four European and one Gurkha) against five of sepoys. They actually had a preponderance in cavalry, though this arm is not of great use in sieges. In the following weeks, however, large bodies of sepoys (sometimes whole brigades) arrived at Delhi from stations that had joined the Mutiny, often accompanied by groups of ghazis or religious warriors. The latter were ill armed and ill

106

trained, but potentially useful in close combat (the only kind in which their swords and knives had military value) as their religious zeal inspired them to seek martyrdom by slaying unbelievers regardless of their own lives. In the assaults of 12, 13 and 19 June, they had been stopped only by artillery and long-range Enfield fire, supplemented by disciplined volleys from troops still using the old muskets.

These ghazis, strictly speaking, were not jehadis or mujehaddin (the Arabic form of the same word) as in orthodox Islamic political theory *jihad* or holy war can only be declared by the king of a country, and even then only when victory is assured. Bahadur Shah eventually called on all his subjects to protect their respective faiths by waging war against the British, but could not declare holy war for Islam without alienating that half of the population of Delhi that was made up, in Muslim eyes, of polytheists and idolaters. The zealots who flocked to Delhi were not welcomed by Bahadur Shah, who had no means of paying or feeding them, and who, though pious himself, was concerned to protect his Hindu subjects against their extremism. At a more earthly level, he disliked their camping out in his beloved gardens.

On 17 and 18 June the mutineers from Nasirabad (two infantry regiments and a horse artillery battery) arrived. In accordance with the usual practice in armies joined by deserters, they were required to prove themselves in battle and, attacking on 19 June, almost reached the British camp. The 9th Lancers, dealing with a threat to the British rear, charged on too narrow a front and found themselves under heavy fire from walls and gardens. As one officer wrote: 'The niggers who had been in the road all joined their comrades behind the hedges, so we could not kill many.' In the confusion they lost six killed, including Lieutenant Colonel Yule, whose body was found the next day with the usual mutilations. The regiment, 493 strong when it marched for Delhi, was by this time reduced to 391 effectives.

The sepoys did not know how close they had come to victory, and withdrew in good order, leaving the British to reoccupy the lost ground. On 22 June another three mutinied infantry regiments arrived, the 36th and 61st which had left Jalandhar on 7 June, and the 3rd, which joined them as they passed Phillur. These entered the fighting on 23 June, the day when Reid thought he might lose Hindu Rao's house. The Bareilly brigade, 2,300 strong under Subadar Bakht Khan, with their Eurasian bandsmen playing 'Cheer, boys, Cheer', and thousands more ghazis in their train, arrived at the beginning of July, soon after Chamberlain reached Delhi with his reinforcements from the Punjab. The Bareilly men attacked cautiously on 3 July and more forcefully on 9 July, with close-quarter fighting in the suburb of Sabzi Mandi, below Hindu Rao's house.

In the interim, Sir Harry Barnard succumbed to cholera on 5 July, a week after the monsoon broke and turned his camp into a quagmire. Sir Thomas Reed, acting C-in-C of the Bengal Army since Anson's death, had reached Delhi at the same time as the field force, but was too exhausted to assume executive command, and had left Barnard in post while he dealt with the Army administration. Now he felt it his duty to take over, but when a force of twenty sepoy regiments attacked the British position on 14 July, it was Chamberlain who led the counter-attack and was badly wounded in the process. On 17 July Reed admitted he was unfit for field service and went back to Ambala, after appointing Archdale Wilson to command the Delhi force with promotion to brigadier general. Two colonels, followed by one of the brigadiers, went with him, either as invalids or in protest at being superseded by Wilson who, as a substantive colonel, was their junior.

After every sortie the British drove back their attackers, but suffered casualties from artillery when they reached the city walls, and from musketry as they returned to their own lines. The consequent attrition, with twenty-five officers and 400 men becoming casualties between 9 and 14 July, began to affect morale and men were heard to complain about useless pursuits that cost lives but never caught the enemy. Some vented their frustration on their own Indian camp followers and shot them when they could not shoot mutineers. Conditions in and around the camp were appalling, with the sour-sweet smell of death from the bodies of unburied animals and enemy dead left to rot where they lay. Flies, thriving in these corpses and in the waste products of thousands of men, horses and baggage animals, bred in millions and carried disease everywhere. They got into men's food, drink, clothes and even into Rotton's Bible, and acted as vectors of the cholera and dysentery that had been with the army all the way from Ambala. The 60th Rifles suffered fewer cases of cholera than other British units, and (with no one understanding the real cause of the disease) attributed it to their surgeon ordering them to wear their serge uniforms to keep warm in the damp and chilly nights. More likely their saviour was Major Reid, who put a Gurkha sentry on the well at Hindu Rao's house. Their morale held up, as did their marksmanship, and they were delighted by reports that the King of Delhi had offered a reward for every rifleman's green jacket brought to him.

Wilson was cautious by nature, as his support for Hewitt's decision not to pursue the mutineers from Meerut had made clear, and he wrote to his wife that he was not sure about his own qualifications for the Delhi command. On the other hand, his victory at Ghazi-al-Din Nagar was to his credit, and the steady methodical approach of a siege artilleryman was very suitable for the task in hand. The city, in practice, was no more invested than Sebastopol had been during the Crimean War, and the British position on the Ridge was even more precarious than it had been at Balaclava. Such difficulty as Delhi citizens had in obtaining supplies was due not to blockade but the depredations of Gujars and other robbers. The gunners with the force were pleased that the command had gone to an officer of their own arm and most others welcomed his appointment, thinking he could only be an improvement on his predecessors.

Wilson appreciated that his army was no longer a mobile force intending to take a city by a sudden rush, but had become a static army needing all the techniques of nineteenth-century siege craft. He began by introducing a system of shifts and reliefs, so that the order 'Stand To' was no longer given to the whole force at each alarm, but only to the one-third warned for duty. This countered the tactic introduced by Bakht Khan on becoming the Mughal C-in-C, of dividing his own command into three and making harassing attacks with each section in turn, to keep the British constantly under stress. Wilson strengthened his own defensive works, cleared away the buildings in the suburb of Sabzi Mandi that had covered enemy attacks, and ordered his troops to stand fast when a sortie was repulsed, rather than pursue a retreating enemy back to the city walls. Seeing poor morale reflected in declining standards of cleanliness and appearance, he also told his new command to smarten itself up, boosting men's personal pride in themselves as soldiers and doing something to improve hygiene. At the operational level, he ordered the arsenal at Firozpur to send him a heavy siege train and repeated his predecessor's request to John Lawrence for reinforcements, making it clear that until they and the siege train arrived he would make no attempt to storm the city. Indeed, he said that if they did not come, he would abandon the siege altogether and fall back to Karnal. While he waited, the sepoys on 23 July attacked a building on the left of his position, called Ludlow Castle by the troops, and were driven back. On 31 July and 1 August they attacked the right of the Ridge and established new battery positions on the British flanks. One of these played with considerable effect upon Ludlow Castle, until a determined sortie of Bengal Fusiliers and Punjab Infantry on 12 August captured its four guns and brought them back in triumph to the British camp. Both sides suffered significant casualties in the affair, with Brigadier Showers and Captain Coke of the Punjabis badly wounded.

Lawrence had previously been inhibited by the situation in the Punjab, where, despite the disarmaments and mutinies, twelve sepoy infantry regiments and various cavalry regiments retained their arms. On 11 June, in order to find troops for Delhi, he had proposed to hand over Peshawar to Dost Muhammad, the Amir of Afghanistan. This idea had some merit, as until 1835, when it was annexed by Ranjit Singh, the entire district had been under Afghan rule, and its inhabitants, mostly Pathans or ethnic Afghans, were never reconciled to rule from Lahore. Indeed, the question of Peshawar was one that had brought on the Afghan War, because Dost Muhammad would only allow the British into his country if they recovered Peshawar for him, and the British, unwilling to alienate Ranjit Singh, decided that the only alternative was one of regime change, deposing Dost Muhammad and installing a rival. By this time, however, Dost Muhammad, having regained his throne, was on friendly terms with the British, and Lawrence saw only advantages in restoring the lost province.

His officers at Peshawar, however, were astonished at the idea and Edwardes argued that no Afghan ruler would be content with only the Vale of Peshawar. Canning was equally opposed to a withdrawal. It would be taken as a sign of British weakness, he told Lawrence, and thus encourage the spread of rebellion to southern India. Every prince would suppose that the British Raj was collapsing just as had the Mughal Raj, and would scramble to take his share. Canning certainly wanted Delhi taken and, supported by the acting C-in-C, Sir Patrick Grant, continued to

1. The death of Brigadier Adrian Hope in the failed attack on Ruya Fort, Rohilkhand, 15 April 1858.

2. Elephant battery on the march, 1858.

3. The Mughal palace-fortress at Agra, capital of the British North-West Provinces, 1857.

BLOWING IN THE KASHMIR GATE DELHI.

4. 'Blowing in the Kashmir Gate', Delhi, 14 September 1857. Bronze relief on the base of Queen Victoria's statue, Royal Military Academy Sandhurst, Camberley. *(By kind permission of the Commandant)*

5. Indian Mutiny memorial of the 9th Royal Lancers, by Carlo Marochetti. North Wall, Exeter Cathedral. (*By kind permission of the Dean and Chapter*)

9. Bronze statue of Sir James Outram, Embankment Gardens, Westminster.

10. Bronze statue of Sir Henry Havelock, Trafalgar Square, Westminster.

11. Bronze statue and monument to Sir Colin Campbell, Lord Clyde, by Carlo Marochetti. Waterloo Place, Westminster.

press the commanders on the Ridge to do so. He did not think, however, that the political consequences of abandoning Peshawar would be outweighed by whatever strength its garrison would bring to the Delhi Field Force.

Edwardes opposed sending any more troops out of the Punjab. Writing on 29 June, he told Lawrence:

> Delhi is not India and if General Reed cannot take it with eight thousand men, he will not take it with nine thousand or ten thousand ... there are two policies open to you: to treat the Punjab as secondary to the North-West Provinces and go on giving troops to General Reed until you break down in the Punjab, or to maintain the Punjab as your first duty and the most important point of the two.

Reed, he said, should be told he could have no more from the Punjab and that he must either take Delhi with what he had or get reinforcements from Calcutta.

A month later, Lawrence was better placed to respond to Wilson's call. On 26 June Nicholson had disarmed the 33rd and 35th Bengal Infantry, part of his Moveable Column, as they reached Phillur after a long and tiring march. The 58th Native Infantry had been disarmed on 7 July at Rawal Pindi (though two companies of the 14th NI there fled and were killed either by mounted police or local villagers after the British put a price on their heads). The plan to disarm the rest of the 14th at Jhelum miscarried, when the detachment of European and Multani troops arrived late, giving the sepoys a chance to seize their weapons and put up a fight. About 150 were killed and another 150 captured. The remaining 120 or so escaped to the territories of the Maharaja of Kashmir, who handed them back to the British.

Pre-empting their own disarmament, the 46th Bengal NI and a wing of the 9th Irregular Cavalry mutinied on 9 July, at Sialkot, looting the Treasury, opening the gaol and killing the station commander and various other officers and Indians who stood by them. Women and children were spared with the exception only of Mrs Hunter, the wife of a Church of Scotland missionary. She had offended Muslim fundamentalists by setting up a little school for girls and was killed along with her husband and baby. As elsewhere, some sepoys protected their officers and families from attack and helped them gather their valuables. Colonel

111

Farquharson and Captain Caulfield of the 46th were offered generous terms if they chose to stay with their regiment. The offer was declined, but the protection was maintained. The next day the sepoys marched away in good order, heading for Delhi.

Nicholson disarmed the rest of the 9th Irregular Cavalry in his column, and pursued the Sialkot brigade with a force of newly raised Pathan cavalry, a troop of horse artillery (with some of its gunners and drivers riding as dragoons) and a wing of the 52nd Light Infantry mounted mostly in ekkas, with a few on the troop horses of the 9th Cavalry. He found them on 12 July at Trimmu Ghat, on the Ravi, 10 miles beyond Gurdaspur. Nicholson's deployment was regarded by the 52nd as faulty and a series of spirited charges by the mutineers almost won the day. For most of the 52nd, it was their first time under fire, and one of their officers noticed his men ducking and looking about for cover as they advanced. British superiority in guns (nine against one) and small arms (eighty of the 52nd had Enfield rifles) forced the sepoys to retreat to the river, where they became trapped on a large island. Nicholson waited for reinforcements and on 16 July, while his artillery kept up a frontal bombardment, the infantry crossed the river undetected and took the sepoys in the flank A few courageous men defended their single gun to the last. 'We saw one brave fellow,' wrote an officer of the 52nd, 'about a hundred yards from the guns, all around him having been killed, loading and firing all by himself, till he was knocked over.' The rest were either shot as they fled or drowned trying to escape across the river. This was the first time that a British regiment wore khaki in combat, though the Guides and other Punjab corps had worn this colour (from the Hindustani word for 'dust') for many years previously.

Lawrence decided that Nicholson and the Moveable Column should go to Delhi. They left Amritsar on 25 July and arrived amid scenes of jubilation on 14 August, reinforcing Wilson with the 52nd and a wing of the 61st Foot, a field battery of Bengal Artillery, the 2nd Punjab Infantry and 600 Punjabi horsemen. The Moveable Column ceased to be a separate command, and Nicholson assumed the role of second-in-command to Wilson. Indeed, some thought that he effectively took over from his less extrovert superior officer, touring the outposts, polishing his image as the immensely tall, black-bearded man of action and encouraging all to believe that, with his arrival, the long-awaited

112

attack on Delhi was imminent. Wilson's appreciation was that, even with Nicholson's reinforcements, his force was inadequate for the purpose. He decided to wait for the siege train and the additional reinforcements Lawrence had promised. Nevertheless, rather than remain entirely on the defensive, he sent William Hodson with the Guides and 200 of the recently raised Hodson's Horse to follow a group of insurgent cavalry that had left Delhi as Nicholson arrived. The two forces met at Rohtak, and Hodson secured a much-praised victory.

Behind them, there were still some Purbiya regiments left in the Punjab. The disarmed 26th rose at Mian Mir on 30 July and killed their commandant, sergeant major and a havildar. They were pursued for a time by the Artillery and 81st Foot, after which the hunt was left to local Punjabi villagers, who killed about 150 of them. Without food or firearms, 280 of the remainder surrendered to Frederick Cooper, the Deputy Commissioner of Amritsar. He decided they should all hang, but as there were not enough trees for his purpose, had them shot by his Sikh police. The bodies were thrown into a well near the Ajnala police station, so that Cooper later reported: 'There is a well at Cawnpore, but there is also one at Ujnalla.' This wording shocked even John Lawrence who referred to it as 'that nauseous despatch'. He was, however, not against exemplary punishment on principle, and forty others of the 26th who fell into British hands were taken to Lahore and blown away from guns.

The siege train heading for Delhi consisted of thirty-two heavy guns and mortars of various natures, complete with ammunition and stores vehicles, drawn by an impressive array of elephants and gun bullocks, but escorted only by one wing of the 8th Foot and another of the Bombay Army's 1st Baluch Battalion. The insurgents, who had been reinforced by the Nimach mutineers, with ten field guns and numerous ghazis, decided to intercept it as it passed through the area held by the British allies, against whom they had had some local successes. During the night of 23 August about 6,000 sepoys, with eighteen field guns in support, marched out of Delhi, but its intentions were speedily reported by Hodson's intelligence agents.

Nicholson followed them with a squadron of the 9th Lancers, 400 Indian cavalry, sixteen horse artillery guns, 800 European infantry (61st Foot and Bengal Fusiliers) and 800 Punjab infantry. He caught up with the Nimach brigade at Najafgarh on 25 August after a march of some 20 miles through the monsoon rains and immediately attacked through flooded ground to achieve a brilliant victory, the first major battle in the open since Badli-ki-Serai. Against 800 sepoys killed, he suffered fewer than 100 total casualties, and captured thirteen guns and the enemy camp. The Bareilly brigade, a mile away from this engagement, made no attempt to take part, and Nicholson did not become aware of its presence until it was too late for his exhausted men to go on. The repeated failure of Bakht Khan's attacks on the Ridge, followed by this defeat in the field, had resulted in his replacement as C-in-C by a military court under the restored supremacy of Mirza Mughal, though Bakht Khan kept control of his Bareilly brigade and its treasure. During his absence the Delhi garrison made a sortie on 26 August, but were driven off before Nicholson's column returned later in the day. The siege train continued inexorably on its way and its leading elements, in a column stretching back for 8 miles, reached Delhi on 4 September. The final reinforcements also arrived, comprising the wing of the 60th and gunners from the artillery depot at Meerut, the 4th Punjab Infantry, and 3,000 Dogras from the army of Maharaja Golab Singh of Kashmir.

Wilson was still hesitant about committing his small army to an assault. His own strength was less than 10,000, only half of them infantry, whereas within the city, so his Intelligence branch told him, there were four times that number of armed men. Half of these were ghazis, not regular sepoys, but a significant threat if their zeal for martyrdom inspired them to defend the city street by street. Moreover, the British Army had a poor record of fighting in built-up areas. Fifty years earlier it had suffered humiliating defeats by Argentineans inside Buenos Aires and by Egyptians inside Rosetta. Although he had been reinforced, men continued to die from disease and attrition. The 52nd, for example, who arrived at Delhi 600 strong, could by this time muster only 245. If there were no more men available from the Punjab, he thought it better to keep his strong position on the Ridge and wait until troops came up the Grand Trunk Road from the east. On 20 August he told his chief engineer, Lieutenant Colonel Richard Baird Smith, that he was trying to explain to the Governor-General that Delhi was defended by 7 miles of walls, with 114 guns mounted on them and another sixty field guns of British manufacture, and was impregnable except to a conventional siege for which he been sent neither the guns nor the men. He thought that the idea of blowing in the gates and escalading the walls, twice rejected, was still impracticable and, if it failed, his army would be lost.

Nicholson did not share this view and, according to Roberts, who was on the staff at the time, intended to lead a coup against Wilson if he refused to order an assault. To avoid any suggestion that, as the senior ranking officer, he wanted to take over the command himself, he thought that Colonel Campbell of the 52nd should be appointed by a council of war. Such an act, undertaken in the presence of the enemy at such a critical time, would have been as much a mutiny as any committed by the sepoys and it is very doubtful that Campbell, a professional soldier of the regular British Army, would have had anything to do with it. The plan, however, was never put to the test as Wilson, encouraged by his principal staff officers and under pressure from Lawrence (who told him that it would be better to lose the army than the Empire, and that as long as Delhi held out the Empire was at risk), published a general order on 7 September telling his troops to prepare to attack Delhi. He ordered that, once inside the walls, care should be taken not to harm women and children and that the troops should not stray in search of plunder. Captured property (to which by the usage of the time the army was entitled after taking a city by storm) would, he said, be fairly distributed by the established rules.

Officially, the army greeted his order with approval, the officers swearing on their sword hilts to respect women and children. Unofficially Lang, who had joined the Field Force, was not so sure. 'The English soldier, once roused, is as bloodthirsty as any man in the world, and seldom have they met a foe who merited their hatred as have the Pandies. The rest of our army is composed of as ruthless a set as could be found – Sikhs and Afghans and ... Gurkhas.' He decided that if he survived the fighting he would get well clear of the city. Others felt that there was little reason to spare anyone, of whatever sex, who had encouraged atrocities against British women and children.

Nicholson continued with his disloyalty, and wrote to Lawrence on 11 September:

> I have seen lots of useless generals in my day, but such an ignorant, croaking obstructive as he is, I have never hitherto met with ... I

115

believe the Meerut catastrophe was more his fault than Hewitt's. And, by all accounts, he was driven into fighting at the Hindun and could not help himself ... He is now allowing the Engineers to undertake active operations simply because he knows the army will no longer put up with his inactivity.

Nicholson added that Wilson was becoming jealous of him, and had refused to show him the plan of assault. Baird Smith, the chief engineer, shared Nicholson's view of their commander, and later wrote: 'I have such contempt for Wilson's military capacity and found him throughout the siege operations so uniformly obstructive ... that I say as little about him as I can.' When Wilson told him: "I have already more than I can manage, and my head gets into such a state that I feel nearly mad sometimes. For God's sake don't drive me so,' Baird Smith passed on the note to Nicholson. 'I am satisfied that Wilson has gone off his head,' he said, and Nicholson reported the same to Lawrence. 'Wilson's head is going, he says so himself, and it is quite evident he speaks the truth.' Wilson himself, in default of the support he was entitled to expect from two of his senior officers, stopped speaking to either of them.

Despite these dissensions, once Wilson had decided on the assault, all the scientific and mathematical skills honed over two centuries of Western siege-craft was brought to bear against Delhi. Baird Smith, wounded and confined to his quarters with dysentery or its treatment (brandy and opium), had to leave the task of selecting a site for the batteries to his deputy, Captain Alexander Taylor. Ground was broken for the first battery on the night of 7 September and by dawn it was ready to receive its armament, four 24-pdrs, five 18-pdrs and a siege mortar. On 12 September all four batteries began a twenty-four hours' continuous bombardment, with horse gunners and volunteers from the British cavalry brought in to assist the foot artillery in the exhausting work of passing ammunition to the guns and manhandling them back to their firing positions after recoil. On 13 September, the engineers (Arthur Lang among them) reported that the breaches both at the Kashmir and Water Gates were, in the technical language of the time 'practicable'. The defenders, however, constructed retrenchments behind the breaches. When their heavy guns could no longer fire from the shattered bastions, they brought them outside and duelled with the siege batteries in the open. In the week following the opening of the bombardment, the British suffered over 300 casualties from enemy fire.

The assault was launched on 14 September with five separate columns, each of between 850 to 1,000 strong, and composed both of European and Indians, the latter making up two-thirds of the whole. Ahead of them the 60th Rifles were deployed as sharpshooters to suppress enemy fire as soon as the siege guns stopped. Before the British troops marched out, Father Bertrand prayed for their victory and their souls, and told them that even the Protestants would take no harm from the blessings of an old man and a clergyman. The first and second columns reached the breaches, though with heavy casualties among the leading files carrying the scaling ladders. While they climbed the rubble under deadly musketry fire, two Bengal Engineers and eight British and Indian sappers crossed the sole remaining beam of the bridge outside the Kashmir Gate. Lieutenant Duncan Home and the powder bag party placed their explosives against the wooden gate before the surprised defenders could stop them, but a sergeant was killed and a havildar wounded. As planned, they took cover in the ditch while Lieutenant Philip Salkeld and the firing party came up to set the fuse. Salkeld was mortally wounded before he could light it and passed the slow match to Corporal Burgess, who completed the mission, only to fall himself just as the charge exploded. Bugler Hawthorne, detached from the 52nd by Colonel George Campbell, commanding No. 3 Column, sounded the advance. In all the noise, Campbell did not hear the bugle, but went forward with his regiment after seeing the explosion. The leading elements opened the shattered gates and the rest surged through to join the columns from the walls.

Once his men were inside the city, things went almost as Wilson had feared. Nicholson, leading the first column, took a wrong turn in the maze of streets, and his men went on without him, guided by Lang and Pemberton of the engineers. They rushed on, cheering and shouting, under intense musketry and artillery fire, and took the Mori Bastion. Lang climbed up to wave to the troops outside, but came under friendly fire from them. 'We tore strips of white, blue and red from dead Pandies clothes, and put up an impromptu flag and then rushed along again,' he afterwards wrote. As they reached the Lahore Gate they were stopped by a barricade with a gun firing canister from behind it. Brigadier Jones commanding No. 2 Column, then arrived to ask where the Kabul Gate was. Lang told him it was far behind them. Jones said his orders were to stop at the Kabul, and decided merely to hold what had been gained thus far. The 1st Bengal Fusiliers at the head of the first column, invincible as long as they were charging forward, found themselves in a stationary firefight against sepoys shooting from rooftops or over walls. After half an hour, ignoring all orders of their officers, they dropped back to the Kabul Gate. Major G.O. Jacob, their commanding officer, led them forward again, but was shot down. With other officers killed or wounded, the fusiliers again retreated. Nicholson re-appeared and launched another attack, but the men saw it was pointless and hung back. Hit by a sepoy marksman, he was carried under protest to a dhoolie and the British position at the Kabul Gate was stabilized only by the arrival of Jones's column.

Major Charles Reid, leading No. 4 Column, was wounded fighting in the suburb of Kishanganj and did not reach the Kabul Gate, where he was meant to join the troops inside the city. Indeed, the counter-attack on Reid's column, led by mounted sepoy officers whose skill and courage attracted British admiration, was the most effective insurgent move of the day. Commanded by Bakht Khan at the head of the Bareilly brigade, it prevented the arrival of the reinforcements that might have taken the Lahore Gate and, instead, drove them back almost to their start line at Sabzi Mandi. For a time it seemed as though the British camp itself, with every available European having been committed to the assaulting columns, was in danger.

Hope Grant of the 9th Lancers, commanding the cavalry brigade, had been sufficiently near to the walls for Nicholson to shout to him from the Mori Bastion that all was going to plan and he was about to attack the Lahore Gate. He now saw Reid in difficulties and drew up the cavalry about 500 yards from the Lahore Gate to protect his flank. There they remained under heavy fire for several hours. Tombs's troop of horse artillery was an easy target and Tombs himself was wounded, with 24 of his 50 men and 17 horses also becoming casualties. Among the cavalry, six officers and forty-two men were hit, with Captain Rosser, the Carabinier who had offered to ride and warn Delhi at the time of the Meerut outbreak, among the wounded. Grant himself was struck by a spent bullet, and eleven officers had their chargers killed under them. The 9th Lancers lost 5 men killed, one officer and 39 men wounded, and 61 horses killed, wounded or missing. When Grant rode along the line to steady them, they told him they would stay there as long as he liked.

By the end of the day Wilson had established his headquarters in St James's Church, just inside the Kashmir Gate. Campbell, wounded in the street fighting, joined him there after reaching the Jama Masjid, the great mosque in the city centre, only to be driven back by ghazis swarming out to meet him. The desperate nature of the fighting was such that everyone was involved. Surgeon Reade of the 61st, who had accompanied his regiment's eighty stormers through the Water Gate breach (most of the 61st were allotted to No. 5 Column, forming the reserve) found himself under fire from a rooftop as he treated wounded in the street. Drawing his sword, he assembled a group of ten men and led them to the attack. Only two of them survived unscathed, but the enemy was driven away and the gallant doctor himself, who personally spiked a loaded 32-pdr, was later awarded the Victoria Cross. Assistant Surgeon Valentine McMaster of the 78th Highlanders was given the same award for his part in the melee. In a war where both sides killed enemy wounded as a matter of course, the convention that medical men were non-combatants had no place.

Wilson himself had always been doubtful about the chances of success. Now, with a lodgement confined to a mere cusp of the walls, his men exhausted and many of his officers dead or wounded, he considered abandoning what had been won and retiring to protect his camp, so nearly lost to Bakht Khan's sortie. His casualties during the day had amounted to 8 officers killed, 162 European other ranks and 103 Indians killed, 52 officers, 510 European other ranks and 310 Indians wounded, many of whom died of their wounds soon afterwards. Of the 1,630 European infantrymen who took part in the assault, one-third of the men and half of the officers were down. Lang, one of the few unwounded engineers (though he had lost his voice through continual cheering and shouting), spent the evening securing the neighbouring houses with his sappers, breaking holes through walls and turning out the residents.

Meanwhile, in the worst traditions of the British Army, the troops took full advantage of finding themselves in the quarter where in more peaceful times merchants had supplied beers, wines and spirits to the Christian community. The officers of the

1st Bengal Fusiliers, in a device that was still being used nearly ninety years later by Soviet political officers in the storming of Berlin, told their men that the drink had been poisoned. An old soldier (one meriting this description in every sense of the term) examined the cork of a brandy bottle and pointed out that it was still sealed, an argument to which his officers had no answer. Rotton was among those who believed that the enemy had deliberately left alcohol so that the troops would indulge 'the national sin of drunkenness' and wrote in his memoirs: 'With all my love for the army, I must confess, the conduct of professed Christians on this occasion was one of the most humiliating facts connected with the siege.' The adjutant of the 75th, however, denied this, and said that he himself was in the city throughout the street fighting and never saw as many as a dozen men drunk, nor indeed did he find a single unbroken bottle in the place, despite trying to get one for himself. An officer of the 52nd Light Infantry wrote: 'An immense number of men were drunk about the town, for they found shops full of beer and spirits, yet we had not a single case of drunkenness in the 52nd.'

Faced with all these problems, and with reports that his European infantry had refused to follow their officers, Wilson considered calling off the attack. Admirers of the Punjab school later claimed that it was only Chamberlain, supported by Baird Smith, who persuaded him to hold on to what had been gained. Nicholson, on his deathbed, thanked God that he still had the strength to shoot him. Another version is that Wilson responded to a note from a fellow-gunner, the Bible-reading Lieutenant Colonel Brind that read: 'God has given you a great victory. See that you don't throw it away.' Yet another is that his staff poured him a stiff drink to steady his nerves.

The British resumed the offensive on 15 September and made some progress, fighting through the houses and over rooftops rather than in the open streets. The troops, European and Indian alike, still advanced only with the greatest reluctance. In a few places, affected by sudden panics, they were driven back by ghazis armed only with swords and knives. The Enfield's superiority in range was lost at close quarters, and reliance was placed on the bayonet. If the sepoys had continued to rely on their musketry, the tactic that suited them best and the British least, the attack might have been halted everywhere. In the event, demoralized by hunger and their defeat at the walls, they failed to mount a co-ordinated counter-attack even while numbers of British soldiers were reported drunk.

On the morning of 16 September, the 61st Foot drove the Nasirabad mutineers from the magazine and, finding several mortars still there, brought them into action against the King's palace. Several thousand armed citizens, ghazis and sepoys gathered outside the gates of the Red Fort and called on the King to lead them to martyrdom. In the afternoon he came out and began to do so, but the crowd came under rifle fire from the magazine and halted. Hakim Ahsanullah, the King's faithful adviser, who had always believed that the British would return, urged him not to go on. If he did so, he might be killed or captured, but, if he did not march against the British in person, he could claim that all his actions had been taken under *force majeure*. Others begged him to die fighting, as befitted his ancestors, even if he thought his cause was lost. The old King, never a man of action, returned to the palace to say his evening prayers. The would-be martyrs then dispersed, many of the citizens turning on the sepoys who had for months made free with their property and now would not defend them. At the Lahore Gate, Bakht Khan gave orders to his regulars to prepare to evacuate the city.

Street fighting continued for another four days. British sobriety was mostly restored by 17 September, when Wilson ordered all the alcohol stores to be destroyed, an act carried out so thoroughly that, as Rotton noted, none was saved for use in the crowded hospitals. The well of British courage took longer to refill and Wilson still had good cause to worry about his troops' reluctance to press home attacks on an enemy they could not see. An officer of the 52nd Light Infantry wrote: 'We were very glad when it was over: that street fighting is the deuce; the stench from dead blackies in the streets and on the tops of houses was awful.'

Large numbers of refugees from the propertied classes streamed out of the gates, heading for Meerut and Karnal along the same *via dolorosa* that British refugees had taken five months earlier, suffering the same robberies and murders, and receiving the same occasional kindnesses from villagers along the way. It was not until 20 September that the British advanced through the almost deserted streets of the city to reach the palace. A few devoted sentries or desperate ghazis were bayoneted, the main door was blown open, and soldiers raced in to be first to sit on the Mughal throne. Alexander Taylor rode his horse up the steps of the Jama Masjid unopposed and Hodson made a triumphal progress round the undefended walls. Wilson moved his headquarters into the palace and entertained his staff to a meal of bacon and eggs in the Diwan-i-Khas, the magnificent audience chamber. The next morning, 21 September, a gun salute announced that Delhi was once again under the British flag.

Thus ended one of the longest, hardest-fought and politically important sieges in the history of the British Army. British casualties from enemy action during the entire campaign totalled 3,877, with 46 officers, 526 European other ranks and 440 Indians killed, and 140 officers, 1,426 European other ranks and 1,299 Indians wounded. Approximately a third of these were incurred during the storming and street fighting. Among individual regiments, the 60th Rifles lost 137 all ranks killed and 252 wounded in this period, amounting to 75 per cent of the six companies that had reached Delhi on 30 May, and 60 per cent of those who arrived as reinforcements at the beginning of September. In the final seven days, they lost 92 killed or wounded, eleven officers among them. The 81st Foot, reduced from the 1,000 who left Firozpur in May to barely 400 effectives in early September, lost 4 officers and 72 men killed or wounded on the day of the assault alone. Cholera, dysentery and heat-related illnesses claimed the lives of many more. The 8th Foot, arriving at Delhi 362 strong on 28 June, could only muster eighty-one when the siege was over. The 9th Lancers, some 400 strong, lost one officer and 26 men killed, 2 officers and 64 men wounded, and 121 horses between 30 May and 20 September. The 52nd Light Infantry, once able to muster forty-five files per company on parade, was now down to eight; the regiment's officer strength was reduced to thirteen, including the two surgeons.

Casualties among the defenders were never properly known. The regular sepoys had certainly suffered several thousands in their numerous sorties against the Ridge and in the various battles in the hinterland, but their officers had enough tactical skill not to reinforce failure and, despite numerous desertions for lack of pay or food, most units remained strong enough to maintain their cohesion. The ill-armed ghazis had taken equally heavy casualties in the open and now, trapped within the city and abandoned by the regulars, they suffered far more when the avenging British caught them.

Many of the Company's officers in the force had lost friends or relatives when the British were driven out of Delhi. Others of a humbler social level, serving as volunteers in the ranks of the Bengal Fusiliers, had suffered in the same way, and an officer of the regiment heard men shouting, 'Where's my wife' and 'My poor children' as they bayoneted their enemies. In the confusion, there was no distinction made between guilty and innocent, and men were killed regardless of whether they had borne arms against the British or had actually sympathized with them. The famous Urdu poet Ghalib, who was there at the time, wrote mournfully of the death of thousands. War poets are notoriously unreliable as reporters, but seemingly harmless people of all kinds were among those killed, just as harmless Christians had been in the previous May. Even if a soldier is so minded, when fighting in built-up areas it is impossible to distinguish between peace-loving individuals just trying to keep out of the way, or partisans who have just thrown away their arms and mingled with non-combatants. The troops who took Delhi were not so minded in any case and none could say whether those non-combatants killed in the storming of their city had not previously taken part in the massacre of Europeans Whereas the insurgents killed people because of their religion, the British did so because of their race and some of Hodson's own agents narrowly escaped death at the hands of their employer's comrades-in-arms.

The British had orders to spare women and children but collateral damage is inevitable in any city under attack, and many had been killed during the bombardment. In some cases, to avoid their being taken by the British or their Punjabi auxiliaries, women were killed by their own husbands and fathers, just as in besieged Lucknow some British officers planned a similar fate for their own female dependants. Nevertheless, soldiers could not be blamed for unintended offences against modesty when a sepoy was caught wearing the full-length veil of a Muslim woman. Attempted escape in female clothing is a common enough device in societies where the fashion is for long dresses and covered heads. Many Europeans had used it earlier in the year, and no less a personage than Jefferson Davis, President of the Confederate States of America, did the same a few years later. Even 150 years later suspected Islamic terrorists were said to have passed through British airports thus disguised.

Barter, the adjutant of the 75th, approached by a householder complaining that British soldiers had entered his women's apartments, went to investigate. The women, said Barter, 'set up a shrill kind of howl at our appearance'. Private Uzell, a grenadier of the 75th, explained that he had only been ransacking the house and had not laid a finger on them. Barter peered under their veils, expecting from the fuss to find them all very beautiful, but 'I never saw a more abominably ugly and dirty-looking set of females anywhere.' He told the householder that the British, unlike his fellow-citizens, did not make war on women, and ordered a sentry to be placed over them to prevent further annoyance. One officer, whose letter home was published in the *Illustrated London News*, said that he regretted the mercy given to 'coolie women ... fiends in female form' who had been involved in the cruel treatment of English women and children, and had tried to loot the British camp. 'Mercy to such wretches is a mistake. They are not human beings.' Every man found in the city was bayoneted on the spot, he said. 'They were not mutineers, but residents of the city, who trusted in our well-known mild rule for pardon. I am glad to say they were disappointed.' The Indian policeman Main al-Din wrote that many leading men were killed when they were taken for rebels.

> In this way God showed his anger ... As innocent Christians fell victims on the 11th May, so the same evil fate befell Mahomedans on the 20th September. The gallows slew those who escaped the sword ... every man who had an enemy was denounced. False witnesses abounded on every side ... The slaughter of innocent helpless women and children was avenged in a way that no one anticipated.

With the re-establishment of British control came the victors' justice. In the general exodus, the King had fled to the mausoleum of his ancestor, the Emperor Humayun, 6 miles outside the city. Bakht Khan, marching by with his brigade, urged him to join them and carry on the fight but, still hoping to persuade the British that he had nothing to do with the mutineers, he once more decided he was too old for war. His whereabouts were reported to Hodson who obtained Wilson's permission to negotiate the King's surrender and to offer to spare his life. This would normally have been the task of Greathed, the civil commissioner with the force, but he had died of cholera on

20 September. Bahadur Shah's favourite wife, Begam Zinat Mahal, who had for several weeks been among members of his family trying to make a deal with the British, now negotiated on his behalf. She obtained Hodson's written agreement to spare his life, as well as that of her father and her son, but made no stipulation about the King's other sons, rivals to her own in the succession she still hoped would come about.

The party then surrendered and was taken back to the British lines, where Wilson was no more pleased than the rest of his army to see the King still alive. He told Hodson he did not want to be bothered with other royal captives. Hodson took him at his word, and on 21 September returned to Humayun's tomb to capture the three princes still there: Mirza Mughal, Mirza Khizr Sultan and Mirza Abu Bakr. After carrying them off in a curtained bullock cart, he ordered them to get out and take off their fine clothes; he then shot them with his own hand. The bodies were left in the road where, so Hodson told a crowd that had gathered, those of European men and women had been similarly exposed. No one in the British force, which had fought with such determination to destroy the House of Timur, its past, present and future, mourned them. Hodson had simply saved the State the cost of a hanging.

Twenty-one other Mughal princes were hanged as rebels, along with the Nawab of Jajjar and the Raja of Ballabhgarh, both of whom had rallied to the King's cause. The Nawab's defence was the familiar one, that he just happened to be present when the mutineers rode in, and he was no more to be blamed for his men joining them than were the British officers whose own sepoys had done the same thing. Mrs Muter wrote that he went to the gallows with a calmness that 'inspired my husband, who commanded the escort, with the deepest respect'. Another lady said she was told that the execution was deliberately botched.

Meanwhile, Delhi became another Badajos. Sikh units proved especially efficient as looters, a word that entered the English language from the Urdu *lutna* (to rob). 'I never saw such fellows for loot,' wrote Barter, 'nothing escaped them'. British, Gurkhas and Indians alike set about plundering everything of value, despite the efforts of the prize agents to have such property placed into a common pool from which could be sold for the benefit of all. Mrs Muter, writing her memoirs many years afterwards, was shocked to find officers admitting such activities in their own memoirs, and said she thought of Joshua, Chapter 7, verse 21 ('When I saw among the spoils a goodly Babylonish garment and two hundred shekels of silver ... then I coveted them'). She herself went to the prize agents to buy some pearls at the request of a friend at Meerut, but on testing them with a needle found that they were only made of wax within a shell. Among the other items she found were Bibles belonging to ladies who had perished in the massacre.

In the end, the prize agents stopped searching the city for valuables and simply resorted to the long-established convention of allowing each street to pay a ransom in lieu of further molestation. By then, anything worth taking had gone, and the surviving residents were not prepared to pay much for what was left. Delhi had been reduced by the fighting to a state of ruin comparable to that of many great European cities in the aftermath of the Second World War. Heathcote of the 60th Rifles wrote at the time: 'The scene of desolation that reigns through the place is fearful to contemplate. When we first came in it was awful: pools of blood, dead and dying men – the streets in some places actually choked with them – broken guns, houses in ruins from the effects of shot ... the silence seems almost overpowering after the incessant din of the last few months.'

When it came to the distribution of prize money, the Government of India argued that the people of Delhi were not belligerents and therefore any property taken from them was not subject to the laws of prize but belonged to the State. Instead, the troops were given six months' field service allowance, leading someone to write on Delhi's walls 'Delhi taken and India re-conquered for 36 Rupees and 10 annas.' The prize agents handed over Rs 3,547,917 (nearly thirty-five and a half lakhs of rupees) to the Government of India, but it took ten years of legal argument and two court cases for the troops to be paid their due.

At Delhi, Rotton conducted a simple burial service for Nicholson on 24 September. He then watched a column, commanded by Lieutenant Colonel Edward Greathed of the 10th Foot, march out after Bakht Khan. On Sunday, 27 September there was a service of thanksgiving, for which Rotton's text was from Psalm 116 ('What shall I render unto the Lord for the benefits which he has done unto me?'). The next day, with a week's leave, he started for Meerut to see his wife and children. Colonel Young, no longer needed in the field, had already gone back to his family and office at Shimla.

Chapter 8

THE RESCUERS OF LUCKNOW.
JUNE–SEPTEMBER 1857

'Hold it for fifteen days!' we have held it for eighty-seven!
And ever aloft on the palace roof the old banner of England blew.

Tennyson, The Defence of Lucknow

The road train with its trickle of European soldiers reached Varanasi on 25 May, bringing the first few men of the 84th Foot and 1st Madras Fusiliers; 150 men of the 10th Foot arrived from Dinapur, followed by another sixty Madras Fusiliers on 2 June. The city was of strategic importance from its position on the Grand Trunk Road's crossing of the Ganges, 460 miles from Calcutta. Members of several princely families, Muslim as well as Hindu, had palaces there, and it was believed that some might seek to rouse the population of the holiest Hindu city in India against Christian rule. On hearing of the mutiny at Delhi the local military officers had advised retiring into the nearby fortress of Chunar, but the Civil Commissioner, Henry Tucker, a noted evangelist, continued to ride through the city accompanied by his daughter and carrying only his whip and a Bible – just as, he said, David had carried only a sling and a stone.

On 4 June news came of the mutiny of the 17th NI at Azamgarh, 50 miles to the north. The recently arrived station commander, Brigadier George Ponsonby, a Bengal cavalry officer, decided to disarm the 37th and told Neill, who had arrived with his Fusiliers the previous day, that he needed all his Europeans for this. As an officer of the Madras Army, Neill held a low opinion of the Bengal sepoys and their officers alike. Anxious to press on to Kanpur, he insisted that the disarmament must take place immediately. The 37th paraded but, fearing they would be attacked, panicked and rushed to recover their arms. Ponsonby, feeling the weight of his sixty-seven years and the effects of the sun, collapsed and Neill, though still not the senior ranking officer, took over. By sunset the three Indian regiments had been dispersed with heavy casualties, though the British too had taken losses. Most of these were Bengal officers killed or wounded as they tried to reassure their men, but the 10th Foot, supervising the disarmament, lost their assistant surgeon and two men killed. The European community spent the night crammed into the Old Mint, the designated safe haven. Most, to avoid the stifling June heat, spent the night on the roof, in various states of dress or undress, in brilliant moonlight, as it was now twenty-six days since the previous full moon had shone down on the events at Meerut.

The Bengal officers blamed Ponsonby and Neill (both of whom were strangers to them and their men) for bungling the whole operation and driving previously loyal regiments into mutiny. Tucker, the Civil Commissioner who, despite the military refusing to spare him a man, had kept the population of the city from joining the disturbances, also thought the affair had been badly handled. Certainly it confirmed the sepoys' suspicion that being ordered to parade in the presence of British troops was potentially a death sentence. It also delayed Neill's march up-country, thus negating his very purpose in persuading Ponsonby to act with such haste. The fury with which the British then set about hanging every man and boy suspected of supporting the mutiny was equally counterproductive, as the civil labour on which the troops depended fled before their vengeance.

Most of the Europeans remained at the Mint, where they and its contents were protected by Sikh guards. A leading member of their faith, Raja Surat Singh, went down to reassure them and joined with other local nobles in supporting the authorities. A large number of missionaries and their families, unable to reach the Mint, were protected by the Raja of Varanasi in his fort at Ramnagar, from where he sent them on to Chunar with an escort of his own militia. This prince maintained his generosity after the war and presented a well to the waterless Chiltern village of Stoke Row as a memorial. Equally chivalrous behaviour was displayed by Hingal Lal, a Rajput land-holder who sheltered a group of European fugitives from a mutiny at Jaunpur on 5 June. On the approach of marauders, he declared that they should cut his throat before he gave up a guest, and placed the ladies and children in an inner room while telling the men to join his own retainers on the walls. No attack was made, however, and on

9 June a party of volunteer cavalry sent by Tucker took them to the Varanasi Mint.

Lieutenant Blake reached Varanasi with the 84th and marched to the Mint 'where all the ladies – in fact everyone – were, and never in my life did I see such a confusion as there – men, women, children, all together, all higgledy-piggledy.' The task of commanding and fortifying the Mint had been allotted to the senior British subaltern. 'I found that this was now me. I did not care much for this, but did it in a way. I told them I was no engineer, but all my arrangements were approved of.' Wondering where his own meals were to come from, he was taken in by Lieutenants Simpson and Palliser of the 13th Irregular Cavalry and the next morning met Simpson's mother and sister at breakfast and liked them both. He was then sent out with his half-company and a British magistrate to collect various parties of European fugitives. At Jaunpur, they found the ruins of the church with 'blood-spattered walls, and blood-stained garments, male and female, lying about' and were joined by the local raja 'a nice-looking fellow in very gorgeous kit. He said he had two young ladies in the fort whom he would send to us.' The Raja was as good as his word, though Blake had to push his way through an increasingly threatening mob to bring them to safety. In subsequent expeditions he found himself passing alone through groups of disaffected sepoys and escaped only through a mixture and bluff and good horsemanship. It was clear that though Varanasi was secure, British control in the surrounding countryside was still in the balance.

The 78th Highlanders, recalled from the Iran war, reached Varanasi by bullock cart on 25 June, and were employed on local punitive expeditions. One of its men wrote that, after various hangings and floggings, they turned about 200 people out of a village and set fire to it.

> I beheld six children from eight to two years old, an old dotal woman, an old man not able to walk without help, and a young woman, about twenty years old, with a child wrapped up in her bosom. I am sure the child was not above five or six hours old . . . I took the woman and her infant in my arms to carry her and her babe out. The children led the old woman and old man.

After a hard struggle he got them out through the flames, but all their possessions were lost and even the few clothes they had on were partly burnt. He then gathered a group of women to help rescue a dying man and his attendant, drawing his bayonet when they protested they had enough to do 'and so they had, poor things'. Away from the fires, 'the old woman of that small family I took out, came to me and I thought she would have kissed the ground I stood on. I offered them some biscuit that I had for my day's rations; but they would not take it; it would break their caste, they said.'

Neill, having supervised numerous hangings of captured sepoys, left Varanasi on 9 June, heading for Allahabad, 74 miles up the Ganges at its confluence with the Yamuna. Almost as holy as Varanasi and just as strategically important, Allahabad was the easternmost city of the North-West Provinces, housing an arsenal, a major treasury and a strong fort. The cantonments, 4 miles away from the city, housed the 6th Bengal Native Infantry, a company of native artillery, and five companies of the Ferozepore Sikhs under Lieutenant Brasyer, who had started his military career in the ranks of the Bengal Artillery. The road train brought several detachments of European infantry through the city, but these were hurried on to Kanpur. The civil authorities ordered all European non-combatants to move into the fort. Apart from seventy-four artillery pensioners recalled to the colours, the only European troops were a hundred civil servants and railwaymen, who had been formed into a volunteer corps, so the Ferozepore Sikhs were sent into the fort with them.

On 6 June the 6th Bengal NI was paraded to hear the thanks of the Governor-General in Council for having volunteered, some three weeks earlier, to march against the Delhi mutineers. But within hours there came news of the bloodshed at Varanasi. The sepoys, taking this as evidence of British treachery, seized their arms and fired on their officers. Colonel Simpson of the 6th was wounded, and eight other officers and three sergeants were killed. Several cadets, newly arrived in India and left behind in the Mess when the officers of the 6th went to investigate the trouble, also perished. The city mob, swelled by convicts from the gaol, joined the insurgency with the usual looting and burning. Christians of any kind, including six drummers of the 6th who went out to bury their dead officers, were murdered, along with Hindu pilgrims caught up in the rioting. The next day the sepoys of the 6th, many appalled at the disintegration of their regiment, dispersed to their home villages. Government was assumed by a pious young Muslim, Maulavi Liakat Ali, in the name of the King of Delhi. He administered Sharia law and, in accordance with its provisions, allowed Christians their lives if they accepted Islam. He had, however, no military experience and, despite all his piety and wit, had little control over the fighters who rallied to his cause. After the war he evaded British justice for fourteen years, but was eventually exiled to a penal settlement, despite pleading that he had saved several European lives, including that of Amelia Horne.

Conditions inside the fort did little credit to the British authorities. Widows and orphans were denied rations on the grounds that they were non-combatants. There were worries about the Sikhs, whom it was feared would rise on news of the attack on their co-religionists at Varanasi, but Brasyer maintained his influence over them. Volunteers and Sikh groups sallied out of the fort on foraging expeditions that, after some street-fighting with the Maulavi's men, degenerated into plundering. A civil servant turned volunteer officer noted that his railwaymen, several of whose colleagues had been killed in the rising, were 'as bloodthirsty as any demons need be'. The same writer said that the Sikhs were in every way their equal in excess. 'Such scenes of drunkenness I never beheld. Seiks were to be seen drunk on duty on the ramparts unable to hold their muskets. No one could blame them, for they are such jolly, jovial fellows, so different from other sepoys.' A Baptist missionary, Mr Owen, took a sterner view, noting in his diary for 10 June: 'The Europeans began to plunder. The Seiks, ever ready for anything of the kind, instantly followed the example. The thing has gone on from bad to worse, until it is now quite impossible to restrain the Seiks, untamed savages as they are ... Everything is as badly managed as can be. Indeed, there seems no management at all.'

With nothing but the summer heat to stop him, Neill arrived with an officer and forty-three fusiliers in the afternoon of 11 June, paraded the Volunteers and condemned their lack of discipline. The Sikhs, who had been selling them stolen liquor at cheap rates, were moved out of the fort to prevent them from dealing with the fusiliers. They nevertheless continued, as Neill put it, to run in and out of the sally-ports like cats. To keep them loyal, he bought up their liquor and sent them out to forage in neighbouring villages instead of European-owned warehouses in the city. Such liquor as remained was either bought by the commissaries or destroyed.

On 12 June another detachment of Neill's regiment arrived so that he was able to muster 270 fusiliers. With two steamers at his disposal, he evacuated the women and children, nearly a hundred all told, from the overcrowded fort on 15 and 17 June. The Maulavi fled the city and the British avenged the massacre of 6 June as they had elsewhere.

All these distractions, and the disappearance during the Allahabad disturbances of 1,600 draught bullocks collected for Army use, fatally delayed the rescuers' advance. The onset of the monsoon brought little relief from the heat, and the overcrowded Allahabad fort became a breeding ground for germs. On 18 June the first cases of cholera were reported. Eight men were buried that night and twenty the next day. By 22 June, when the outbreak began to decline, seventy fusiliers had died. The rest of their regiment and the headquarters of the 84th Foot arrived, but it was not until 30 June that Neill's second-in-command, Major Sydenham Renaud, marched for Fatehpur, en route to Kanpur with 800 cavalry and infantry. The next day the steamer *Brahmaputra* left Allahabad carrying a hundred infantry up the rising Ganges towards Kanpur.

As Renaud left, Brigadier General Henry Havelock arrived. An officer of the British Army, he had transferred at an early stage to the 13th Foot for service in India, where an officer without wealth could hope to obtain promotion without purchase, through succession to a battle casualty. He had served in the First Burma War, in the Afghan War (where he was part of 'the illustrious garrison' that held Jalalabad after the retreat from Kabul), in the Gwalior campaign of 1843, and in the wars against the Kingdom of Lahore. His command of a division in the recent war against Iran had brought him much credit, and Sir Patrick Grant, with whom he travelled on the same steamer that brought Grant from Madras to be C-in-C, India, introduced him to Canning with the words 'Your Excellency, I have brought you the man.' He was at this time aged sixty-two, slight of stature, and with face and hair, as he said himself, as grey as his first charger.

A committed Christian years before this became the fashion, he was married to the daughter of an eminent Baptist divine, Dr Joshua Marshman, co-founder with the more famous William

Carey of the Baptist Missionary Society's centre at Serhampur (located in the Danish enclave near Calcutta when the East India Company denied missionaries residence in British India). He became a Baptist himself and had some success in preventing drunkenness among his soldiers. As well as his Bible, Havelock studied his profession and the lives of the great commanders, Napoleon among them. From him, he copied the habit of addressing his troops in grandiose language, even to the extent of beginning his speeches with 'Soldiers ...' just as Napoleon began with 'Soldats ...' He also studied the major languages of the country in which he spent his career, Persian and Hindustani, which led some to think that he was too well disposed towards its inhabitants.

Sir Patrick Grant, who selected him for command of the field force heading for Awadh, remembered that Field Marshal Lord Hardinge, a Napoleonic veteran who had served as Governor-General, had said, 'If ever India should be in danger, the government have only to place Havelock at the head of an army, and it will be saved.' Calcutta society was not so sure and one newspaper referred to 'that singular fossil, Col. Havelock, from the cretaceous or pipe-clay period'. Some members of Canning's Council even questioned his appointment, and Lady Canning wrote that Havelock was 'not in fashion, but all the same we believe he will do well'. He left Calcutta on 25 June with the two regiments that had served under him in Iran, the 64th Foot and 78th Highlanders (complete with feather bonnets, kilts and bagpipes), with orders to pick up Neill at Allahabad, relieve Kanpur and reinforce Lucknow. The full extent of the insurgency in Awadh and the North-West Provinces was still not fully appreciated in Calcutta, though it was known that Jhansi had fallen.

This was Havelock's first independent command, a position to which, like any soldier, he had long aspired. To his wife he wrote that he had prayed since his schooldays of holding command in a successful action. At his first meeting with the equally devout and ambitious Neill he made his authority quite clear. Neill was forbidden to issue any orders while Havelock was present. On 2 July a message reached them from Sir Henry Lawrence that Kanpur had fallen. Neither at first believed it but, when confirmation came a day later, Havelock ordered Renaud's advance party to halt and wait for him to arrive with his main force. Renaud who, as he marched, had out-Neilled Neill by his zeal in burning villages and hanging suspected rebels, was told, 'Burn no more villages, unless occupied by insurgents.' Even Neill himself, in ordering him to 'destroy all places en route to the road occupied by the enemy' had said, 'but touch no others; encourage the inhabitants to return'. Havelock telegraphed Grant to say that news of the fall of Kanpur had been confirmed by a post-rider who had witnessed the events. Grant told Neill to order Renaud to halt, if the report was assessed as reliable. Neill acknowledged, but added that in his opinion Renaud's force was strong enough to deal with any opposition even if the reports about Kanpur were true, and should press on to Fatehpur. By doing so he challenged Havelock's judgement, despite the latter's greater experience of war. He also forgot, or, unlike Havelock, perhaps had never read, Napoleon's maxim that the first duty of a soldier is obedience.

At Kanpur, Nana Sahib formally took over the government and on 1 July was crowned Peshwa at Bithur. On 9 July his general led an army of 500 horsemen (mostly from the 2nd Bengal Light Cavalry), 3,000 infantry (half of them regular sepoys) and twelve guns towards Fatehpur, 40 miles south-east of Kanpur, intending to arrive there before Renaud, who was still advancing on the city. Havelock learned this on 10 July, three days after beginning his own advance from Allahabad. The first rains had passed and, despite the heat, he quickened his pace so as to reach Renaud's camp during the night of 11 June, producing a combined force of 435 men of the 64th Foot, 376 of the 1st Madras Fusiliers, 284 of the 78th Highlanders and 190 of the 84th Foot. Most of the infantry had the new Enfields, having used them in Iran or been issued with them before leaving Calcutta. With them were six 9-pdr guns of the Royal Artillery under Captain Francis Maude, formed from the garrison of Sri Lanka, the first men of the Royal Regiment to reach India in a hundred years, and two field guns of the Bengal Artillery, eighty-eight artillerymen all told. The cavalry amounted to twenty European volunteers and 500 of the 13th Bengal Irregular Cavalry.

The two armies met at dawn on 12 July. In a classic encounter battle, the Bengal cavalry drove in the volunteers while the sepoy infantry and artillery advanced in column behind them. They then discovered Havelock's entire force in front of them, with the guns deployed in the centre (as Napoleon, himself an artillery-man, would have advised) and protected by a company of the 64th with their Enfields. Havelock was able to report that the whole battle was decided in ten minutes by the rapid and accurate fire of his guns and riflemen. The sepoy infantry, who always preferred a firefight to a bayonet charge, finding their muskets hopelessly outranged, broke and fled. Maude, having silenced their advanced battery, repeatedly moved his own guns forward and for a time found himself behind the main enemy line while he engaged fresh targets. One such was an enemy commander directing his troops from an elephant, which Maude killed with a shot from a gun he laid himself. The commander, said by some to have been Ramchandra Panduranga, Tatya Tope, one of Nana Sahib's senior aides-de-camp, survived and later became one of the most successful guerrilla leaders of the war. But the incident further disheartened the insurgents, and when Maude turned his fire on those making a stand around their main battery they abandoned the guns and fled back through Fatehpur.

The European infantry, most of whom had just marched 24 miles, were too exhausted to pursue. Havelock reported 5 killed (though another 12 succumbed to the heat) and 4 wounded. Two more were injured by a wounded bullock that attacked them in the packed streets of the city. The insurgents suffered about 150 killed and the loss of their guns. The victors sheltered from the midday sun and, after restoring themselves with grog and biscuit, were allowed to take souvenirs from the city. Havelock issued an order of the day thanking his soldiers for their exertions and attributing the victory to the rapidity of the artillery fire, the power of the Enfield rifle, British pluck, 'and to the blessing of Almighty God, and to the most righteous cause of humanity, truth and good government in India'.

On 14 July he resumed his advance, and the next day, after a 20-mile march to the village of Aong, fought two brisk actions on the Pandu Nadi River, taking five guns and driving the enemy from their position. Once more casualties were slight, though they included Major Renaud, who was badly wounded in the left thigh and died after an amputation. A cavalry attack on the British rear echelon was driven off by a collection of about a hundred invalids and logisticians. The British advanced again on 16 July, the men learning as they marched that the women and children who had survived the massacre of the Kanpur garrison were being held in captivity there. Four miles short of Kanpur, the rebel army stood on an entrenched line with five heavy and two light guns dispersed in the villages through which it ran. Havelock decided to turn the enemy's left flank with a march of several miles through difficult terrain and the noonday sun. At about 2.00 p.m. Maude brought his guns into action under enemy fire, but was unable to silence their heavier pieces and the British infantry, reduced to a mere 900 effectives by heat, fatigue and an issue of heavy porter in place of the usual rum, were pinned down by sepoy volleys.

At this point Havelock ordered the 78th to advance against a village on the extreme left of the enemy line, containing a battery of three guns. One eyewitness later wrote that the Highlanders 'rose, fired one rolling volley as they advanced, and moved forward with sloped arms and measured tread, like a wall'. With their pipes playing them on, they began their charge about a hundred yards short of the objective 'like a pack of hounds racing in to the kill ... There was not a shot fired nor a shout uttered, for the men were very fierce and the slaughter was proportionate.' The British then attacked in echelon all along the line, driving the sepoys from each position in turn, but suffering casualties from artillery fire in the process. In the gathering dusk, they heard rather than saw fresh enemy troops joining the battle, and found the sepoys making a stand around their remaining heavy guns. It was reported that Nana Sahib himself had come out to inspire his troops. With his gun teams and gunners exhausted by the difficult ground, Maude had not kept up with the advancing infantry, and all four European battalions were stopped by the enemy artillery.

Havelock, whose charger had been killed under him, found a remount and told the 64th, 'Get up, my lads, and take those damned guns.' One of the volunteer cavalry remembered that 'Up we got with a cheer; it was more like a howl, and charged up, giving them a volley at eighty yards, and ran in.' Havelock, in his despatches, described the approach to contact as covering 300 yards, during which the sepoy gunners changed from round shot to canister as the British approached, and served their pieces with a determination and accuracy he had seldom witnessed. It was not enough to prevent their capture, however, in an act for which his son and ADC, Lieutenant Havelock, was awarded the Victoria Cross. Maude, marvelling that the enemy cavalry had not attacked his guns as his weary bullocks tugged them through the mud, reached the scene in time to hasten the enemy's flight. Enemy losses were estimated at 250, along with their position and all but two of their guns. The British, through prudent use of cover, lost only one officer, five European soldiers and one Sikh killed, though another hundred or so were wounded. During the night they bivouacked on the outskirts of Kanpur, waiting for their tents and rations to come up, and with nothing to drink but contaminated water, but cheered by the thought that the next day they would rescue their kinswomen.

After the massacre at the boats, the surviving British women and children were held prisoner in the Bibighar or Ladies' House, built by a former British Resident of Kanpur as the home of his Indian mistress in the days before such liaisons were frowned upon. Subsequently they were joined by the few survivors of the Fatehgarh massacre and various other captives. No one knew quite what to do with them and several died of gastro-enteric illnesses while their fate was decided. One option was to hold them for ransom. Another was to use them as hostages against a British return to Kanpur. However, it seemed that neither of these options were open. At a council of war held following their defeat on 15 July, one of those who had fled from the field said that it was impossible to negotiate with the British, who were coming on like madmen and slaughtering all in their path – soldiers and civilians, men and women alike.

This was not too far from the truth, for a series of bloody assizes had left bodies dangling from roadside trees, with women and children left to die of hunger or exposure when their villages were put to the torch. One man with the temerity to ask for compensation for his burnt property was promptly hanged as a rebel sympathizer. Writing from Varanasi on 29 June, the Reverend James Kennedy wrote: 'Such is the state of things here that even fine delicate ladies may be heard expressing their joy at the vigour with which the miscreants are dealt with.' The result was that the British troops being hurried after Neill and his 'Blue Caps' came to be regarded as demons in human form. Most British civilians, including Mr Kennedy, felt they were the safer for it, but local people fled from their approach and the line of the Grand Trunk Road became a virtual desert 10 miles wide.

Certainly the British were advancing at unimaginable speed, having at this time marched over a hundred miles through the monsoon during the eight days since their main force left

Allahabad. At Kanpur, it seemed that the only thing to do was to kill the white captives so that the white soldiers, with none left to rescue, would lose heart and go back. The regular sepoys refused orders to shoot women and children, but eventually a group of five psychopaths, some Hindu, some Muslim, two of them butchers from the bazaar, went into the house and used their swords on everyone there. The next morning, 16 July, while Havelock advanced towards another victory, seventy-three women and 124 children (some still living) were dragged out and thrown down a well.

In the evening, British spies entered the city and discovered what had happened. On 17 July Nana Sahib blew up the Kanpur magazine and retreated to Bithur. Havelock's men, arriving at the Bibighar later in the day, found so much blood there that it was still wet, with evidence of the genocide scattered all around. A week later, left in command while Havelock advanced towards Lucknow, Neill ordered condemned prisoners to lick a part of the floor before their execution, irrespective of their personal involvement in the massacre. This ritual pollution was intended to pursue them beyond the grave, so that he would have his vengeance in this world and the next. Every soldier passing through Kanpur on the way to Lucknow was shown the well and the bloodstained prison-house.

Due to Canning's rejection of Elphinstone's offer to send a fast steamer to catch the previous mail, news of the mutiny did not become known in London until 27 June, the same day that Kanpur fell. The first reaction, as is usual in any British military disaster, was to blame the commanding generals. 'Where was the C-in-C?' demanded the Conservative spokesman on India in the Lords. 'Why was he not in the midst of his army?'

Benjamin Disraeli, Conservative leader in the Commons, expressed astonishment that an ancient capital city had been allowed to fall into the hands of rebellious soldiery, and demanded Canning's resignation. At a private party he was more humorous. 'I said that for my part I had great confidence in George Anson, because he had seen the Great Mogul so often on the ace of spades that he would know how to deal with him. All the world laughed very much, and Mrs Anson sent off the joke to the General. Alas! Alas!' The Duke of Cambridge went to talk over the news with Palmerston, the Prime Minister, and thought it 'certainly most alarming and painful' though, according to

Disraeli, everyone was shocked by the cavalier attitude initially adopted by the ministers. 'Her Majesty is sorely afflicted,' he wrote to Lady Londonderry and, in the Commons, he called for a new relationship between the Queen and British India, and the abolition of the East India Company.

A fortnight later news came of Anson's death and within the day the Secretary for War, Lord Panmure, invited Lieutenant General Sir Colin Campbell to succeed him. Campbell, then aged sixty-five, had been an officer in the British Army since 1808. He had served under Wellington and Moore in the Peninsular, and under Gough in the Opium War and the Second Sikh War. In 1852 he conducted a successful campaign on the Punjab frontier, but condemned the Punjab system of border control as guerrilla warfare carried out by civilians. Dalhousie, always resentful of any criticism of his show province, responded by accusing Campbell of 'excessive caution', effectively of cowardice. Campbell resigned in protest (forbidding any expression of support by his officers) and returned to England, but took the field again in the Crimean War, commanding the 'thin red line' at Balaclava and being appointed GOC of the First Division in succession to Cambridge. When command of the British Army in the Crimea was given over his head to a Guards officer, he went home but was cajoled by the Queen and Prince Albert into continuing to serve. He left England the day after his meeting with Panmure, and after travelling through France by train and crossing Egypt to Suez, reached Calcutta on 13 August with the news of his own appointment.

Canning would have preferred Sir Patrick Grant to retain the command, at least while completing his task of organizing the logistics necessary for a prolonged campaign. Moreover, Grant knew how the Indian military machine worked, and was able to manage with a headquarters staffed by deputies, because all the principal heads of department had been with Anson at the time of the outbreak and were therefore with the army at Delhi. Canning admitted that Campbell would be a better field commander (Grant had been much criticized in the press for concentrating on logistics instead of leading his army to victory) but thought that he did not understand the political importance of securing places such as Patna, the headquarters of the vital Opium Revenue on which Indian finances rested, or the restless small states south of the Grand Trunk Road. Campbell was opposed to diverting resources from the aim of destroying the enemy's main force, but in any case, until his own staff and the promised British reinforcements arrived, could do little but continue Grant's policy of building up the logistics system.

Reinforcements from home were not easily found. The Regular Army at this time was its own reserve, and the only way of bringing those on the peacetime establishment up to strength was to raise new recruits, who (as the Crimean War had shown) were of limited value in the field, or by calling on men to volunteer for transfer from their own units to those ordered on service. Panmure informed Parliament on 29 June that there were 10,000 men about to embark as part of the normal system of annual reliefs and that an additional 4,000 would be sent in response to Canning's appeals. It was soon realized that, even with the troops diverted from the China expedition or sent by various colonial governors, more would be needed. Cambridge wrote in his journal for 3 August: 'Four more regiments of Infantry and one of Cavalry, and 1,000 Artillery are ordered out to India. This will still further reduce our force at home, and how we are to get the men to replace them I cannot tell, but we must do our best. This all gives a great deal of trouble, and we are very hard-worked.' One of the units moving in the normal course of relief was the 88th Foot, the Connaught Rangers. Veterans of the Crimea, they embarked at Portsmouth before news of the Meerut outbreak reached England. After months at sea without touching land, they reached Calcutta to be baffled by a signal telling them that Delhi had been taken. They were hurried to Raniganj, issued with a few necessaries (in the dark) and joined the bullock train to Kanpur.

Eventually Parliament was obliged to increase the Army establishment, and second battalions were authorized for the senior twenty-five Regiments of the Line, with additional battalions for the two Rifle corps, to replace the same number of units sent to India either from home or the Mediterranean. Cavalry, which did not have a battalion system, was more difficult to produce, and rather than raise new regiments, it was decided to convert battalions of the Military Train, many of whose men had served in the cavalry and all of whom knew about horses. The Company departed from precedent by raising six regiments of Bengal European Light Cavalry, and also raised another three Bengal European Infantry regiments, with officers from mutinied native regiments. The first units from England reached Calcutta in October 1857. As the need for urgency was realized, sailing troopships were replaced by steamers, and the Turkish government repaid British support in the Crimean War by allowing British troops to use the overland route through its Egyptian territory.

On 27 June, after the massacre, a large force of insurgents marched from Kanpur towards Lucknow. Two days later they reached Chinhat, 7 miles away from the city. Urged on by Martin Gubbins, his warlike Financial Commissioner, Lawrence decided to meet them, believing that a bold attack such as the British had so often made in their Indian campaigns would achieve success, hearten his own men and demoralize the insurgents. His force was notionally a strong one: 300 Europeans of the 32nd Foot, 170 loyal sepoys, 36 European Volunteer horse, 84 Oudh Irregular Cavalry, 10 field guns (4 manned by Europeans, 6 by the Oudh Irregular Force) and a howitzer, drawn by an elephant. In practice, the battle proved a disaster for the British, who were late starting and marched out without the 32nd being given breakfast. After various halts under a burning sun, they encountered a well-led enemy force, much stronger than Lawrence had expected.

The infantry deployed to meet it and the artillery began a duel in which the howitzer shot to good effect, though neither side's field guns had the range to do much damage. The insurgents then brought their guns forward, as part of a general advance, with formed regiments headed by their colours, and took both flanks of the British position. The cavalry were ordered to charge, but only the European volunteers did so. The Oudh guns were driven into a ditch and their detachments rode off with the teams and ammunition wagons. Lawrence sent the 32nd against the village of Ismailganj, on his left flank, which he had neglected to occupy, but by this time it was in enemy hands. The British came under heavy musketry fire, the sepoys' favourite tactic, and were driven back with the loss of their commanding officer, Colonel Case, who refused an attempt at rescue by one of his captains and ordered him back to his company.

After sepoy musketry defeated a second attack, Lawrence ordered a retreat. The gunners fell back with their limbers crowded with wounded. The howitzer's elephant had bolted and the more placid bullocks provided for use in just such an emergency had been allowed to stray. When the sagacious pachyderm was recaptured, he refused to be hooked up to his gun, which, together with the stranded field pieces, had to be abandoned. Lawrence's casualties totalled 365, including 115 killed (three officers and several senior NCOs among them) in the 32nd alone. The road back to Lucknow was lined with the bodies of British infantry killed not by enemy action but by the effects of heat. Some of the survivors owed their lives to loyal sepoys of the 13th Bengal NI who left their own wounded comrades and rescued British troops.

Lawrence, for all that he held a military rank, was in practice an administrator and had no experience of high command in the field. Politically, his decision to attack might have been sound but, leading the force in person, his execution was faulty. The consequences of his defeat were just as Anson, Barnard and Wilson had feared would follow any rash action on their part before Delhi. The illusion of British invincibility in the field was shattered. Waverers joined the insurgency or fled. The mutineers followed him to Lucknow and by the evening of 30 June the city was under siege. A brief panic subsided when the insurgents failed to follow their victory with an immediate assault while the garrison was still confused and demoralized. Lawrence used his semaphore to send a message to the Macchi Bhawan, which he no longer had the men to defend, ordering its commander to spike his guns and blow up the ammunition before retiring to the Residency at midnight. The 32nd had its headquarters there and lost its documents and band instruments.

When a shell burst in his office on 1 July, his staff urged Lawrence to move to a more sheltered location, but he said that gunners never hit the same place twice. The next day they did and he was mortally wounded by another shell. Mrs Harris, wife of an Anglican chaplain, nursed him through his final hours, noting in her diary: 'His screams are so terrible, I think the sound will never leave my ears; when not under the influence of chloroform, he is quite conscious.' He died on 4 July, mourned by everyone in the garrison. Despite his defeat in the field, for which, on his deathbed, he blamed only himself, he had made full provision for their defence. In his final hours he continued to give instructions for its conduct, appointing Major John Banks to succeed him as Chief Commissioner, and Brigadier Inglis, colonel of the 32nd, as military commander. Executive command of the 32nd passed to its senior surviving captain.

Inglis was better placed to stand a siege than had been Wheeler at Kanpur. His defences, though still incomplete, were stronger and his garrison larger. His European forces included the 32nd, still nearly 500 strong, a company of the 84th, 89 Bengal artillerymen, 51 Eurasian drummers and 133 officers of mutinied regiments, totalling some 800 regular soldiers. There were another 150 Europeans capable of bearing arms who were enrolled as volunteers, including the masters and senior boys of La Martinière School, to this day one of India's most prestigious seats of learning. Not all volunteers were British subjects. Among them were M. Duprat, a former officer of the Chasseurs d'Afrique, who now became a gunner, and Signor Barsotelli, a veteran of the recent campaigns in Italy. Alongside them were 712 loyal sepoys and native officers, who held their own section of the walls. Gubbins suggested disarming them, but Inglis refused to lose half his bayonet strength and the idea was abandoned. There were 1,280 non-combatants of various ethnic groups and social classes, 600 of whom were women and children, and 680 were men, including domestic servants and civil labour of various kinds. There were even some state prisoners, including the brother of the former king and other noblemen of doubtful allegiance. The defences had a perimeter of about a mile and enclosed some 37 acres filled with private houses and gardens. There were ten major strong points, mounting fifteen guns and seven mortars.

None of the defences, however, were proof against artillery, and there was a constant attrition of soldiers and civilians to round shot and musketry. Women and children mostly lived in underground rooms. In the intervals between the bombardments, they came out for air and hygiene, but still suffered casualties from enemy action. The shelters were infested by rats and vermin, and Maria Germon, the wife of a captain of the 13th Bengal NI, declared she had seen a bandicoot (a rat-like animal) the size of a small pig. The wife of a cavalry officer, whose two-year-old son died of fever at the beginning of the siege, just before her own nineteenth birthday, recorded that one 'huge horror' ran up her dress, but was frightened away by her screams. Bustle, the pet dog of the junior chaplain, the Reverend James Harris, might have helped, but when Lawrence ordered all loose dogs to be hung, Mrs Harris put the dog in with the horses. He pined so much that she brought him back, but those with whom she shared her cellar objected and a nearby sentry, Private Metcalfe of the 32nd, looked after him until the end of the siege. Some of the senior families had goats, which subsisted on shrubs and plants in the Residency gardens, but they produced insufficient milk even for their owners' children and there was none to spare for others, who died for lack of it. There was the odd cow and enough sheep to keep up a scanty supply of mutton.

The senior chaplain was the Reverend Henry Polehampton. When the 52nd Light Infantry was at Lucknow he wrote of them: 'I never had a truer Christian among any of the congregations I addressed than in that regiment', and stayed with them as long as he could until they were succeeded by the 32nd. He was wounded by a musket-ball on 7 July and died of cholera on 19 July, leaving Harris to cope with the task of visiting the sick and burying the dead, six or seven at a time on the worst days. The smell from the shallow graves grew so bad that services had to be conducted from a distance and on one occasion Harris returned home and retched for two hours, causing his frightened wife to fear he had contracted cholera himself. The Roman Catholic padre, Father Bernard, seems to have confined his ministrations to his own flock. A man of narrower mind than Father Bertrand at Delhi, he refused to conduct the funeral of the gallant Chasseur d'Afrique on the grounds that he had denied the existence of Providence.

The garrison had more surgeons than were normally provided for 3,000 people, as they included those of the mutinied regiments. One of these was Dr Brydon, who had survived the retreat from Kabul in the Afghan War and would later be immortalized in Lady Butler's painting *The Remnant of an Army*. At Lucknow he was just as vulnerable as everyone else, and was wounded by a stray musket-ball as he sat at dinner. In the overcrowded hospital they carried out the usual battlefield surgery of their time, probing gunshot wounds and amputating shattered limbs, but most of those with major trauma died of shock or sepsis. Conditions were as bad as in the Crimea, without even the few trained nurses who reached there, and the sick and wounded were comforted only by lady volunteers. Smallpox, cholera and gastro-enteric diseases flourished.

Although the insurgents at first seemed content to rely on their artillery, both men and women for weeks slept in their clothes for fear of a sudden assault. Some ladies kept phials of prussic acid or laudanum beside them, and others agreed that their husbands would keep their last bullets for them, so they should not be taken alive. Gubbins refused to have any part in such arrangements, saying that the time had not come for such desperate plans. Among the ladies of the 32nd the widowed Mrs Case and her friend Mrs Inglis determined that they would accept God's will rather than commit suicide. Some anxieties were allayed when it became known that the Kanpur massacres had not involved sexual assault. Clothes began to wear out, and inflated prices were paid when the effects of the dead were auctioned. 'Luckily, crinolines are not necessaries,' wrote the teenage cavalry wife. She was shocked by a doctor's wife whose clothes wore so thin as to become almost transparent, and noted that 'most of us had scanty wardrobes ... but we managed to cover ourselves.'

During July three major *taluqdars* (local land-holders) joined the insurgents with contingents of their own retainers. Their men were armed mostly with bows and no match for the British in the field, but they were skilled at tunnelling, and the insurgents now resorted to mining. Captain Fulton of the Bengal Engineers dug counter-mines using volunteers from the 32nd. A mine that had eluded him was sprung on 19 July, but was in the wrong place and the accompanying assault was beaten back after a day's fighting. The defenders suffered twenty-five casualties, but the attackers lost many more.

The attrition continued. The 32nd recorded 170 men killed or hospitalized during the first month. Banks was shot on 20 July and as the next senior civil servant, Ommaney, the Judicial Commissioner, had died of wounds on 5 July, the indefatigable Inglis concentrated all authority in his own hands. On 29 July the garrison was cheered by the sound of distant gunfire, and sentries reported they could see a relieving column, but the guns were merely saluting the ex-king's twelve-year-old son. On 6 August the boy was declared Wali (governor), thus discarding the royal title that the British had bestowed upon their client king and emphasizing that, as in former times, the ruler of Awadh owed allegiance to Delhi.

On 10 August another mine was sprung, but again the assault was driven back. A third mine, on 18 August, opened a breach

145

30 feet wide, but the British brought up a gun, and a later sortie allowed them to regain the lost ground and repair their defences. On 5 September another attack was beaten off, but explosions from mines and continual battering from enemy artillery began to bring down buildings that sheltered the troops. Fulton, the soul of the defence, was killed on 14 September, leaving a widow at Shimla with six children. However, the hot weather and the monsoon had both been survived, and on 19 September, for the first time in eighty days, there were no funerals and no admissions to hospital. The question was whether Inglis, with food supplies failing and his bayonet strength reduced to 350 Europeans and 300 Indians, could hold on until relief came.

After recovering Kanpur, Havelock ordered Neill to remain there with 220 men, while he himself crossed the swollen Ganges at Mangalwar on 26 July, en route to Lucknow. He advanced on 29 July with elements of the 64th Foot, 78th Highlanders, 1st Madras Fusiliers, the Ferozepore Sikhs and ten field guns, some 1,500 men in all, and after 3 miles made contact with the enemy at Unao. The flooded ground forced him to make a frontal attack and sepoy musketry fire inflicted many casualties before the 64th made a bayonet charge. The sepoys fell back on their supports, who launched a counter-attack in mass formation, headed by their colours and drummers. It was now their turn to be shot down as they advanced on a narrow front and they were driven back with the loss of fifteen guns. After a brief rest, Havelock advanced through the monsoon rains another 8 miles to Bashiratganj, where the enemy had rallied. A frontal attack by the 78th with artillery support dislodged them, but the 64th, sent to cut off their retreat, had been delayed, and most of the enemy escaped back to Lucknow.

Havelock calculated that he had inflicted about 400 casualties on a force 6,000 strong, but had suffered eighty-eight. Battle, cholera and dysentery reduced his effective strength to 1,364. Lucknow was still 30 miles away, he had fired away a third of his ammunition, he had many sick and wounded who could neither be left nor evacuated without an escort that would fatally weaken his main force, and on that very morning he had learned that a sepoy mutiny at Dinapur had interrupted the flow of reinforcements on which he had counted. With no teams to pull the captured guns, he had them put beyond use, and started back on 31 July to a defensive position at Mangalwar. He reported this decision to Grant, the temporary C-in-C at Calcutta, and outlined the various options that would be open to him if he were reinforced.

Many of his men, fearing that their sacrifices would once more have been made in vain, resented the decision, and Neill's Blue Caps openly said that their colonel (now a brigadier general) would not have turned back. Neill himself told Havelock that this retreat would weaken British prestige, and he should have brought in the guns as evidence that he had taken them. As there were no European reinforcements available, he should press on to Lucknow without delay and then 'Return here sharp, for there is much to be done.' A furious Havelock told him that he had no need of such advice from an officer under his command, and that only the needs of the service prevented him from putting Neill under arrest. 'There must be an end to such proceedings at once ... You now stand warned. Attempt no further dictation.'

He was in contact with Lucknow through the agency of Angad Tewari, a pensioned sepoy who several times made the hazardous journey through insurgent lines and who first returned there on 22 July with cheerful news of Havelock's initial successes and promise of an early relief. It was this that led the British garrison to mistake the celebrations for the new Wali as the sound of their arrival. On 4 August, however, after retreating to Mangalwar, Havelock's chief of staff had to send Inglis another message, saying 'You must aid us in every way, even to cutting your way out, if we can't force our way in. We are only a small force.'

Neill sent a company of the 84th and seven guns across the river, and on 5 August Havelock again advanced to Bashiratganj and recovered it after an artillery battle. Enemy casualties amounted to some 300 against Havelock's losses of two killed and twenty-three wounded, but cholera and other illnesses cost him another hundred out of his 1,010 Europeans. He reported to Grant that there were three strong positions, with fifty guns and 30,000 men, between him and Lucknow, and a quarter of his artillery ammunition had already been fired away; the whole province had risen in arms against the British so that he was faced by local forces as well as by regular sepoys; and his men were demoralized by constant combat against vastly superior numbers. He told Grant that if he went on, his column would be

147

sacrificed without helping Inglis, who would be doomed anyway if the column was wiped out, as would Kanpur, held by only 500 Europeans, half of them sick. Lucknow, in his view, was more expendable than his own force, the only one in the field apart from that at Delhi. To keep it in being, he once again fell back to Mangalwar.

At the same time, Neill reported that 4,000 men (including sepoys who had mutinied at Sagar in Bundelkhand on 29 June) had reached Bithur and threatened Kanpur. Unless supported, he said, he would have to stay within the entrenchments, and the whole country would rise, with the steamer bringing much-needed ammunition from Allahabad unable to proceed. Havelock fought a brisk action at Burhia-ka-Chauki to cover his withdrawal and crossed over to Kanpur on 13 August. His force was now down to a total of 1,415, including 335 in hospital. Even Neill realized it was so weakened that, without reinforcements, it could not reach Lucknow. It could, however, go to Bithur, and on 16 August Havelock, with 750 Europeans and 250 Sikhs, stormed its defences and took the city. Havelock reported 250 casualties, and cheered his exhausted men by asking if they themselves could achieve so much with their small numbers, what further triumphs could be expected when the troops on their way from China, the Cape, and England arrived? 'You will be acknowledged to have been the stay and prop of British India in the time of her severest trial.'

The flow of reinforcements so desperately needed by Havelock had been disrupted by the mutiny of the sepoy brigade at Dinapur, Bihar, on the Ganges 120 miles below Varanasi. The local commissioner, William Tayler, was convinced that the many Wahabi residents in the nearby city of Patna were planning a rising. He argued that the British should strike first, by arresting the leading Wahabi clerics (which he did) and disarming the sepoys at Dinapur (which the divisional commander Major General George Lloyd, refused to do, as he had only the 10th Foot with him). A riot in Patna on 3 July, when a British official was murdered, was followed by a series of trials, conducted by Tayler with scant regard for legal niceties, after which nineteen men were hanged. Nineteen others were acquitted by a higher court when their cases were reviewed, much to Tayler's disgust. He was eventually removed from his commissionership, giving him a grievance that led to his resignation. He thereafter waged a pamphlet war against the Bengal authorities, gaining the sympathy (then and later) of those who shared his view of himself as the saviour of Patna.

At the time, supported by the local indigo planters, Tayler continued to press Lloyd for disarmament, and eventually secured a compromise whereby on 25 July the sepoys were ordered to hand in the percussion caps without which their muskets could not be used. Still unsettled by the destruction of the Varanasi brigade, they fired on their officers and fled up the River Son (Soane) to Ara, 25 miles away. On 27 July the mutineers entered Ara, plundered the treasury, opened the gaol and offered their services to the local chieftain, Kunwar (Koer) Singh. A much-respected Rajput nobleman then in his seventies, he had fallen into debt and was in danger of being forced off his ancestral land. The sudden prospect of regime change offered him a way out of his troubles, and he now joined the rising with large numbers of his own clansman. On Tayler's advice, the local Europeans had already sent their dependants to Dinapur, and they themselves now defended a building known as the billiard room, with a garrison of fifteen European and Eurasian volunteers (mostly railwaymen) and fifty Sikhs.

News that they were under attack obliged Lloyd to send a relief force. After various difficulties in navigating the Son, this was reduced to 300 men of the 10th Foot, seventy Sikhs and a dozen volunteers. Led by Captain Dunbar of the 10th, they ran into a night ambush half a mile outside Ara. Dunbar was killed and his men fell back in confusion, repeatedly firing contrary to orders and suffering casualties from their own as well as enemy fire.

The next morning they retreated the 12 miles back to their river-steamer, under constant fire all the way. There were no medical evacuation arrangements, the only surgeon with the force was wounded and casualties who could not keep up were left to their fate. A few officers were saved by the Sikhs, and Private Dempsey, a grenadier of the 10th, won the Victoria Cross for carrying the mortally wounded Ensign Erskine in his arms. Assistant Magistrate Ross Mangles received the same award for carrying a wounded soldier on his back, one of the only two serving civil servants ever to be so decorated. At the river, discipline collapsed as men scrambled into boats or threw away arms and equipment to swim out to the steamer. Ensign Battye of the 10th recalled the loss of the officer commanding the Sikhs. 'I saw him disappear in midstream before I entered the water. He cried out "My God, I'm sinking!" That cry rings in my ear ... an alligator may have seized him, as there were several of them about.'

As the steamer arrived back at Dinapur, onlookers were surprised to see it go straight to the hospital wharf. When the extent of the disaster became known, a crowd of wives of the 10th rushed to Lloyd's bungalow, where he was obliged to barricade himself in, though it was Dunbar, who had called in his scouts and disregarded reports that the enemy were watching him, whom they should have blamed. Seven officers and 184 men had failed to return, and of those who did, 3 officers and 63 men were wounded. At Ara, the siege of the billiard house continued. The Sikhs refused appeals to desert and make common cause against the British, even when offered Rs 500 each. When water ran short, they dug a well 18 feet deep. When meat was needed, they crept out, led by Jemadar Hukm Singh, and drove in some sheep. When the sepoys tried a mine, Hukm Singh counter-mined, and when ammunition ran short he threw brick-bats at them from the roof.

Major Vincent Eyre of the Bengal Artillery, a veteran of the Afghan Wars, had reached Calcutta from Myanmar with his company in June. On their way upriver to Allahabad they saw the cantonments at Dinapur burning as the sepoys mutinied. He reached Buxar (Baksar), 45 miles from Ara, on 28 July, and marched three days later to its relief, with 3 guns and 40 men from his own company, 150 men of the 5th Fusiliers (another unit newly arrived from Mauritius), and some volunteer cavalry, 216 in all. On the way he learned of Dunbar's defeat and was the target of similar jungle ambushes, but successfully countered them with his superior firepower. Kunwar Singh met him in force at Bibiganj on the night of 2 August and pressed the fusiliers hard, but a bayonet charge drove in the insurgents' right flank and allowed Eyre to relieve Ara the next day, having suffered casualties of two killed, fifteen wounded and one dead of cholera.

He was reinforced from Dinapur on 9 August by 200 men of the 10th and a hundred Sikhs, and pursued Kunwar Singh through the jungle to his stronghold at Jagdishpur. On 12 August, British superiority in artillery and long-range rifle fire once again brought them victory and Kunwar Singh was dislodged at the cost of only six men wounded. Eyre blew up the fort and its contents and also a Hindu temple that Kunwar Singh had ruined himself to build, though the destruction of the latter was subsequently condemned by the C-in-C, India, as 'a mistaken view of the duties of a Commander at the present crisis'. The 10th, in return for their own wounded having been killed in the retreat from Ara, showed no mercy, and captured sepoys were hung after a drumhead court martial. Eyre and his men, commended for their success, were recalled to join the reinforcements heading for Kanpur.

The 54-year-old Major General Sir James Outram, hailed by Sir Charles Napier as 'the Bayard of India, *chevalier sans peur et sans reproche*', for his services in the Afghan War, was an officer of the Bombay Army with a distinguished record both as a diplomat, administrator and commander. His chivalry was no mere affectation and his sympathy for the amirs of Sind, displaced by British expansion, later brought him Napier's displeasure. It extended equally to the ordinary British soldiers, and as a member of the Governor-General's Council he wrote that 'the British soldier, even of the roughest stamp, is, if wisely and kindly treated, susceptible of a culture – physical, intellectual, moral, and professional – far in excess of that which is generally supposed to be attainable by him.' The soldiers' wives received similarly chivalrous consideration. 'The women should feel, and their husbands and husbands' comrades should see, that the most trifling matters affecting their comfort and happiness engaged their officers' constant and solicitous attention. They should be addressed as if it were assumed that every woman was in feelings a lady, and in moral tone all that her best friends could wish.'

After hurrying back from his victory over Iran he arrived at Calcutta on 31 July and was given command of the combined Dinapur and Cawnpore divisions (both vacant as Lloyd had been removed and Wheeler killed), with the appointment as Chief Commissioner of Oude, a post he had held before, at the time of the annexation. He reached Dinapur on 15 August to find that seven companies of the 90th Perthshire Light Infantry, four days further upriver, had been recalled because of the recent mutiny and now had cholera among them. Deciding there was no reason to keep them cooped up on their boats, he sent them on again, and would have done the same with a company of the 5th Northumberland Fusiliers, except that he needed them for local defence. The 'lax discipline and exasperated feelings' of the 10th, still angry at the fate of their wounded, had been responsible for the murder of loyal sepoys in the garrison, and they could not be trusted to do duty in the town.

Four days after his victory at Bithur, Havelock telegraphed to Sir Colin Campbell, the newly-arrived C-in-C, with a situation report. He said that his force had been losing six men a day to cholera and was now reduced to 700 effectives, exclusive of lines of communication troops. If reinforced with 2,000 Europeans, he would resume the offensive and was sure that, with his superiority in artillery, nothing could stand against him. On the other hand, without the promise of speedy reinforcements, he would retreat to Allahabad.

The message he sent to Lucknow on 4 August had taken eleven days to reach Inglis, who replied that it was impossible to leave the defences. He had 120 sick and wounded, 220 women and 230 children, and no transport for them or the 23 lakh of rupees of treasure and 30 guns he would have to abandon. He would therefore place his force on half rations and hoped these would last until 10 September. This reply reached Havelock on 23 August and he immediately telegraphed it to Campbell in support of his request for more troops. On 29 August he sent a message to Inglis to say Campbell had promised that reinforcement would come within twenty or twenty-five days, and that he would then be ready to march on Lucknow. 'I can only say, do not *negotiate* but rather perish sword in hand.'

Outram had originally planned to march directly on Lucknow, following the more northerly road from Varanasi through Jaunpur. Inglis, however, was clearly in desperate straits and the nearest force to him was at Kanpur, from which Havelock said he would retire unless reinforced. Military theory might dictate that Lucknow and its few hundred regular troops were expendable. Politically and morally it was unthinkable that the garrison there, with so many women and children among them, could be left to share the fate of Kanpur. If Lucknow were to fall while troops were being concentrated into the mass that would ensure victory, the dust of blame would certainly settle on the skirts of the British government. Thus Brigadier General Havelock received his reinforcements, but with them came a major general who out-ranked him, just as he outranked Neill. Campbell, who knew what it was like to lose a command, made a point of officially praising him for 'the energy, promptitude and vigorous action' that had marked his conduct of the recent operations.

Outram, with his usual chivalry, wrote to Havelock: 'I shall join you with reinforcements, but to you shall be left the glory of relieving Lucknow, for which you have already so nobly struggled.' Until the relief was achieved, he said, he would serve militarily only as a volunteer under Havelock's command, and go with the column in his civil capacity as Commissioner. This decision, nobly meant, did not work well in practice. It is, indeed, doubtful if Outram had the constitutional right to hand over command in this way, though both Canning and Campbell signified their agreement. In practice, his position as Commissioner placed operational decisions in his hands, and Havelock found it necessary to defer to him as if he were the military commander. The outcome might have been happier if he had responded to Outram's chivalry with a corresponding gesture of his own, and insisted on serving under him; but it is hard to surrender a command and the arrangement was meant to be short-lived.

Outram reached Kanpur on 15 September with the last batch of reinforcements, some 1,400 men in all. Leaving Lieutenant Colonel Wilson of the 64th to guard Kanpur with his headquarters and invalids, the main force crossed the river on 18 September, just over 3,000 strong. Outram commanded the cavalry, made up of fifty sowars of the 12th Bengal Irregular Cavalry and a hundred gentlemen volunteers. The infantry, comprising elements of the 5th Fusiliers, the 64th Foot, 78th Highlanders, 84th Foot (less the company already inside Lucknow), all by this time armed with Enfield rifles, the 90th Light Infantry, 1st Madras Fusiliers and the Ferozepore Sikhs, were formed into two brigades under Neill and Colonel Hamilton of the Highlanders respectively. Three batteries of artillery, under Olpherts, Maude and Eyre, went with them, brigaded under Major Cooper.

Mangalwar offered a brief resistance, but Unao and Bashiratganj were undefended and every bridge along the way had been left intact. After marching though three days of continuous rain, the column reached the Alam Bagh, a walled enclosure of several acres beside the road 2 miles south of Lucknow, where the insurgents waited for them. While the artillery bombarded the frontal defences, one of Havelock's two infantry brigades waded through a water obstacle to take their right flank and Neill led the other in an advance that captured the Alam Bagh in a few minutes. Outram, at the head of the cavalry, pursued the retreating sepoys and captured five guns before he was stopped by superior numbers at the city's southern canal. Returning to the main force, he heard the news that the British had recaptured Delhi.

Leaving 300 unfit men to guard the Alam Bagh, Havelock resumed the advance on 25 September. With the British Army's aversion to fighting in built-up areas, his plan had been to outflank the city, make two passages of the River Gomati (Gumti) and approach the Residency from the north. Outram advised that, with the recent rains, this route was too boggy for the artillery, and accordingly the army took the direct route through the city. Determined resistance was encountered at the Char Bagh bridge over the canal ravine, but the position was eventually taken by a bayonet charge. Captain Willis, commanding the 84th, addressed his men, 'telling them I expected great deeds from them, their comrades were in front, in the garrison, anxiously expecting them to relieve them, and the poor wives and families in Calcutta looked to us to succour their husbands and fathers. So we set up a cheer ... and charged up the street, driving the niggers out of the houses.'

With Outram leading one brigade by a separate route, Havelock pressed on through the maze of streets until the two groups met at the massive Kaisar Bagh. There, in the fading light, Outram urged an overnight halt to allow the rear of the column, with its baggage and heavy guns, to catch up. Havelock used his last period of command to decide to go on, as the Residency was almost in sight, enemy fire had slackened and the worst of the street fighting seemed over. The final rush, however, provoked an equally determined resistance from the insurgents. Firing from rooftops and houses, where the British infantry could not reach them, they inflicted the heaviest casualties of the day.

In the confusion, a column of dhoolies with the wounded lost its way and came under attack. Some bearers carried their loads to safety but others fled, leaving about forty helpless men to be put to death. Surgeon A.D. Home and Assistant Surgeon William Bradshaw of the 90th escaped with five of their patients and nine survivors of the escort and conducted a desperate defence in a nearby building until rescued the next day. Both were awarded the Victoria Cross, as were three soldiers with them. The 78th was awarded a regimental Victoria Cross and allowed to select the representative who wore it, a provision that still exists in the regulations but is no longer used. They chose Assistant Surgeon McMaster, who in addition to his medical duties had carried the Queen's Colour in the final rush to the Residency. It was said that the 9th Lancers wanted to use the same provision to honour a regimental *bhisti*, or water-carrier, but Indians were not at this time eligible. Surgeon Robert Bartrum of the Bengal Medical Service had been with the dhoolies. His wife, Katherine (Kate), and their baby son were inside the Residency where, with both of them dressed in the cleanest clothes she could find, they waited for him for two more days, until Dr Bradshaw came to say that Bartrum had been killed beside him. In war, not all journeys end in lovers' meetings.

In the gathering dusk, Havelock and Outram led the way through an embrasure into the blocked-up Baillie Guard post, followed closely by men of the 78th. Mrs Harris, like the other ladies, had no idea they were so near, and was taking the evening air when:

> Suddenly, just at dark, we heard a very sharp fire of musketry quite close by, then a tremendous cheering; an instant after, the sound of bagpipes, then soldiers running up the road, our compound and veranda filled with our *deliverers*, and all of us shaking hands frantically, and exchanging fervent 'God bless you's' with the gallant men and officers of the 78th Highlanders ... the state of joyful confusion and excitement is beyond all description. The big rough-bearded soldiers were seizing the little children out of our arms, kissing them with tears rolling down their cheeks and thanking God they had come in time to save them from the fate of those at Cawnpore. We were all rushing about to give the poor fellows drinks of water, for they were perfectly exhausted.

Tea was made for a party of thirsty officers, but without milk or sugar, and there was nothing to give them to eat. In the crowd she was suddenly seized by both hands and 'warmly greeted' (the term a Victorian lady, especially a chaplain's wife, would use, in a published journal, to mean 'kissed') by one of her old friends among the rescuers, while 'utter strangers beamed upon each other'.

The blood-price had been heavy. Between leaving Kanpur and taking the Alam Bagh, Havelock had lost 207 casualties. In the streets of Lucknow, he lost 11 British officers killed and 108 men killed, 22 officers and 317 men wounded, and 77 men missing (mostly from the abandoned dhoolies), a casualty rate of about 25 per cent. Casualties included some of the loyal sepoys within the garrison, bayoneted by Highlanders who took them for the enemy. Among the killed was Neill himself, shot at close range while his brigade passed under an archway. Cooper, the artillery brigadier, had also fallen. Outram was wounded slightly, and Colonel Robert Campbell, commanding the 90th, mortally. Few of the seriously wounded in the once again overcrowded hospital lasted long. The chloroform was finished and Chaplain Harris conducted nineteen funerals on 26 September. Campbell, after an amputation, became increasingly ill, and was nourished by a daily egg from one of Mrs Inglis's hens. The bird had been offered to her at Rs 5, which she thought too much, but Colonel Inglis bought it. It began to lay just in time to save it from being eaten and continued to do so until Campbell died on 12 November. The hen never laid again, but was kept as a pet.

After the initial euphoria, it was realized that Lucknow had not been relieved, but only reinforced. Outram had intended to evacuate the Residency immediately and had therefore left all his forward maintenance supplies (including the chloroform) at the Alam Bagh. Only after arrival did he appreciate that there was no transport to be procured from Lucknow city, as it remained in insurgent hands. Even with transport, fighting his way back through the streets against the same level of resistance as that encountered on the way in, encumbered by the women, children and wounded, was out of the question. Unable to leave, he had to stay, though as his men had brought nothing more than was in their packs, they had to be fed from the resources of an already starving garrison. Lieutenant Blake of the 84th, appointed to command the grenadier company after its captain was killed in the street fighting, wrote that his men had no food at all for the first day after they arrived. 'At last I saw a native coming along with four goats. I asked him to sell one, he refused so we took it.' His men milked it and then killed and roasted it. Blake enjoyed his share and also the milk, which the men insisted he should have, as there was not enough to share among them all. They then all went to join the other units collecting souvenirs from the Old Palace, which was found to be full of coins and other valuables. Pay parades, with the military chest left at the Alam Bagh, were impossible.

Outram immediately used his extra numbers to extend the perimeter and recover lost ground. They had to be fed and rations were reduced still further. The providential find of a large store of grain laid in by Sir Henry Lawrence, about which his commissaries knew nothing, allowed Outram to calculate that, with care, food could be eked out until 1 December. In the usual way of garrisons under siege, unfamiliar herbs and novel diets helped vary the monotony, and careful household managers made the best of things. Mrs Inglis found some arrowroot for sick children and took provisions from her own store to the families of her husband's soldiers. A large goat and two kids disappeared and some of the Fusilier sentries were held responsible. Certainly there were cases where hungry soldiers took chapatis and left rupees in their place. Rats and kittens, the usual siege fare, were not resorted to, but one of the doctors shot 150 sparrows to make a curry. Mrs Germon wrote that most of his dinner guests enjoyed it, but she could not be persuaded to try it herself. As the nights became colder, soldiers and civilians alike grew hungrier, and wondered when they would hear the pipes of Campbell's beloved Highlanders.

Chapter 9

THE DELIVERERS OF LUCKNOW. SEPTEMBER 1857 TO MARCH 1858

Fortunatus nunc sum – I am in luck now.

An officer of Sir Colin Campbell's staff

With the eyes of the world on Lucknow, Campbell left Calcutta on 27 October to command the relief in person. The hot weather was over and European troops could move without the risk of heat-related casualties that had taken so heavy a toll earlier in the year. Ahead of him went the 53rd Foot, released from Calcutta by the arrival of more British troops and the formation of citizen volunteers (reluctantly authorized by Canning at the end of June). With them, carried steadily forward at 25 miles a day by the bullock train, despite repeated attempts by anxious local officials to detain them, were the 93rd Highlanders, diverted from the China expedition, and the last three companies of the 90th, delayed by shipwreck. Also ahead of him was the first party of a naval brigade of 329 seamen and fifty-six marines, under Captain the Honourable William Peel of the steam frigate *Shannon*, a veteran of Sebastopol and a son of the former Prime Minister. Their equipment included not only the four 24-pdrs and four 12-pdr rocket tubes normally carried for service with landing parties, but six 68-pdr guns of the ship's main armament on locally-made field carriages. They had left Calcutta in river-boats on 18 August, but the underpowered steam engines of the time made slow progress against the monsoon-swollen Ganges and it was not until 3 October that they reached Allahabad. From there they went by land, in a long train of heavy guns, ammunition tumbrels and logistic vehicles of all kinds, drawn by elephants and some 800 gun-bullocks, the 'cow-horses' as the sailors called them, with a horde of the monkeys, parrots and other creatures that seamen commonly keep as companion animals.

The anxiety of the local governments was by no means unjustified. South of the Grand Trunk Road large and well-armed insurgent forces, those of Kunwar Singh among them, were still in the field. In Bundelkhand, Canning's worries about 'the wild jungly rajas' were borne out when the ruler of Rewa came under pressure from his nobles to join the revolt. The Dinapur mutineers had reached Nagod in September, where the 50th Bengal NI mutinied and joined them. On 18 September the 52nd Bengal NI, further south at Jabalpur, deserted en masse. A combination of all these bodies would have forced the British in this region to retreat south across the River Narmada (Narbada). Canning was prepared to risk this and refused all requests to divert Campbell's stream of reinforcements into these areas. He insisted, however, that troops were found for the protection of Varanasi and Bihar, the centre of the vital opium revenue, and 320 men of the 10th Foot and 170 of the 17th Madras NI were held back accordingly. The recently arrived Madras sepoys, brigaded with Madras Europeans, were happy to demonstrate that they had nothing in common with their Bengal counterparts, though it was rumoured in the bazaar that they had said they would join them if faced with overwhelming numbers.

Help also came from Gurkha troops despatched by Jang Bahadur, the chief minister of Nepal. Canning had refused to accept them when they were first sent, as he suspected Jang Bahadur of having his own designs on Awadh. Moreover, he had not wished the British to seem in need of assistance and accordingly the Gurkhas had been recalled. When the revolt spread, he had to change his mind and at the end of July they crossed the frontier en route to Gorakhpur, 120 miles east of Lucknow. Moving at a rate of 6 miles a day, they were too late to influence the siege, but took over the defence of Jaunpur and Azamgarh, the districts lying between the Gomati and Ghaghara (Gogra) rivers north of Varanasi.

A further cause of anxiety had been the defence of Agra. There, on 5 July, the garrison commander, Brigadier Polwhele, had led out his troops, the 3rd Bengal Europeans, 200 volunteer cavalry and two guns, to meet a combined force of mutineers from Nimach and Kota. In an encounter at Shahganj, his artillery ran out of ammunition and he retreated to Agra fort with forty-nine officers and men killed and a hundred wounded. The city mob rose and thirty European civilians, men and women, were

159

murdered. The rest of the 4,000-strong Christian community, including American missionaries, French nuns, Italian priests, Parisian entertainers, Armenian traders and all the civil servants of a great provincial capital, fled into the fort, though at first Indian Christians were shut out. All men of military age and European descent were required to join the Volunteers if they wished to remain. Some of the refugees had lost all they owned; others brought in their servants and business stocks with them, and the fort, though overcrowded and insanitary, was never short of food from the outside. The victorious mutineers did not attack, but continued on their way to Delhi. Though most of the city remained in rebel hands, communications with Calcutta were not interrupted. Messages arrived removing Polwhele from command and announcing that J.P. Grant, a member of the Governor General's Council, had been appointed Lieutenant Governor of the Central Provinces, a new local government created from the south-eastern parts of the North-West Provinces as temporary expedient while Colvin was shut inside Agra. Colvin never left Agra, as he died there on 9 September, worn out, it was said, by his many burdens.

His senior officers continued to quarrel among themselves, the regulars with the volunteers, the civil with the military, and even the Protestants with the Catholics. In early October, they feared a possible junction between mutineers from Delhi, Mhow, (where on 2 July the garrison had joined a mutiny of the Maharaja Holkar of Indore's forces) and Gwalior. There, the Maharaja Sindhia had taken the Gwalior Contingent into his own service, reasoning that if the British won, they would be grateful to him for keeping a division's worth of regular troops out of the fighting; or if they lost, such an army would stand him in good stead in any war of succession. The Mhow and Indore men joined him at Gwalior but, when he failed to lead them against the British, departed for Agra in early October.

Greathed's column from Delhi consisted of two troops of horse artillery and a field battery, the 9th Lancers, 500 Punjab Cavalry, 1,200 Punjab Infantry, and the 8th and 75th Foot, who were barely able to muster 450 British bayonets between them. Indeed the 8th, in the three months it spent at Delhi, at one time had been reduced from 362 to eighty-one effectives. Lieutenant Barter, the adjutant of the 75th, thought his regiment should not have been selected to go with Greathed at all, as they had only

250 men left out of 928 and 5 officers out of 28, whereas the 61st, which was originally chosen, seemed to have 12 officers and 400 men. Their surgeon, however, reported them unfit for field service, and Barter overheard their officers gleefully congratulating him on his decision, which meant the 75th had to go in their place. They fought various actions along the way, defeating the Jhansi mutineers at Bulandshahr on 28 September. At Aligarh, the cavalry formed into a line to pursue fugitives into the fields as if beating crops for game. One officer of Lancers wrote: 'A scene commenced which baffles all description – peafowl, partridge and Pandies rose together: the latter gave the best sport.'

By now Greathed was a mere 40 miles away from Agra and a series of urgent messages from the authorities there made him hurry to the city's rescue, with the Europeans carried in carts or on elephants. His men crossed the Yamuna by Agra's bridge of boats early on 10 October and marvelled at the clean white caps and red tunics of the troops on the ramparts. The crowd that watched them come were equally astonished at the appearance of the bearded, sun-bronzed, khaki-clad veterans of Delhi. One lady told her companion, Charles Raikes of the judiciary, 'Those dreadful-looking men must be Afghans.' Barter, when he heard of it, thought this an ungracious welcome for men who had marched 57 miles in twenty-four hours to their rescue. Raikes himself only realized they included British regiments when he saw a clay pipe in the mouth of a man in the rear company. 'My heart bled to see these jaded miserable objects, and to think of all they must have suffered since May last to reduce fine Englishmen to such worn, sun-dried skeletons.'

Colonel Cotton, who had replaced Polewhele as the local commander, assured Greathed (disregarding assessments by the senior Volunteer officers) that there were no enemy in the area. Greathed, glad to give his exhausted men a rest, decided not to post picquets until the evening, and ordered the column to bivouac on the racecourse outside the city while they waited for their baggage train. The cooks started breakfast, while the officers and men threw off their equipment and relaxed. Some slept, others took the chance of a bath. Horses were unsaddled and gun teams unharnessed. Some officers went to visit friends in the fort. Arthur Lang, the Engineer, joined a group of friendly ladies for breakfast. Barter went with two other officers to find family graves from when they had previously been stationed there.

161

Wandering about, he heard the sound of firing and supposed it was men cleaning their arms or shooting pigeons. He then encountered a formed body of 200 rebel sepoys and realized that a battle had started.

Neither side had known of the other's presence – the insurgents because Greathed reached Agra so quickly, the British because they relied on Cotton's faulty intelligence, and both sides because of the high grass on the racecourse and crops in the surrounding fields. The result was a soldiers' battle, with the insurgent gunners ranging on the British lines and insurgent cavalry riding into their camp, while British bugles sounded the alarm and officers rushed back to their men. Roberts, who had come with the column from Delhi, saw civilians become mixed up with the approaching baggage train as they fled back to the fort. Loose horses and followers streamed in all directions. Greathed reached the firing line three minutes after the alarm and found the artillery already in action, the Lancers in their saddles, though in every kind of dress, mostly in shirt-sleeves, and the infantry drawn up at their emergency positions of assembly. Individuals caught in the open duelled for their lives with bayonets, swords and lances.

Barter found some Punjab cavalry saddling their horses and tried to borrow a mount to get back to the 75th, but none could be spared. He ran on and saw his regiment form square and repel a series of cavalry charges. Insurgents were heard shouting to each other that their opponents were the *bhala-vale* (lit. spearmen) from Delhi, a force thought still to be miles away, and the 9th Lancers subsequently adopted the soubriquet 'The Delhi Spearmen'. As in other battles, many sepoy officers displayed great courage and determination, but the element of surprise had been lost and, with their artillery as the decisive arm, the British were able to fight the insurgents off. 'Had not our fellows been used to get ready and fight at a moment's notice, nothing could have saved us,' wrote Barter.

Within the fort, the gunfire had at first been taken for salutes. The 3rd Europeans, with band playing and colours flying, came out with a battery of guns to join the fight, but by then it was mostly over. Cotton, who as the senior ranking officer assumed command (though Greathed was not at first clear he had done so), pursued the retreating enemy and captured their camp and fifteen guns. Lang was scathing about the Agra troops compared

162

with those from Delhi, though he also wrote that the 75th 'behaved so much as usual that Gordon, who commands them, actually said to me that they were so unsteady that he was beyond words disgusted with them.' He was even more critical of the Agra Volunteer Horse, though admitting that they did good work during the pursuit, in which he claimed to have killed twelve men with his own sword.

British casualties were remarkably small, totalling eleven killed and fifty-six wounded. The Moti Masjid, or Pearl Mosque, an architectural gem even by comparison with the nearby Taj Mahal, served as the hospital and Mrs Raikes and other ladies nursed the wounded round the clock for several weeks. Never in the whole time, according to her husband's account, 'did the soldiers utter a word that could shock the ears of their gentle nurses'. Greathed (nicknamed 'No-head') and Cotton were less tenderly treated. Command of the column was given to Hope Grant, who arrived from Delhi on 18 October, and who led it on to reach Kanpur a week later. Crossing into Awadh in response to Campbell's orders, he halted at Banthira, on the bridge over the River Sai at Bani about 6 miles south of the Alam Bagh, and made contact with the defenders. Supplies and ammunition were delivered safely, but the cavalry escort was routed by a swarm of hornets.

The column from Allahabad (the 53rd, 93rd Highlanders and the naval brigade with the siege train) was delayed by the decision of its commander, Lieutenant Colonel Powell of the 53rd, to leave his camp and march 16 miles in search of the Dinapur mutineers, who were reported as being either about to cross into Awadh or to attack Fatehpur. The two forces met at Khajuha (Kudjwa), 25 miles south-east of Kanpur on 2 November, in a fierce engagement that was almost a British disaster. Powell himself, engaging some 4,000 men (half of them sepoys in uniform) and five guns with a mere 500 men and two guns, was killed and 20 per cent of his force became casualties before the insurgents retreated. Captain Peel, as the senior ranking officer, took command and captured their camp and guns, but broke off the pursuit with his men too exhausted to continue. Campbell, while paying tribute to Powell's personal courage, officially observed that 'he had exceeded his duty' in leaving the siege train whose safety should have been his main concern, and was particularly displeased that British sappers of

163

the Royal Engineers (the first to serve in India) had been used as infantry, despite his repeated instructions to the contrary.

After they reached Banthira, Arthur Lang remarked on the fraternization between Highlanders and the Punjabis of his own column. Walking back to his tent after the pipers had finished playing for the Officers' Mess, he found groups of Afghans, Sikhs and Highlanders trying on each others' headdresses, 'each jabbering away in the other's language, not in the least understood by one another, but great friends'. He was glad to see the seamen of the naval brigade, though 'they seem so strange and out of place, rolling about up here, using their sea language among the niggers, driving bullock gharis and swearing because "she tacks about and backs and fills so".'

From Lucknow, Outram was able to maintain contact with Kanpur by notes concealed in quills and carried by his Indian spies. Possibly remembering from his Latin lessons that Julius Caesar had used a similar device when besieged by the Gauls, he wrote in the Greek script. When an officer who had clearly been less attentive at school objected, he replied: 'You ask me to write in the English character. So would the enemy wish me to do. As the only security against their understanding what we write in case our letters fall into their hands, the Greek character must be used.' He refused to send letters to his wife, saying that all private communications were forbidden to others and that he could not, in honour, take advantage to write privately himself. The besiegers remained active and for the first fortnight after the reinforcements arrived there were alarms every night. Mining and countermining continued with, in the words of Captain Willis of the 84th: 'the niggers beating us hollow at this work: they are the most indefatigable brutes behind walls in the world, and if their courage equalled half their ingenuity we should be beaten out of this place within a week. They are up to every dodge.'

The Gwalior Contingent, responding to personal pleas from Tatya Tope, had finally decided to leave Sindhia and join Nana Sahib's army at Kalpi. This city, on the Yamuna, was barely 40 miles south-west of Kanpur, and Outram now urged Campbell to deal with this new threat before relieving Lucknow. He promised to make his supplies last until the end of November, though warned that his own troops would be less physically able to co-operate with the relieving column when it did come, and that he

164

would be able to move fewer guns. This was because most of the gun bullocks would by then have been eaten and he was ready to eat his starving horses.

Campbell decided to maintain his aim of relieving Lucknow. The political need to rescue the garrison and non-combatants who had already endured so much was imperative, and the troops would significantly add to his field strength. On 9 November Campbell marched from Kanpur and took personal command of the force at Banthira. The base at Kanpur, well-protected by the field fortifications constructed during Havelock's command there, was left to Major General Charles 'Redan' Windham, a veteran of the Crimea, with the headquarters of the 64th Foot and detachments of the 5th and 84th, recovered invalids and enough seamen to work his guns, totalling 550 men. All other reinforcements passing through were to be sent after the C-in-C, except for 500 of the 27th Madras NI and six guns of the 2nd Madras Brigade under Brigadier M. Carthew, expected to arrive the following day. Windham was ordered to be ready for any enemy movement from Kalpi, but otherwise to strengthen his defences and remain inside them, making as great a show of force as he could, unless under actual bombardment.

On 10 November, Thomas Kavanagh, an uncovenanted civil servant, arrived at Campbell's tent after passing through the insurgents' lines in disguise. Outram's usual messenger, Kanauji Lal, in normal times a court bailiff, had been reluctant to take him and Outram was inclined to agree, but eventually appreciated that Kavanagh would be useful as a guide. Kavanagh smeared his face and hands with lamp-black and was sent off into the night with a final daub from Outram himself. After several narrow escapes from village dogs and suspicious sepoys, the two messengers reached the British camp and were taken to Campbell. Outram's advice was the column should take the route round the outside of Lucknow as Havelock had originally planned, and it was this course that the relieving column followed when it resumed its advance on 13 November. Kavanagh was awarded the Victoria Cross and Rs. 20,000, and promoted to assistant commissioner. Kanauji Lal was made a revenue officer, with a reward of Rs. 5,000 and substantial land-holdings.

Brushing aside the insurgents around the Alam Bagh, Campbell occupied the Dilkhusha Bagh (Garden of the Heart's Delight) and La Martinière on the night of 13 November. With reinforcements continuing to reach him from Kanpur, he now had an army of some 5,000 men, including 200 of the Military Train serving as dragoons and forty-four guns from the naval brigade and the Royal, Bengal and Madras Artilleries. The infantry, organized into three small brigades, included the 8th and 75th Foot and the 2nd and 4th Punjab Infantry from Delhi; elements of the 53rd and 84th Foot from Calcutta; the 64th Foot and 78th Highlanders from the Gulf; and the 5th Northumberland Fusiliers, 23rd Royal Welsh Fusiliers, 82nd Foot, 90th Light Infantry and 93rd Highlanders from the diverted China expedition.

Following a feint against the western side of the city, Campbell crossed the undefended canal near its junction with the Gomati on 16 November and advanced to the Sikandar Bagh. The sepoy defenders had no guns, but allowed the Punjab cavalry at the head of the British column to approach along a narrow ravine to within musket-shot before opening fire. The cavalry retreated but became mixed up with the horse artillery and British infantry following them. The horse gunners rode up one of the banks and came into action 60 yards from the Sikandar Bagh's thick wall, supported by rifle fire from the infantry. Campbell rode up to judge the situation and was hit by a spent bullet that had killed a grenadier of the 93rd. He decided to counter the sepoy muskets with heavy artillery and after half an hour's bombardment opened a breach through which the infantry attacked. When the only gateway was taken (through the bravery of Kumara Khan of the 4th Punjab Infantry), the sepoys were caught in a trap in which their preference for missile action was of no avail against the shock action at which their adversaries excelled. Apart from a handful who escaped over the walls, all the 2,000 defenders were killed and the British fought on for another quarter of a mile to reach the mausoleum of Shah Najaf.

This was attacked by the 93rd Highlanders with close support from Middleton's Battery of the Royal Artillery and the heavy naval guns, of which Campbell wrote in his despatches: 'Captain Peel behaved very much as if he had been laying the *Shannon* alongside an enemy's frigate.' The guns, however, were unable to breach the tomb's thick walls and no scaling ladders were available. Once again, accurate sepoy musketry caused heavy casualties, especially among the mounted staff officers (Kavanagh, riding with them as a guide, was one of several whose horse was shot under him) and Campbell, always parsimonious with his soldiers' lives, decided to fall back. Before the orders could be given a group of the staff moved through the undergrowth alongside the building and found a crack in the wall. Climbing through, they discovered that Peel's rockets, brought up when he could not breach the walls, had landed inside and the defenders had fled. The rockets were generally disliked, as they were liable to cause casualties from friendly fire, but on this occasion their worth could not be denied and the force then halted for the night along a line from the Sikandar Bagh through Shah Najaf's mausoleum to another large building, formerly the mess-house of the 32nd Foot, half a mile to the south.

The British plan was for Outram to make a sortie and join Campbell when the relieving force reached the Moti Mahal (Palace of the Queen), a quarter of a mile beyond Shah Najaf's mausoleum. In preparation for this, Captain Willis and the 84th were detailed to storm the Harn-Khana, or Deer Department, alongside the palace, once the engineers had exploded a mine to breach its wall. '[We] were all drawn up and ready for the sally', he later wrote:

> Unfortunately the powder had been down the mine thirty-six hours – the General not thinking Sir Colin would have taken four days from the Alambagh to our position, and there appeared to be a doubt as to the mine exploding, added to which the Engineer officer told me, just as I was about to start, that the distance to the wall was so great that they could not get a candle to burn down the mine, and therefore after a certain point could not tell whether the end of the mine went as far as the end of the place intended to be breached.

Disliking this, Willis asked the chief of staff if he should wait to see if the mine breached the wall, but was told to attack anyway. When the mine went off, 'away we rushed, followed by the men ... cheering away as hard as we could – there is nothing like shouting on these occasions.' They reached the wall to find that the mine had exploded 10 yards short, merely causing a large crater. Unable to climb the high walls with his 8-foot ladders, he led his men along to where he knew the 18-pdrs had been making a breach throughout the morning, and entered the building there. For the next few days he remained under constant alarm from counter-mining until 19 November, when men of the 90th (led by the future Field Marshal Sir Garnet Wolseley), who had come with Campbell, fought their way into the Moti Mahal just as their comrades from the Residency entered it after springing a mine. British casualties had amounted to 122 killed and 414 wounded.

Havelock and Outram came out to greet their Commander-in-Chief while enemy shot continued to fall nearby. Campbell had already decided to leave Lucknow as soon as he could, and those who had made space in their homes for fugitives from outside the perimeter now realized they were about to become refugees themselves. Mrs Harris was glad to go, but faced ruin by having to leave behind all her possessions. Campbell found his patience tried by ladies seeking permission to bring out extra trunks and boxes. Two of the younger ones told him they would be back soon, provoking him to say, 'No ladies, no. You'll be good enough to do nothing of the kind. You have been here quite long enough, I am sure; and I have had quite enough trouble in getting you out of it.' Russell of *The Times* reported that 'in order to make a proper effect, most of the ladies came out in their best gowns and bonnets' and suspected them of applying a little rouge. Captain Goode of the 64th, in a letter published in *The Times* the following January, wrote: "The ladies had to walk out; and I went to see them, expecting to find them looking very miserable. Instead of that, they looked quite well, dressed up in white gloves; and made me feel quite ashamed of my dirty appearance, as I had been sleeping on the ground, in the dirt, for several nights.'

The 600 sick and wounded were evacuated during 18 November, followed the next day by the 450 women and children, the surviving state prisoners and the contents of the State treasury. Guns and supplies that could not be moved were destroyed and the long columns, screened by canvas where they passed from the narrow streets across open ground, made their way out to the Dilkhusha Bagh. Mrs Harris was in a group that came under fire and took refuge with officers of the 90th, who gave them water and wine. At another halt they were given tea with milk and sugar, biscuits and bread and butter, 'long untasted luxuries', and on reaching camp, the officers of the 9th Lancers had a supper waiting for them. Mrs Harris lost her dog Bustle on the road, but he subsequently reappeared. The young cavalry wife, travelling on her own while her husband was with his men, went into labour and was helped by an officer of the Lancers who brought Surgeon Brydon to attend her (she had a little girl).

While Peel's heavy guns bombarded the Kaisar Bagh to give the impression that the British intended to attack, the last of the garrison left its fires burning to deceive the enemy and marched out in silence on the night of 23 November. Passing through successive lines drawn up by Campbell to protect the evacuation, they reached the Dilkhusha unhindered. Havelock, already desperately ill from dysentery, died there the next day. He had been Sir Henry for four days, as Campbell brought the news of his KCB, but never lived to know that he had also been awarded a baronetcy and a pension. He was buried at the Alam Bagh when the whole force retired there the following day.

With the women and children rescued, many of the troops wanted to stay and hold the city they had won. Outram, as Chief Commissioner, also wished to stay there, and thought that two brigades would enable him to do so. Campbell, however, declared it a false position and judged that the best way to dominate the district was to keep a division at the Alam Bagh. Accordingly, he left Outram there with 4,000 men, made up of the 5th Fusiliers, 75th Foot, 78th Highlanders, 90th Light Infantry, 1st Madras Fusiliers and a regiment of Punjab infantry, with 200 artillerymen and the Military Train cavalry, a month's supplies, twenty guns and ten mortars. The 400 Madras infantry and two guns left at the Bani bridge also came under Outram's command.

Campbell himself marched out of the Alam Bagh on 27 November, and crossed the Bani bridge later that day, though the rear of his 4-mile long column did not arrive until after dark. There, he heard heavy gunfire from the direction of Kanpur, from which no messages had come for several days. He decided to hurry on and the convoy and escort moved out at 9.00 a.m the next morning. He then received a series of messages from Windham saying that Kanpur was under attack and he had been driven back into the entrenchments. Campbell pressed on with all speed and halted within 5 miles of the Ganges. The tail of his column, with the heavy guns, baggage, and non-combatants, hurried after him and arrived in some confusion after dark. Campbell himself crossed the river in the twilight and reached the entrenchments, where he took personal command.

169

During October the first infantry reinforcements from England had landed at Calcutta, including the 34th and 38th Foot, 42nd Royal Highlanders, 45th Foot, 3rd Battalion 60th Rifles, 88th Connaught Rangers and the 1st and 2nd Battalions of the Rifle Brigade. Elements of the 34th, 88th and Rifle Brigade, together with the rear companies of the 82nd, reached Kanpur, where Windham retained them in view of the increasing threat from Kalpi, and thus raised his strength to about 1,700 men. At the same time that Campbell left Kanpur for Lucknow, Tatya Tope left Kalpi and moved towards Kanpur. On 17 November Windham decided to make a show of force as authorized by Campbell, and advanced to the western side of Kanpur. Tatya Tope's troops were not fully concentrated and Windham asked Campbell for permission to attack one or other of their two leading groups, so defeating them in detail and preventing them from getting into the city. His messages never arrived, so on his own initiative he attacked one of the groups on 26 November and forced it to retreat with the loss of three guns.

On occupying their ground, however, he saw that they were the leading division of Tatya Tope's main force and accordingly, heavily outnumbered, he fell back towards the city and the bridge of boats. The next day Tatya attacked, using his heavy artillery to full effect, and drove Windham into his defences, where some of the demoralized British infantry took the chance to break into the liquor stores and drink themselves insensible. It was said that some of these were new recruits, but some of them were in units that Windham had led to disaster at the Redan two years previously. The situation was saved only by the arrival of four companies of the 3rd Rifle Brigade, who had disembarked from England earlier in November and reached Kanpur just in time to join their 2nd Battalion in covering the retreat.

On 28 November Tatya Tope attacked again. Brigadier Wilson of the 64th led a charge against the main enemy battery, but fell mortally wounded. His men reached the enemy guns but were left unsupported and fell back with heavy casualties, some from friendly fire. Brigadier Carthew also found his troops firing into each other as dusk fell and sent for reinforcements just after Campbell rode in. They were sent but Carthew then joined the general retreat to the entrenchments. Campbell, who was present when the reinforcements were sent, demanded an explanation, remarking that 'no subordinate officer, when possessing easy means of communication with his immediate superior, is permitted, according to the principles and usages of war, to give up a post which has been entrusted to his charge without a previous request for orders.' As Windham had sent the reinforcements requested, Campbell judged Carthew might have taken this as evidence that its retention was considered essential. 'His Excellency refrains from remarking on the very serious consequences which ensued.' He did, however, remark that troops did not fire into each other if they had been properly posted and their officers duly instructed of the respective positions.

Making a quick attack without a proper appreciation, Windham had suffered a defeat in the field comparable with those at Chinhat and Agra. He lost not only a battle but a city, and with it all the stores carefully collected for the next campaign, together with tentage, rifle ammunition, and the personal baggage and greatcoats (needed in the coming cold nights) of his own and Campbell's men. British casualties amounted to 317, including Lieutenant Colonel Woodford of the Rifle Brigade killed. Carthew claimed that Windham had said, on the evening of 27 November, something like 'Well gentlemen, when we can hold out no longer we must retire to the entrenchment.' Windham agreed that, having decided to hold as much of the city as he could, with a large convoy of women, children, sick and wounded expected, he had said that everyone should hold their positions for as long as possible before retiring at the last. Campbell eventually decided that his first impression had been erroneous and expressed regret at his hasty remarks. At the time, however, he was under some strain, for though the arrival of his army allowed him to save the bridge of boats, he had to leave Kanpur city in insurgent hands while the long convoy was brought safely over. Only when he had despatched the last of what he described as his 'incumbrances' to Allahabad and safety on 6 December did he feel free to turn against the enemy.

Reinforced by the steady bullock trains, Campbell now had a force of over 6,000 men. The cavalry, under Hope Grant, consisted of the 9th Lancers and elements of four Indian regiments, 600 in all. The infantry, divided into four brigades, were 5,000 strong, comprising elements of the 8th Foot, 23rd Royal Welsh Fusiliers, 32nd and 38th Foot, 42nd Royal Highlanders, 53rd, 64th and 82nd Foot, 88th Connaught Rangers, 93rd Highlanders, the 1st, 2nd and 3rd Battalions of the Rifle Brigade,

171

and two Punjab regiments. There were thirty-five guns of the Royal, Bengal and Madras Artilleries and the naval brigade. Most of the infantry had come from the United Kingdom, the 38th having embarked at Cork on 30 July and reached Calcutta on 16 November, the 42nd sailing on 4 August and arriving at Calcutta in late October, the 34th embarking at Portsmouth on 24 August, and so on.

Against these Tatya Tope had an army of some 15,000 men and forty guns, in two divisions. The Gwalior Contingent, well armed and well trained, held his right flank, on the open ground south of Kanpur. The left flank, resting on the Ganges, and the centre, posted in the city's narrow streets, were held by the troops of Nana Sahib, 10,000 strong, under his brother Bala Sahib. Some of these were regular sepoys from various stations, but most were recruits in newly formed regiments. On 6 December, appreciating that the centre was virtually invulnerable and Bala Sahib's flank could not be turned, Campbell masked these positions and threw his main force against the Gwalior men so as to defeat them in detail before they could be reinforced from the centre. Windham was left behind to guard the entrenchments. The insurgent guns opened a heavy fire on the advancing British, but the attack was pushed rapidly on, Peel's sailors, finding that their 'cow-horses' were too slow to keep up, abandoned them and called on the infantry to help man the drag-ropes. 'There was the sight beheld,' wrote Campbell 'of 24-pounder guns advancing with the line of skirmishers.'

The Gwalior Contingent, over-confident from their earlier victories, were taken by surprise and fled back towards Kalpi, abandoning most of their guns and being pursued for 14 miles before the British cavalry abandoned the chase. Their camp was taken with food still heating on the fires, bullocks still tied beside their carts and patients still in the hospital. From the beginning of this war, both sides killed enemy sick and wounded as a matter of course and none were spared now. It was reported that the insurgents had placed barrels of rum in front of their line in the expectation that thirsty British soldiers would break ranks and consume them, but Campbell warned the 93rd Highlanders that they had been poisoned and the barrels were overturned on his orders.

Campbell's chief of staff, Major General W.R. Mansfield, commanding the diversionary attack, saw Bala Sahib's troops abandon their positions, but was reluctant to commit his own forces to fighting in built-up areas. Another version of events is that he did not see them as he was very short-sighted, too vain to wear spectacles with uniform, and would not ask others what was happening. Bala Sahib hurried the troops away towards Bithur, where Nana Sahib had briefly re-established his capital. Two days later, 9 December 1857, Hope Grant intercepted them with his own cavalry brigade, eleven guns and 2,000 infantry as they tried to cross the Ganges at Serai Ghat. After a short engagement he captured fifteen guns and pushed on to Bithur, where he destroyed Nana Sahib's palace and several temples. Campbell thus dispersed the last army large enough to challenge him in the field at the cost of thirteen killed and eighty-six wounded, trifling except for those included among them.

With Lucknow evacuated and Kanpur secured, Campbell was free to commence mobile operations in the central Doab or 'Two Rivers Land' between the Ganges and Yamuna. A force of 1,900 men under Brigadier Thomas Seaton had left Delhi on 9 December with a 19-mile-long convoy and, after a series of minor engagements as he passed down the Grand Trunk Road, re-established British control over Mainpuri, 100 miles north-west of Kanpur, on New Year's Eve. Brigadier Robert Walpole moved from Kanpur with 2,000 men, heading first south-west towards Kalpi, then north-west to Etawa and finally due north to join Seaton at Biwah on 6 January. Campbell himself, after his transport returned from Allahabad, left Kanpur on 24 January with 5,000 men, intending to pick up his other two columns en route to Fatehgarh. This was the last centre of insurgency in the Doab, the government having been assumed by the Nawab of Farrukhabad, the descendant of its former rulers, following the mutinies there in the previous June. On 2 January, Campbell recaptured Fatehgarh and Farukabad, while the insurgents fled across the Ganges into Rohilkhand, not stopping to destroy their stores or the bridge of boats. Walpole and Seaton joined him two days later.

With the restoration of British civil government came the usual mass executions. Some officers, Captain Peel among them, expressed their disgust, but the local commissioner, 'Hanging' Power, had known many of the Europeans involved in the Fatehgarh massacres, and showed little mercy. The troops coming from Kanpur had all looked into the well there, and responded in the same way as Arthur Lang. 'Every man across the river whom I meet shall suffer for my visit to Cawnpore. I will never again, as I used to at Delhi, let off men whom I catch ... I think now I shall never stop, if I get a chance again.' Many soldiers took a cowardly pleasure in abusing condemned prisoners. Others helped themselves to valuable souvenirs from the Nawab's abandoned palace.

Campbell had already planned his next move. The recovery of Lucknow and the rest of Awadh would, in his appreciation, require an army of 30,000 men. He could not form this without leaving the Grand Trunk Road, essential for the passage of reinforcements from both the Punjab and Calcutta, at risk. His plan was therefore to use his existing army during the rest of the campaigning season to attack Rohilkhand and Bundelkhand, where the enemy was weakest. At the same time, two columns of troops from the Bombay Army and the Hyderabad Contingent would march eastwards from Mhow, which had been recovered for the Maharaja Holkar of Indore on 2 August. Securing the line of the Narmada for 250 miles to Jabalpur, they would then advance north to meet Campbell at Kalpi on 1 May. In the 1858–9 season, with his flanks secured and his army concentrated, he would wage the decisive campaign in Awadh.

Canning overruled him on the grounds that, as long as Lucknow remained in insurgent hands, it would show there was a viable alternative to British rule and thus encourage all those still fighting against it. It might, indeed, inspire anti-British elements in other parts of India to join the rising, even at this stage. He also feared that, left undisturbed, the insurgents in Awadh would take the offensive, invading Bihar or neighbouring areas of the newly created Central Provinces. They had, indeed, already occupied parts of Jaunpur and Azamgarh, defended by the Nepali Gurkhas. The new Lieutenant Governor, J.P. Grant, warned that, without European troops, the British would have to pull back to the Ganges, with the loss of the opium revenue. At the end of November 1857 Canning had dispatched Major General Thomas Franks to hold these two districts with 2,300 Europeans and 3,200 Gurkha allies, with the protection of Varanasi as his primary mission.

Campbell accepted that as head of government, Canning had the right to determine the direction of the campaign, and a new plan was devised to meet his wishes. Campbell and his main force would remain at Fatehpur, giving the impression that he intended to invade Rohilkhand, while supplies and reinforcements gathered at Kanpur. He would then march back from Fatehpur to Kanpur and cross into Awadh with three divisions to relieve Outram at the Alam Bagh. Franks's force, renamed the 4th Division, would advance north-westwards from Jaunpur, and Jang Bahadur's 8,000 Gurkhas would move due west from Gorakhpur so that all three columns converged on Lucknow simultaneously.

At the same time, Canning moved his capital from Calcutta to Allahabad. J.P. Grant returned to his place on the Council and Canning took over the government of the Central Provinces in person. The official reason for the move was that it brought the Governor-General closer to the operations in the field, where some of his critics had long argued he should be, despite the fact that the telegraph line gave him control irrespective of his location. Not all his Council agreed with the idea and it was limited to six months from 30 January 1858, with some departments left at Calcutta.

By 8 February, Campbell had concentrated his main force across the Awadh border at Unao. After a final conference with Canning at Allahabad, Campbell reported on 12 February that he would be ready to advance in six days time but, as Jang Bahadur had yet to move, he was minded to wait for him. Canning agreed, as much for political as military reasons as, if excluded from his share of the glory, Jang Bahadur would 'break with us and go back to his hills within a week. The loss of this help would be very inconvenient, but to find ourselves on bad terms with him would be much more so.' On 28 February Campbell left Kanpur to join his army at Banthira.

While they waited, Outram remained at the Alam Bagh. Though he was able to maintain contact with Kanpur, he did so with some difficulty and, when Campbell planned to postpone the reconquest until 1858–9, considered re-establishing his token centre of government elsewhere in Awadh. With the decision to give priority to Lucknow, he kept his position and fought off a series of major attacks made with increasing numbers and determination as British intentions to return became clear, but every time beaten back with heavy losses. One attack was led by an individual in the guise of the Hindu monkey god Mahavira, and another by the Maulavi Ahmadullah Shah, who had been

175

imprisoned at Faizabad for preaching sedition and released by the sepoys when they mutinied on 8 June. He subsequently became a leading figure at Lucknow, though the royal family were Shi'as and he was a Sunni. A man of great holiness and courage, he condemned the slaughter of women and children as contrary to Islamic principles and a distraction from the aims of the revolt. On 21 February Outram used his cavalry reinforcements to engage the attackers in the open. At the Alam Bagh, as at Delhi, the bravery and superior numbers of the insurgents were negated by their own poor generalship and defeated by British firepower.

The popular idea that Indian ladies took no part in public life was disproved as much at Lucknow as it had been at Jhansi and Delhi. The beautiful Begam Hazrat Mahal, Queen Mother of the young Wali, and effectively Regent on his behalf, constantly urged her generals to attack the Alam Bagh and on one occasion scandalized the members of the *darbar* (council) by tearing off her veil and haranguing them on their cowardice. On 25 February, riding an elephant, she appeared in the field and encouraged the attacking troops. On the British side, intelligence from Angad Tewari and other agents ensured that Outram always knew the insurgents' plans. On 3 March, Campbell advanced from Banthira, joined forces with Outram and occupied the Dilkhusha Bagh.

Campbell had by this time assembled 18,277 men. The cavalry division, under Hope Grant, consisted of two brigades, one containing the 9th Lancers and three Indian regiments, and the other the 2nd Dragoon Guards and 7th Hussars (mounted on horses taken from sepoy cavalry units) and two Indian regiments, totalling 3,169 men. The artillery, under Archdale Wilson, consisted of the naval brigade, three troops of horse artillery (one British, two Bengal) and seven companies of foot (six British, one Bengal), 164 guns, including the siege train from Delhi, and 1,745 men in all. The infantry, in three divisions each of two brigades, amounted to 12,498 bayonets, under Outram. The 5th Fusiliers and 84th Foot were brigaded with the 1st Madras Fusiliers; the 78th and 90th with the Ferozepore Sikhs; the 34th with the 38th and 53rd Foot; the 42nd and 93rd Highlanders with the 4th Punjab Infantry; the 23rd Fusiliers with the 79th Highlanders and 1st Bengal Fusiliers; and the 2nd and 3rd Rifle Brigade with the 2nd Punjab Infantry. The 825 sappers were commanded by Major Robert Napier of the Bengal Engineers, who had reached Lucknow with Outram and remained with him at the Alam Bagh. Brigade commands were given to officers with Indian experience in preference to more senior officers arriving from England, despite complaints by the latter at this breach of military protocol. With the army went a baggage train 25 miles long, with a string of 16,000 camels, 12,000 draught bullocks and 60,000 non-combatants providing civil labour.

Franks's 4th Division marched to Lucknow via Faizabad. They were opposed by the Wali's troops and fought three successful actions before halting at Sultanpur. Reinforced by the 3rd Sikhs, they resumed their advance the next day and on 4 May made contact with Campbell, 8 miles away. Jang Bahadur, in personal command of 9,000 Gurkhas, arrived on 11 March, thus bringing up the total allied force to the 30,000 which Campbell had stipulated. Since the departure of the British, Lucknow had been fortified by lines of earthworks on the east side, where Campbell had made his previous attack. Behind these the Kaisar Bagh remained as a citadel, and between them the streets were blocked by barricades and strong points, with every palace, mosque and mausoleum pierced for cannon and loopholed for musketry. Whatever their weakness in the field, the sepoys were formidable behind walls and knew how to make good use of them. Their numbers included some 30,000 regulars drawn from elements of over 100 mutinied regiments of the Bengal Army and various contingents, fourteen new regiments raised by the Wali's government, and the Bareilly brigade under General Bakht Khan. They were supported by another 50,000 volunteers, Ghazis, local townsmen and the taluqdars' militias.

Fulfilling the first duty of a chief engineer when a fortified place was to be attacked, Napier examined the enemy defences. He reported that, on the north, Lucknow was protected only by the Gomati and that from there the British could outflank the defences resting on the south side of the river. Campbell, as parsimonious with his men's lives as he was with his personal comforts, seized this opportunity of minimizing the fighting in built-up areas, and sent Outram over the river with Hope Grant's divisional headquarters, a brigade of cavalry and the 3rd Infantry Division. They crossed on pontoon bridges during the night of 5/6 March and after advancing for 4 miles encountered hostile cavalry. These were driven away by artillery fire and pursued by the 2nd Dragoon Guards, fighting in their first Indian combat. The dragoons came under enemy gunfire in their turn and withdrew after losing their senior officer, Major Percy Smith.

Outram bivouacked for the night of 6/7 March 4 miles north of the city, near to the site of Lawrence's defeat at Chinhat. He was surprised there early on 8 March by a strong insurgent force, with enemy round shot landing in his camp at the same time as the alarm was sounded, but the attack was not pressed home. The next day Outram emplaced his heavy guns on the north bank of the river and forced the insurgents to abandon most of their outer defence line. At the same time Campbell captured La Martinière on the south bank, allowing his troops to advance to the abandoned defences along the canal protecting Lucknow's south-eastern side. On 10 March, guarded by Hope Grant's cavalry, Outram shifted his camp closer to the river and constructed batteries for the bombardment of the Kaisar Bagh. Campbell captured Banks's House, at the southern end of the outer defences and prepared to bombard the Moti Mahal, half a mile south-east of the Kaisar Bagh. The next day, 11 March, Outram, advancing along the north bank of the Gomati, reached the iron bridge opposite the Residency and the stone bridge half a mile upstream of it. On the south bank, the 93rd Highlanders and 4th Punjab Infantry stormed the Moti Mahal, killing some 800 of the defenders who were trapped inside. In the process, William Hodson, the nemesis of the House of Timur, received his own death wound as he hunted mutineers through the maze of rooms and corridors. The Sikandar Bagh and Shah Najaf's mausoleum fell with little resistance and the insurgents retreated to a line from the Kaisar Bagh through the 32nd's old mess-house to the river bank.

Jang Bahadur arrived the next day, obliging Campbell to receive him in person, in full dress uniform, while the troops continued to fight their way forward. On 13 March the Gurkha contingent entered the city and on 14 March the 10th Foot and Ferozepore Sikhs took the lesser Imambara Mosque, between the Moti Mahal and the Kaisar Bagh. Franks, commanding this sector, decided to continue the advance and called in reinforcements from neighbouring positions, though Campbell had planned to stop at this point. The Kaisar Bagh's defenders, after days of bombardment from Outram's guns, suddenly withdrew, leaving several ladies and other members of the ex-King's family behind.

As the British and Punjabi soldiers swarmed in, they found themselves surrounded by the accumulated riches of a dynasty and turned from fighting to plunder. Across the river Outram saw his enemies fall back and asked permission to cross the bridges. Campbell's reply, through Mansfield, was that he could do so only if it would not cost a single man. As the bridges were still defended by insurgent artillery, Outram took his orders at face value and held his position while a mass of sepoys fled westwards.

The reply, in effect, meant that Campbell was determined to maintain his aim of a deliberate advance along both sides of the river, and the next day, 15 March, this was resumed according to plan. While the infantry, supported by heavy guns, continued to fight their way north-westwards through the city, Hope Grant and one of his cavalry brigades was sent north, in case fugitives were heading for Sitapur, 50 miles away. Likewise, the second brigade, under Colonel William Campbell of the 2nd Dragoon Guards, while remaining on the south side of the river, moved to block the road to Sandila, 40 miles away to the north-west. Both formations were recalled on 16 March, when Campbell discovered that there were still large numbers of insurgents holding out in the city. Outram was at last allowed to cross to the south bank and attack the Residency. The defenders there, estimated as several thousand strong, left their positions and dispersed. Some struck south and made a counter-attack on the Alam Bagh, in an action that lasted for four hours before they broke off the engagement. Another large group crossed the iron bridge, which had been left virtually undefended. An even larger body crossed upstream of them and circled north of the city. With no British cavalry there to stop them, they joined forces and escaped eastwards along the Faizabad road.

Others continued to hold out in the city, with Begam Hazrat Mahal moving between the various posts to encourage them. The advance continued during 17 and 18 March until almost the only major building not in British hands was the Musa Bagh, near the river a mile beyond the north-western city limits, where a force of 9,000 insurgents had gathered. On 19 March Outram attacked with two infantry divisions while Colonel William Campbell was posted to cut off the enemy retreat and Hope Grant held the north bank to prevent any fugitives crossing. Colonel Campbell, however, lost his way and was not in the correct location when the insurgents, after coming under fire from Outram's guns, abandoned the Musa Bagh.

Most therefore escaped into the country, though two troops of the 9th Lancers pursued them and captured twelve guns before being halted by enemy artillery. Begam Hazrat Mahal, the young Wali and their retinue escaped from the city to carry on the fight elsewhere. The princesses captured in the Kaisar Bagh displayed equal spirit and assured William Russell, who went to visit them, that their men would soon be back. The Maulavi defended a house in the city centre against repeated attacks by the 93rd Highlanders and 4th Punjab Infantry until 21 March, when he exfiltrated with his men through the British lines.

Campbell's recovery of Lucknow deserves to be recognized as one of the British Army's greatest feats of arms. During twenty days of methodical advance, they fought their way through a strongly held fortified city and occupied the last major capital in insurgent hands for the loss of sixteen officers and 111 men killed and 595 wounded. Among the casualties was Captain Sir William Peel, with a knighthood for his services in this campaign to add to his Crimean VC. Wounded in the thigh, he seemed to be making a good recovery, but died of hospital-acquired smallpox. Enemy numbers and enemy losses were only estimated, though the body count in the Begam's palace alone greatly exceeded the total number of British dead. That the operations took three times longer than the storming of Delhi owed much to Campbell's careful planning, but much also to the spirited leadership of his opponents. He was criticized at the time and by later writers for having mishandled his cavalry and thus allowed so many of the enemy to flee but, as a man who had seen many wars, he had no interest in prolonging the slaughter for which so many vengeful expatriates thirsted. It was said that Mansfield echoed this view by asking what was the use of intercepting desperate men whose only wish was to escape. Campbell had achieved the aim that Canning, for political reasons, had imposed on his own preferred military strategy. With the last enemy capital taken in accordance with the Governor-General's instructions, the enemy leaders in flight and their army scattered, there seemed no good reason to risk his soldiers' lives further.

His soldiers continued to take every chance of collecting souvenirs, smashing many objects of cultural or intrinsic value in the process. Prize agents were appointed, but most men preferred to rely on their own efforts, especially as all knew that the government was doing its best to cheat the conquerors of Delhi out of their prize money. William Russell, the Irish-born scourge of the British military establishment, filled columns of *The Times* with lurid stories of officers failing to control their men or joining them in the misappropriation of property found in the royal palaces. Censoriously, he wrote of the precious stones and pearls that later found their way to the United Kingdom: 'It is just as well that the fair wearers (though jewellery, after all, has a deadening effect on the sensitivities of the feminine conscience) saw not how the glittering baubles were won, or the scenes in which the treasure was trove.'

Chapter 10

THE PERIPHERY.
COUNTER-INSURGENCY
OPERATIONS, JANUARY 1858 TO
DECEMBER 1859

Be this thy mission ... hold sway over the peoples and impose the
way of peace, spare the defeated and war down the proud.

Virgil, Aeneid, vi. 851

Canning's next decision meant that, instead of a series of mopping-up operations, conducted in the next campaigning season when Campbell had originally intended to take Lucknow, the British were suddenly faced by a whole new rebellion, requiring them once more to fight on through the hot weather and the monsoon. As a collective punishment for the support that so many taluqdars of Awadh had given to the cause of their deposed king, Canning issued a proclamation that all except for six named individuals would have their land-holdings resumed. Other than a promise of life and liberty to those who were not personally implicated in murder, the only concession offered was that dispossessed taluqdars should depend on the justice and mercy of the British government. In view of its previous dealings with Awadh, he might as well have said they should depend on the mildness of the summer sun or the gentleness of the monsoon rain. The result, as Outram and John Lawrence warned him would be the case, was to drive those who had previously been in arms to a more determined resistance. Those who had been neutral, or had helped British fugitives, took up arms themselves rather than suffer the loss of their place in the world. The insurgents who had been driven from Lucknow, instead of quietly dispersing to their homes, remained in the field with renewed hope.

Canning had prepared this proclamation long in advance and only waited for the recovery of Lucknow before issuing it, on the grounds that such leniency as it contained would otherwise be regarded as evidence of British weakness. He sent it to London for approval, unaware that Palmerston's administration had fallen on 12 February 1858 and the Conservatives had returned to office after a generation in opposition. The new President of the Board of Control, Lord Ellenborough, a former Governor-General of India, wrote to Canning on 24 March saying that, once Lucknow was taken, Awadh should be treated with the conventions appropriate to a country conquered after defending itself to the last in a desperate war, rather than those applicable to the suppression of mutiny and rebellion. He was appalled when he received on 12 April the terms of the Awadh declaration, sent long before Canning knew of the change of ministry. It was especially unexpected given that Canning had previously insisted that no one be punished without due process, if only to avoid alienating the many respectable Indians who supported the maintenance of British rule (a policy pilloried in *The Times* and *Punch* as 'The Clemency of Canning'). In a minute denouncing Dalhousie's annexation of Awadh as based on fraud and deception, Ellenborough said that hostilities there 'had rather the character of legitimate war than of rebellion'. Canning was told that the ministers wished to see British rule in India rest upon the willing obedience of a contented people. 'There cannot be contentment where there is general confiscation.'

Due to an error on parliamentary procedure, the draft of this despatch was circulated among MPs for several weeks before it reached the Secret Committee of the Court of Directors. The subsequent scandal threatened to bring down the minority 'Derby-Dizzy' government. To save his colleagues Ellenborough resigned, though the Prime Minister, the Earl of Derby, supported his judgement by telegraphing to Canning that a clear distinction had to be made between the taluqdari militias and sepoys previously in the British service. Canning considered resigning, especially as the news of these proceedings soon reached India and thus prolonged the resistance in Awadh. After a few days, however, he decided, as senior officers in well-paid appointments generally do, that it would be in the public interest for him to remain in post. *The Times* suggested that the ministers had tried to provoke his resignation so that they could lay their hands on a valuable piece of patronage.

While Campbell marched to Lucknow, the second front was opened according to plan. Major General Sir Hugh Rose, then aged fifty-six and more practised as a military diplomat than a field commander, had arrived in India for the first time on 19 September, to command of the Bombay Army's Poona Division. He was resented by those who saw him as an inexperienced interloper, and at first the inevitable consequences of the friction of war on any plan was taken as evidence of his mismanagement. On 17 December he took over the newly formed Central India Field Force, consisting of the 14th Light Dragoons (who had returned to Bombay from the Persian Gulf in May 1857), the 86th Foot, the 3rd Bombay Europeans, the 3rd Bombay Light Cavalry and 25th Bombay NI, elements of the Hyderabad Contingent, a siege train and four horse or field batteries, with sappers and miners from Madras and Bombay, totalling some 6,000 combatants organized in two brigades.

Rose, with the 2nd Brigade, left his base at Mhow, 10 miles south-west of Indore, on 6 January 1858. His first task was to relieve Sagar (Saugor), 200 miles away to the north-east, a mud fort held by seventy European gunners and the 31st Bengal NI since the mutiny of two other sepoy regiments in the original garrison eight months earlier, and containing 150 European women and children. On the way, he demolished the insurgent stronghold at Rahatgarh, despite a surprise attack by Mardan Singh, Raja of Banpur. This prince had previously supported the British, hoping that they would return his ancestral district of Chanderi, seized from the previous raja by Sindhia and then administered by the British to fund the Gwalior Contingent. When they did not, Mardan Singh decided to recover it irrespective of their approval and did so with the aid of the local nobles. After the fall of Rahatgarh he retreated to Barodia, but was again defeated by Rose's column and was himself wounded. Sagar was relieved on 3 February and Rose was later joined there by a Madras brigade from Jabalpur, 80 miles to the south-east. While he waited, he collected supplies, bullocks and baggage-elephants, and augmented his siege train with heavy guns from the Sagar arsenal.

On 27 February he advanced northwards. Mardan Singh, with his ally the Raja of Shahgarh, tried to hold the hill passes between Sagar and Bundelkhand, but was outmanoeuvred at the cost of some British casualties, including Rose's horse shot under him.

184

Mardan Singh fell back, adopting a scorched-earth policy, and the British reached his capital only to find it deserted. Meanwhile the 1st Brigade (previously the Malwa Field Force), advancing on a separate axis, recaptured Chanderi for Sindhia. After marching 120 miles in twenty days, Rose's main force had almost reached Jhansi when, on 20 March, urgent messages arrived from both Canning and Campbell. After his defeat at Kanpur on 6 December, Tatya Tope had rallied with the Gwalior Contingent at Kalpi and now suddenly struck southwards against Charkhari, a small Bundela state whose raja supported the British. The raja, holding out in Charkhari fort, 80 miles east of Jhansi, appealed for help and Rose was ordered to his relief.

Rose, supported by Sir Robert Hamilton, the Governor-General's Agent in Central India, who accompanied his march, decided to maintain his aim. He reasoned that to leave a strong fortress and garrison in his rear would boost insurgent morale by giving the impression he feared to attack it. If the British laid siege to Jhansi, Tatya Tope would leave Charkhari and come to its assistance, whereas even if they headed for Charkhari, it might fall before they arrived. Accordingly, operations against Jhansi began on 21 March, the same day that Campbell completed his capture of Lucknow. The first siege batteries opened fire on 25 March and the remainder the next day, when the 1st Brigade joined Rose's camp. The fort, built on a granite outcrop within a walled city 4½ miles in circumference, was one of the strongest in Central India, and had a garrison of about 12,000 troops, with over thirty guns. Many were regular soldiers from Jhansi's former army, disbanded at the time of the British annexation. All trees and buildings around the city had been levelled to deny the besiegers their raw materials and to give clear fields of fire.

The Rani, since the massacre of the previous June, had been in correspondence with the British authorities, denying any responsibility for what had occurred and claiming that such support as she had given the sepoy mutineers was in response to *force majeure*. This was, however, much the same story as that told by the King of Delhi and Nana Sahib. Lurid tales of sexual assault had no more foundation here than elsewhere. The widely believed story (the subject of a touching poem by Christina Georgina Rosetti) that, after a spirited defence, Captain Skene, the British political agent, finding further resistance useless, shot first his wife and then himself, was quite false. Nevertheless, sixty people had been very cruelly killed and the British were not prepared to take the Rani's words at face value. She was instructed to assume the government of Jhansi state pending the restoration of British rule, when they would investigate what had occurred. In the meanwhile, she had to face incursions from her neighbours, the rajas of Datia and Orchha, who had their own claims on Jhansi territory. In a spirited response, she made alliances with the rajas of Banpur and Shahgarh, reassembled her late husband's army and called on the local land-holders to join her with their militias. They had driven out the invaders and now, with the apparent return of the good old days, stood ready to treat the Central India Field Force in the same way. As the British showed no sign of allowing the Rani to retain possession of Jhansi, she decided to defy them in arms rather than tamely submitting to their return.

As Rose expected, Tatya Tope left Charkhari and marched to relieve Jhansi. He arrived late on 31 March with some 20,000 men, including Mardan Singh's troops, and over twenty guns. After crossing the River Betwa, they lit a huge beacon to signal their presence to the defenders, who acknowledged it with shouts and gunfire. During the night, leaving his siege works held by a third of his force and a contingent of Orchha troops, Rose redeployed the remainder, about 1,900 strong, to meet the anticipated attack. The next morning the insurgents' first line advanced and began a firefight. Rose, meeting them with his 2nd Brigade, pinned them with his field artillery and ordered his infantry to lie down while his cavalry and horse artillery attacked on both flanks. Rose himself led a charge by a troop of the 14th Light Dragoons. The insurgent firing line crumpled and fell back to its reserve, 2 miles in the rear, where Tatya Tope had his command post. With the British closely following, the retreat become a rout before the second line was reached. Tatya Tope's artillery opened fire, but was countered by the advancing British guns. The 1st Brigade, marching towards the sound of gunfire, drove a force of about 3,000 insurgents from a village with a bayonet charge, but in the heat of the day the men were too exhausted to pursue them and they withdrew in good order. Elsewhere, the British cavalry pressed Tatya Tope's retreating men hard, and captured their guns before they escaped back across the river, covered by smoke and flames from forest fires burning behind them. British casualties totalled less than 100, against an estimated 1,500 among their opponents.

Rose resumed the siege, where a masking bombardment had prevented the defenders from sallying out to support their intended rescuers. The engineers had already reported a practicable breach and efforts to close it with wooden palisades had been defeated by red-hot shot. Women as well as men, inspired by the Rani's proclamation that, even if defeated, they would earn eternal glory, laboured on the walls and the Rani herself was observed encouraging them. Accurate shooting by the British siege gunners had dismounted most of her guns, but nevertheless, when Rose launched a moonlight assault at 3.00 a.m. on 3 April there were still enough left, with other improvised explosive devices, rockets and missiles of various kinds, to bring it to a momentary halt. The engineers led the way to the city wall and while one column entered the breach, two others scaled the ramparts. The first two officers were killed as they led the way over the walls, but their men followed and fought their way through fiercely defended streets and houses to reach the palace, designated by Rose as the point where all three columns were to meet. A group of fifty Afghans of the Rani's bodyguard held the palace stable yard until flames drove them out.

Fighting in the city continued into the following day. The 86th and the Bombay Europeans, fighting to avenge their massacred compatriots, gave no quarter to any male of military age, and their comrades of the Bombay Native Infantry followed their example. The estimated number of those killed varied from three to five thousand, with many others subsequently executed. British casualties amounted to about 40 killed and 200 wounded, including 2 killed and one wounded out of the 7 Engineer officers, always among those most at risk in siege warfare. The 86th lost men to suicide bombers who blew up buildings inside the palace as the British entered.

During the day the Rani was persuaded by her advisers that the battle was lost and that she could do more for her cause by escaping to carry on the fight elsewhere. Wearing a breastplate, sword and pistols, she rode in the midst of her Afghan cavalry with the infant maharaja on her saddle-bow, and escaped with members of her household and a baggage elephant through the sector held by the Orchha troops. Rose seems deliberately to have left an opening there, with a view to allowing the Rani to leave rather than hold out in the citadel, which could only be stormed with heavy losses. They encountered an outlying picquet, but rode on for 21 miles towards Kalpi before halting. The Rani's father and her finance minister became separated from the main party and sought refuge with the Raja of Datia, who sent them back to his British friends at Jhansi, where they were later hanged.

Rose had given strict orders against looting, but much destruction of valuable cultural property went on nevertheless. Everyone knew the story of how Mahmud the Iconoclast, the first great Muslim invader of India, had refused to accept an offer of ransom for the holy Shivalingam of Somnath, saying he would not stand forth on Judgement Day as one who took money to spare an idol, but then found it full of precious stones when he destroyed it. In the temples of Jhansi, images of Hindu deities were broken up, and the gold and jewels adorning them carried off by the victorious troops. Despite Rose's orders to spare women and children, many were killed by collateral damage and others by their own husbands and fathers, as some of the British at Lucknow had planned to do, for fear of the usual consequences when a city was stormed. There were, however, other cases in which British soldiers, finding widows and orphans without food, gave them their own rations. The Rani's scorched-earth policy had had little effect on the British, who received supplies from Sindhia and Orchha, but the ordinary people of Jhansi starved and Rose subsequently fed them with government grain seized as lawful contraband.

The next morning, 4 April, when the Rani's escape was discovered, a squadron of light dragoons and Bombay light cavalry was sent in pursuit. They found the Rani at breakfast and one officer almost reached her before a bullet wounded him. Forty of her Afghan troopers sacrificed themselves to protect her flight and the British, with their own horses failing, could not overtake the rested mounts on which the rest of her party escaped. Late on 5 April, escorted by a party of Tatya Tope's cavalry, she reached the headquarters of the Peshwa's army in Bundelkhand, commanded by Nana Sahib's nephew Panduranga Sadashiv, Rao Sahib, at Kalpi, 85 miles north-east of Jhansi.

While Rose recovered Central India, another column, the Rajputana Field Force, marched on 28 February from Disa, in northern Gujarat, to aid the Maha Rao of Kota, where the garrison had mutinied, killing three British officials, in October

1857. The troops included the 72nd Highlanders, the 83rd and 95th Foot, two regiments of Bombay cavalry and two of infantry, and the 8th Hussars, veterans of the Crimea. With the Hussars were Captain and Paymaster Henry Duberley, and his 27-year-old wife Frances (Fanny), the blue-eyed, fair-haired heroine who had been the only officer's lady to stay with her regiment before Sebastopol. Not everyone admired her for this, and one officer, disregarding the problems of camp life in Victorian costume, described her as a 'nasty dirty creature', though adding 'not that I believe all that is said about her'. Nevertheless, she was a great favourite with the troops and was now allowed to escape the dust of the rearguard by riding at the head of the column in her grey linen habit and low-crowned broad-brimmed hat with white veils floating behind.

Kota, on the River Chambal dividing Rajasthan from Central India, was reached after 300 miles on 27 March. Following their mutiny, most of the regular Kota Contingent had departed, first to Agra and thence to Delhi, but insurgents had retained possession of the town. The Maha Rao, with the loyal remnant of his own army, had recovered his palace-fortress, where the British now joined him. After bombarding the town they stormed its main gate at noon on 30 March. Lieutenant Cameron of the 72nd Highlanders won the VC for killing three men in single combat inside the gatehouse before being disabled himself. His superiors decided not to risk more lives by fighting inside this building and ordered the Royal Engineers to blow it up. The city streets were well protected with barricades and guns, with a number of wheeled 'infernal machines', each of forty-five barrels of gunpowder, but apart from a few determined martyrs, no one made a stand. British casualties totalled sixteen killed and forty-four wounded, with the insurgents losing about 400. Some seventy pieces of artillery fell into British hands and the infantry took the chance to look for souvenirs of more personal value. Meanwhile, most of the defenders, heavily laden with loot themselves, streamed out to the town undisturbed by the British cavalry, who had been deployed at a ford 7 miles away, and kept there, by a series of orders and counter-orders, throughout that day and the next night. Mrs Duberley rode into the town the following day to find the streets 'so strewn with plunder that our horses positively walked over cushions, garments, bedsteads, sofas and Persian MSS'. Despite her experience of war, she was shocked to see dogs and pigs feeding on the dead, and noted that where horses and men lay together, the humans were eaten first.

With Kota, 150 miles west of Jhansi, thus secured, Rose gathered fresh supplies and on 25 April advanced towards Kalpi. After a week's marching through drought-stricken country he halted and was joined by the 71st Highlanders, part of the reinforcements released from the Mediterranean by the formation of Cambridge's new second battalions. Unlike the troops sent directly from the UK, who were still wearing blue or scarlet serge, the 71st had been given loose khaki uniforms, but still suffered many heat-related casualties and were driven to use a concoction of honey and ghee to keep their bagpipes operational. Discovering that Tatya Tope had constructed strong entrenchments across his path of intended movement, Rose turned the insurgents' flank and drove them back after a hard-fought action at Kunch on 7 May, inflicting some 500 casualties and capturing nine guns. British casualties from enemy action amounted to twenty-four, but the Indian sun brought down many more, with Rose himself collapsing several times from the heat. The 14th Light Dragoons lost 5 men killed in action and one officer and 17 wounded, with 2 more men dead and another 150 hospitalized from the effects of the heat.

Rose's success was the more creditable since many of the Enfield rifles jammed as the result of sub-standard ammunition, a hazard to which British troops in hot countries would still be exposed 150 years later. In the subsequent advance, heat and thirst put the 2nd Brigade out of action for three days, but by 15 May the force reached the village of Gulauli, 6 miles east of Kalpi. From there he made contact with Colonel Maxwell, 30 miles away on the far bank, detached from Campbell's main army with an all-arms brigade including the 88th Connaught Rangers and a camel corps containing elements of that regiment and the Rifle Brigade.

Kalpi was the last arsenal still in insurgent hands. The troops there were estimated to total 20,000, among them the Gwalior Contingent and other mutinied units which had retreated in good order after their defeat on 7 May and still maintained their regimental cohesion. Their leaders included Rao Sahib, Tatya Tope, the Rani of Jhansi and the Nawab of Banda. Banda had been ceded to the Company by a former Nawab in 1812 in return for a guaranteed stipend, but when British authority collapsed his descendant, still Nawab by title, decided to resume his ancestral lands. He protected European refugees who reached his court and gave them safe conduct to British-held territory, but later became leader of the insurgency in his part of Bundelkhand and supported Nana Sahib (to whom he was distantly related) as the new Peshwa. On 19 April he had been defeated by Major General Whitlock's Madras Division, advancing northwards from Jabalpur in accordance with Campbell's original plan. The Nawab lost 500 men and four guns, but retired to Kalpi with 4,000 men still under command.

On 16 May Rose concentrated his formations with Gulauli on his right flank, despite a large-scale insurgent attack on the rearguard and baggage train of the 2nd Brigade. More troops from Kalpi then attacked various points along Rose's line in succession, but were driven back in turn. The next day the insurgents again threatened Diapura, a village on his left flank from which they had nearly dislodged the 71st Highlanders the previous day, but did not press home their attack. Maxwell arrived on the bank of the Yamuna opposite Kalpi on 18 May and deployed his artillery to bombard the city and cover the ground between it and Gulauli. On the night of 20 May his camel corps forded the river to reinforce Rose, who then shifted his position in readiness to attack on 22 May. Rose placed a mortar battery and three field guns on his right flank, from which the 86th Foot, 25th Bombay NI and the Bombay Europeans were deployed in a skirmishing line down to the river, facing the ravines that protected the east side of the city. The rest of his infantry and artillery were placed on their left, with Maxwell's camel troopers on the flank. The cavalry were placed on Rose's extreme left, where the ground was best suited for this arm.

The insurgents, as his intelligence had already informed him, planned to attack on the same day, having sworn on sacred water from the Yamuna to conquer or die. While their cavalry threatened Rose's left flank, their infantry advanced through the ravines. This gave them good cover, but reduced their ability to employ the missile-action tactics the sepoys always preferred. British guns were hurriedly redeployed to meet this threat and, when his own batteries were silenced, Rao Sahib considered abandoning the attack. The more determined Rani of Jhansi refused to agree and led her own Afghan bodyguard to join the sepoys advancing against the British left. The outnumbered

191

British riflemen were forced back and the gunners in the mortar battery drew their swords as enemy infantry seemed about to overwhelm them. Rose arrived in person with the camel corps at the critical moment and led the dismounted riflemen and rangers in a bayonet charge that drove the sepoys back to the ravines. The whole British line then advanced and the insurgents, under fire from Maxwell's guns across the river, retreated into the city. Despite the strength of their defences, with a rock-cut citadel dominating the entire area, the insurgent leaders decided to abandon them and the British marched in unopposed on 23 May.

Rose evacuated his sick and wounded across the Ganges to Kanpur and replenished his ammunition from Campbell's trains. Contact between the two armies had been established just three weeks later than originally planned nine months previously. The Central India Field Force ceased to exist as a separate command on 1 June 1858 and Rose, about to depart on sick leave, issued a farewell order praising his men for their achievements. With no more exaggeration than usual on such occasions, he said they had marched a thousand miles through mountain passes and jungles and over rivers, taken a hundred guns and the strongest forts and never experienced a check.

Campbell then asked Canning for a decision on what the army was to do next. The choice, he said, was between completing the reconquest of Awadh or re-establishing British control of Rohilkhand. The latter course, he advised, posed little risk, but required the use of large bodies of troops advancing from several directions. He preferred the former, as the province was still in a state of active rebellion (mostly due to Canning's proclamation, though he did not say as much) and Lucknow itself might once more be cut off unless the surrounding districts were firmly in British hands. He proposed leaving Rohilkhand until the 1858–9 campaigning season, and meanwhile ensuring that Awadh was thoroughly pacified. Canning once more disregarded the opinion of his C-in-C on political grounds. Rohilkhand was the last region where an insurgent government still held sway. Khan Bahadur Khan, who had taken over when the British were driven out, had declared his loyalty to the King of Delhi and received an imperial grant recognizing his authority as Nawab. His officials had collected taxes and dispensed justice, but inter-communal disturbances between Hindus and Muslims had weakened his regime, and the business community, on whom the tax burden mostly fell, sympathized with the British. Nevertheless, he raised an army of over 30,000 men (the Rohilas, descended from Pathan mercenaries who had settled in this region, had a strong martial tradition), though he had no regular sepoys or trained military officers to command them, and the Europeans who fled to the nearest hill station, Naini Tal, had resisted their attacks for nearly a year.

Campbell had every reason to be concerned about Awadh. North of Lucknow, Maulavi Ahmadullah Shah had rallied his men and was still in the field despite being defeated by Hope Grant on 13 April. To the west, Kunwar Singh, after fighting in the battle for Kanpur on 6 December 1857, had gone to recover Azamgarh for the young Wali. This district had fallen to Jang Bahadur's Gurkhas, but when these left to join Campbell, Kunwar Singh seized Atrauli, a village one day's march from Azamgarh city. The Azamgarh garrison advanced to meet him but was defeated. Kunwar Singh took the city and drove off a British force from Ghazipur when it tried to recapture it. For a time it seemed that the insurgents might once more threaten Varanasi and the opium revenue. Fortunately for the British, the newly arrived 13th Light Infantry under Colonel Lord Mark Kerr happened to be at Allahabad en route to Lucknow. It was promptly despatched a hundred miles north-eastwards, with a troop of the 2nd Dragoon Guards and four guns, to recover Azamgarh. Kerr recaptured the city but was ordered to stand on the defensive until Brigadier General Sir Edward Lugard and 3,000 men fresh from the capture of Lucknow on 21 March arrived to join him.

Kunwar Singh fell back to his home province, Bihar, fighting a series of well-conducted rearguard actions and crossing the Ganges with a brilliant deception plan, spreading the disinformation that, for want of boats, he would wade across with relays of elephants. The pursuing British arrived to find that the boats collected by Kunwar Singh had ferried all but 200 of his men to the far bank, just before the arrival of steamers with troops from Dinapur and Ghazipur. He was, however, wounded by British gunfire – according to legend he cut off his shattered hand with his sword and threw it as an offering into the river. His army was reduced to 2,000, with no artillery, but he still fought his way back towards his ruined home at Jagdishpur. Captain Arthur Le Grand of the 35th Foot advanced against him from

Ara with 300 men, made up of two weak companies of his own regiment, six gunners with two 12-pdr howitzers, a naval brigade composed of seventy-five merchant seamen from ships at Calcutta, and 100 Sikh infantry. On 23 April they were astonished to find themselves facing an army of sepoys, some still wearing red coats, formed up in regular columns.

Lieutenant Richard Parsons of the 35th charged forward with his skirmishers and drove the enemy back into the surrounding jungle, but then came under heavy musketry fire. Looking back for artillery support, he saw that the rest of Le Grand's column had fallen into an ambush. Most of the gunners had been shot down and the infantry were falling back, losing men to unseen marksmen as they went. Parsons recalled his men and followed, manhandling one of the abandoned howitzers until it snagged against a tree-stump. By this time British cohesion had collapsed. The 35th, still in the serge uniforms in which they had arrived from Europe, and with no breakfast after a 19-mile night march, were no longer in a state to fight. The dhoolie bearers abandoned their loads and joined the flight. 'The most terrible part of the engagement,' wrote Parsons, 'was our inability to remove our wounded, nearly all of whom were left where they fell ... their cries, in some cases to be saved, but in most to be shot, were piteous in the extreme. What could we do? Nothing!' Those killed in the 35th included the assistant surgeon, the colour-sergeants of both companies and ninety-eight others out of the 150 men involved. The Sikhs, unaffected by the heat, kept on firing as they retreated and suffered many fewer casualties. The British lost their two guns, three officers and 130 men, though Parsons insisted that if Le Grand had handled his command properly they could have won in spite of it all. Kunwar Singh's last victory echoed that gained by his troops over Dunbar and the 10th Foot in much the same area the previous July.

Kunwar Singh died of his wounds the next day, but his brother, Anwar Singh, continued in arms. Lugard had followed him from Awadh and, with two other forces, one coming west from Dinapur and another north from Sasaram, drove him out of Jagdishpur. Anwar Singh then retreated to the forests, from where he governed with the support of his Rajput clansmen. The British made roads through the jungle in order to catch him, but he divided his army into small bands, making it easier to obtain supplies and evade the slow-moving regulars. Using classic

194

guerrilla tactics, he emerged from his forest hideouts to release prisoners from gaols, burn government buildings and punish villagers and land-holders who showed loyalty to the British. At one time it was feared he would attack Varanasi, at another Ghazipur, and at yet others, Ara. The British surrounded his jungles and sent seven columns into them, but he once more evaded contact. Only when the British took to using mounted infantry did they gain the mobility needed to come up with his men and destroyed most of them in an encounter on 20 October. Even then Anwar Singh escaped with a few followers to reach the Kaimur hills between Western Bihar and Central India before the campaign officially ended.

Using the same method of operations that he had employed to recover Lucknow, Campbell invaded Rohilkhand with four separate columns converging on Bareilly. On 6 April, Major General Thomas Seaton, at Fatehgarh with the 82nd Foot, moved against insurgents in the neighbouring Doab. On 8 April Brigadier General Walpole, with the 9th Lancers, a brigade of Highlanders, two Sikh regiments and eighteen guns, marched north-westwards from Lucknow to secure the crossing of the Ramganga at Aliganj for Campbell's main force. En route he reached Ruya, the mud fort of Narpat Singh, an elderly Rajput nobleman who had chivalrously responded to an appeal from Begam Hazrat Mahal. An attempt to carry the defences by a quick attack was defeated with the loss of over 100 casualties among the 42nd Royal Highlanders and 4th Punjabis, including three officers. Among these was Brigadier Adrian Hope of the Highland Brigade, shot by an enemy marksman while dealing with the confusion that followed Walpole's decision to call off the assault. Hope was popular with all ranks, and the intrepid news hound Russell, accompanying this column, heard men talk of what would later be called 'fragging' Walpole for his waste of lives. Campbell, always mindful of his men's lives, had given orders that no strongholds were to be attacked without the use of artillery, but some officers deprecated the delays caused by his cautious ways and nicknamed him 'Sir Crawling Camel'. The next day Ruya was found abandoned and Walpole resumed his march, defeating an insurgent force at Sirsa on 22 April.

The third column, starting from Meerut under Major General Nicholas Penny, marched southwards to Bulandshahr and then swung south-east before crossing to the north bank of the Ganges at Fatehgarh on 24 April. Heading for Budaon, they fell into a night ambush in which Penny was killed, but the column maintained its cohesion and pushed on to its planned rendezvous with Campbell at Miranpur Kotra. Campbell, after being joined by Walpole near Aliganj on 27 April, crossed the Ramganga into Rohilkhand and reached Shahjahanpur on 30 April. On 3 May he joined Penny's column (now under Colonel H.R. Jones) and two days later reached the outskirts of Bareilly with some 8,000 men, comprising the 9th Lancers, 42nd, 78th, 79th and 93rd Highlanders, 64th and 82nd Foot, and four native infantry regiments.

The fourth column, the Roorki Field Force under Brigadier General John Jones of the 60th Rifles, crossed the Ganges at Haridwar and captured Najibabad, 30 miles due south on 21 April. There were the inevitable collateral casualties. Major W.F. Carleton of the 60th later wrote:

> Inside the enclosure was a pitiable sight. A young girl – she could not have more than 15, if as much – was lying dead, with a baby, also dead, in her arms [seemingly killed by the blast of a British shell]. It was quite pathetic to see what our men did in the midst of the hubbub. They pulled the clothes from some of the dead bodies lying around and reverently covered up the poor little couple.

John Jones pressed on to Muradabad, 40 miles north-west of Bareilly and waited for news of Campbell's movements. When none came, he advanced again on 3 May and two days later reached Mirganj, 14 miles from Bareilly.

Campbell launched his attack on Bareilly early the same day, 5 May, driving the insurgents from their first position with artillery and then sending forward the 42nd and 79th Highlanders, preceded by Sikh infantry. The latter reached a group of ruined buildings only to come under a heavy fire that drove them back in disorder to the 42nd. The Scots opened ranks to let them pass through, but then mistook a band of pursuing Ghazis for more Sikhs and allowed them to approach the British line. Campbell, close beside the Highlanders, his favourite troops, told the men to stand steady, close ranks and bayonet the Ghazi swordsmen as they came on. Even so, the Ghazis, whose determination to die for their faith gave them an advantage over anyone disposed to stay alive, for once pressed home their charge. Campbell himself, riding between his companies, saw a Ghazi pretending to be dead (a common ruse) and ordered a Highlander to bayonet him. The thrust was turned by the Ghazi's quilted tunic and the man was about to attack Campbell when a Sikh decapitated him with one blow of an Indian sword. Walpole, his bridle seized by Ghazis, was rescued by men of the 42nd despite their previous threats against him. Eventually 133 dead Ghazis were counted, against twenty wounded on the British side.

At the same time a strong force of Rohila horsemen circled round the British line and attacked the baggage train, always a favourite target for cavalry. Campbell, in his cautious way, had left a brigade of infantry to guard the rear, and the Rohilas were driven off by fire from the horse artillery and a counter-charge by the 9th Lancers. Nevertheless, they created a panic among the camp followers and unarmed transport drivers, whose elephants, camels, ponies and bullocks scattered in all directions. Campbell halted his advance until satisfied that the baggage was safe and then decided that, with the heat of the day, his men were too exhausted to fight in Bareilly's built-up areas. After reaching the cantonments of the former Bareilly brigade, he bivouacked for the night, while Jones's Roorki Field Force reached the northern edge of the city.

The next day, 6 May, both forces advanced into Bareilly, but Khan Bahadur Khan and most of his troops had slipped away during the night and the city was finally occupied on 7 May with resistance only from a few suicide squads. Campbell issued his usual stern warnings against plundering and proclaimed an amnesty for all citizens not directly implicated in the murders associated with the mutiny of the previous year. The troops found little left to plunder, but a group of riflemen found a dozen young women whose husbands or fathers had thrown them into wells to prevent them falling into infidel hands. Some still had their heads above water and a pair of riflemen, after climbing down to rescue them, restored them to a grateful elderly female.

For a short time it seemed that the war had ended almost exactly a year after it had begun. Then news came that Maulavi Ahmadullah Shah had moved from Awadh into Rohilkhand and attacked the weak garrison left at Shahjahanpur. Warned of his approach by their Intelligence, the British moved their camp inside their entrenchments beside the town gaol and stood on the defensive. The town and its suburbs fell to the Maulavi, who executed every inhabitant found to have co-operated with the

British, and began a bombardment of the gaol. Campbell sent Brigadier Jones of the Roorkee Field Force (remustered as the Shahjahanpur Field Force) to the rescue. They arrived on 12 May and made a successful junction with the garrison, but in the meanwhile the Maulavi himself had been joined by Begam Hazrat Mahal and Shahzada Firoz Shah with their respective forces.

Firoz Shah, a pious young member of the Mughal royal family, had returned to India in May 1857 from a pilgrimage to Mecca. In June, as British control over west-central India weakened, he unfurled the banner of Islam and gathered an army, mostly of impoverished Muslim settlers from Afghanistan and southern Baluchistan. He seized the city of Mandisore, where he was proclaimed king, and declared jihad against the British. Only one of the neighbouring princes acknowledged this new raj, but by September he had a force over 17,000 strong that in November laid siege to Nimach. This was abandoned when the British launched their Central Indian campaign, but by then Firoz Shah himself had gone to Gwalior, where he took command of the mutinied Indore Contingent. He had been with the insurgents at Lucknow and, after escaping with his men, moved into Rohilkhand, where he retreated before the Roorkee Field Force as it approached Bareilly. Of all the insurgent leaders, he was the one who most strongly condemned the slaughter of European women and children, as being contrary to Islam and a weakening of the moral strength of the revolt.

They attacked the Shahjahanpur entrenchments on 15 May but Jones drove them back and held out for three days until Campbell himself arrived. Cautious as ever, Campbell decided that he was too weak in cavalry to take the offensive before further reinforcements arrived on 23 May (the same day that the Central India Field Force occupied Kalpi). The Maulavi, pursued by Jones, then retreated 25 miles westwards to Mohamdi, where he put up a stout defence before heading back into Rohilkhand. On 5 June he reached Pawayan. A year previously the local raja had done little to protect European fugitives but now, aware that the British had put a price of Rs 50,000 on the Maulavi's head, and with no desire to espouse a lost cause, closed his gates against him. The Maulavi tried to push the gates down with his elephant, but was shot by one of the raja's men. His head was sent to Shajahanpur and delivered to the magistrate while the latter was at dinner. Firoz Shah and Begam Hazrat Mahal meanwhile reached the unsubdued districts of northern Awadh.

After abandoning Kalpi, the leaders of the Peshwa's army debated where to go next. The Gwalior Contingent and the other sepoys favoured moving north into Awadh, where most had their home villages. The Rani of Jhansi suggested returning to Bundelkhand, but Tatya Tope argued that supplies would be difficult to find in Awadh, and that most of the Bundela chiefs were on the British side. Rao Sahib said they should march west to Gwalior and then strike into the Deccan, reviving the old Maratha Confederacy and opening a new theatre of war while the British were still fighting in Awadh. Old men could remember when the Mughal emperor was a puppet in Maratha hands and had to be rescued by the British. Now that the British seemed in decline, Sindhia might at last be persuaded to abandon his policy of prevarication and declare for the Peshwa. If he did so, the hope was that other great Maratha princes would rise and join in sweeping the British into the sea. Even if he did not, the appearance of an army some 11,000 strong, still with twelve guns, might encourage his nobles to rise against him and fight for the Peshwa's cause.

Accordingly, they made a rapid march to Gwalior, where Rao Sahib asked Sindhia only for a contribution of treasure to pay his troops, supplies to feed them, and an unopposed passage through Gwalior territory to the Deccan. Sindhia always believed the British would win and was sure that they would soon arrive in pursuit. Despite the pleas of his chief minister, to the effect that he should be the bamboo rather than the oak, and after hearing that the Peshwa's army was starving and could be dispersed with a single salvo, he put himself at the head of his own army, 8,000 strong with twenty-four guns, and marched to Baragaon, 8 miles east of Gwalior. Since the beginning of the war he had been trying to replace his Purbiya regulars with Marathas, so that the former, who came from the same villages as the Bengal sepoys, had no reason to remain loyal, while the latter stood to gain if a new Peshwa restored the old Maratha Confederacy to power.

When the armies met, Muslims in the Peshwa's army raised the green flag to shouts of 'Din, Din'. Sindhia's Purbiyas, followed by his Hindu Marathas, fraternized with them. His bodyguard remained loyal and suffered some sixty casualties, but when the rest of his army refused to fight, Sindhia abandoned the field and rode north, first to his feudatory, the Rana of Dhaulpur, and thence to his British friends at Agra. His chief minister arranged the escape of the royal ladies from Gwalior to the fortress of Narwa and then joined his master at Dhaulpur. In Gwalior, existing officials were left in post and Sindhia's treasury was used to pay the arrears and bonuses due to the troops (his own as well as the Peshwa's), with shares for the Rani of Jhansi, the Nawab of Banda and Rao Sahib himself. In a glittering ceremony, Nana Sahib was once more proclaimed Peshwa, with Rao Sahib as his viceroy. Rao Sahib wrote to the Queen Mother, Baiza Bai, urging her to return to the city and take charge of the government, saying that he only wished to meet her before going on. Baiza Bai, who had ruled Gwalior during her son's minority, was too experienced in statecraft to be drawn in and forwarded his letters to the British.

Rose's designated successor, Colonel Robert Napier, previously Campbell's chief engineer, was still on his way to take over the Central India Field Force at Kalpi. In his absence, Rose resumed command and marched for Gwalior on 6 June. Campbell could scarcely complain at Rose's sense of urgency, but nevertheless censured him on the grounds that, having resigned claiming ill-health, he had no right to reappoint himself and thereby deny Napier his own chance of a battlefield command. On arrival, Napier loyally served as Rose's second-in-command and ten years later commanded his own army in the successful Abyssinian campaign. Rose had already sent part of his 1st Brigade to watch the Peshwa's army after its retreat from Kalpi, but no one had anticipated the descent on Gwalior. Now he ordered the garrison of Jhansi to join him, while the Hyderabad Contingent, hearing the news on their way home, turned back on its commander's own initiative.

At the same time, Campbell ordered a force of cavalry and infantry from Agra, and the Rajputana Field Force (including two troops of the 8th Hussars, 1st Bombay Lancers, 95th Foot and 10th Bombay NI) to converge on Gwalior. The summer of 1858 was exceptionally hot even by local standards, with temperatures of 100 degrees F being common. In the hospital tents, thermometers exploded as the mercury expanded beyond the capacity of their bulbs. Continual marching, even though undertaken at night, exhausted the troops, already weakened by lack of fresh provisions. Captain Henry Duberley, with the

8th Hussars, reported sick with a sprained ankle only to be diagnosed with incipient scurvy. Fanny Duberley, riding side-saddle, developed a major abscess, serious enough for her to need chloroform while it was lanced by the regimental surgeon. Inside her double-roofed tent the temperature reached 119 degrees F. Unable to ride and often fainting from pain and heat, she was carried along at the head of the column in a litter, and credulous villagers supposed that it was the preserved body of a dead Englishwoman whom the troops were coming to avenge.

A week later she got up to watch a battle at Kota-ki-Serai, 4 miles south of Gwalior, where on 17 June the Rajputana column defeated a strong insurgent force of all arms. In the hospital lines she saw the ambulance dhoolies coming in.

> The first contained poor Berry, a bandsman of the 8th Hussars, whose leg was so fearfully shattered that immediate amputation at the hip was necessary ... more and more came – some dying of sunstroke – the doctors have full employment. Lieutenant Riley, killed by sunstroke within a few minutes of having ridden a dashing charge, was brought in, and with poor Berry was consigned to a hastily made grave.

European manpower in this war was so scarce that bandsmen fought in the ranks from the very beginning and suffered casualties like ordinary soldiers. One musician lost a hand, but told an officer who commiserated with him on his loss of livelihood that he would have himself fitted with a hook and become a trombone player.

Casualties among the insurgents included the Rani of Jhansi. Accounts of her death vary, although most say that, an excellent horsewoman, she was dressed in the uniform of her bodyguard and leading them in combat. The version favoured by the 8th Hussars was that one of their troopers, unaware of her identity, wounded her with his sword in their first charge and shot her when she fired at him from the ground as they rode back. Another is that her camp was surprised by the Hussars and that she was mortally wounded when her horse refused a jump as she tried to escape, while a few of her bodyguard held the British off. Sir Robert Hamilton concluded that she and a female attendant had been hit while observing the battle early in the day, and that the final ceremonies of her hastily arranged cremation were still uncompleted when the Hussars charged in. At the time, few in the British camp regretted her demise, seeing her as the Jezebel of India, responsible for the massacre of so many Europeans whom she might have saved. Later they gave a grudging respect for her personal courage and determination. Among her own subjects she became a folk heroine, as much for her defiance of her Bundela neighbours as of the British. She later became a nationalist and feminist icon, and in 1942, when the Japanese-sponsored Indian National Army was formed to spearhead the march on Delhi, its women soldiers became the Rani of Jhansi battalion.

Unaware of this blow to enemy morale, the British moved up onto higher ground where they spent the night under desultory bombardment from insurgent artillery. With no cooking fires allowed, there was no dinner and Mrs Duberley set off in the darkness to find something to eat. She found her husband and another officer on the sick list also looking for food and eventually reached the regimental mess, though it produced no more than two overheated bottles of beer. A renewed bombardment the next morning was briefly silenced by counter-fire from a British heavy gun, until its trail shattered when recoiling and allowed the watching insurgent artillerymen to resume their work.

On 18 June, Rose and his 1st Brigade joined the Rajputana force, suffering nearly a hundred casualties among the 86th from the heat as they marched. On 19 June the insurgents made a sortie from Gwalior in force, but were taken in the flank by Rose's infantry and driven back, losing five guns which were promptly turned on them as they retreated. The Duberleys, who had gone out to watch, noticed the guns suddenly fall silent. Then a staff officer came by 'riding with speed to order our two troops of the 8th and Blake's Horse Artillery to charge down to a village by the fort. As they started my little horse sprang away. I sang out to Henry – "I must go!" – "Go along then!" said he, eager for an excuse, and away we went at a rushing gallop right to the fort.' At the end of the day they returned to camp, promising to send camels with provisions for their regiment, as none had eaten since breakfast.

Rose gave the retreating insurgents no time to rally and took the city while Rao Sahib and Tatya Tope retreated to the north-west. In the dusk, Sindhia, who had joined Rose's column, stood at the gates supervising the distribution of beer and champagne to the British soldiers. The next day he was escorted back to his palace, despite fire from a dozen men who had reoccupied the fort and were determined to die as martyrs. Meanwhile the brigadier commanding the Rajputana force, concerned for the health of the only lady within his command, arranged for the Duberleys to be given a suite in the palace.

Word spread among the men of her regiment and in a letter to her sister Selina in England she later wrote:

> Before I started, as I was sitting on a box having a good cry, I was startled to find a deputation of the non-commissioned officers of the regiment who came to express their sorrow that I was sick. They said many kind things and said that many and many a man had been saved from giving way to sickness because he could not give in as long as I was seen daily riding at the front of the column ... Well, I was much gratified, of course.

The regimental village concept clearly had a practical as well as an emotional effect; for all that Campbell, the crusty bachelor, regarded women in the battle zone as encumbrances. The Queen Mother, Baiza Bai, still handsome and forceful even in her seventies, told Fanny Duberley that she herself had ridden in a battle when young, having been at Assaye 'when Wellesley Sahib drove us out of the field with only the saddles on which we rode'.

Napier pursued the Peshwa's army with the 2nd Brigade and on 22 May he caught them at Jawra Alipur, 35 miles north-west of Gwalior. Insurgent morale had been weakened by the string of British successes and their line gave way after a troop of Bombay Horse Artillery engaged its left flank. In the 6-mile pursuit, the insurgents lost an estimated 300 against British casualties of 4 killed and 8 wounded, and abandoned 25 guns. Tatya Tope and Rao Sahib, still with a few thousand men following them, crossed the Chambal and headed into Rajasthan. Rose finally handed over his command to Napier and retired to Pune (Poona) on sick leave. Canning meanwhile ordered salutes to be fired at every station in India to mark the recovery of Gwalior.

Awadh alone remained to be reconquered and Hope Grant had countered several threats while Campbell conducted the Rohilkhand operations. Minor operations in July and August included the recovery of Sultanpur (lost by the British in June 1857). There were, however, no more cities to be taken and no more large armies in the field, and Campbell kept most of his troops in cantonments until the approach of the 1858–9 campaigning season. Only a sudden attempt in October by insurgents to seize the small post of Sandila, 30 miles north-west of Lucknow, demonstrated that the British could not relax their guard.

On 2 November 1858 Campbell (ennobled as Baron Clyde of Clydesdale the previous August) marched northwards into Awadh from Allahabad. In his usual methodical way, he despatched other columns from Fatehgarh, Shahjahanpur and Azamgarh in the east, with the aim of driving the insurgents across the Ghaghara and the Rapti into the fever-infested jungle hills of the Terai, bordering Nepal. Aware that every chief in Awadh had his own stronghold, Clyde allotted heavy guns to each column. The mud fortresses crumbled before modern Western siege craft, while the few leaders who attempted to make a stand in the field were defeated in detail. The campaign became one of incessant marching rather than fighting. By the end of the year, with the loss of eighteen killed and eighty-four wounded, the British had restricted their opponents to a narrow strip of territory in the Terai.

Clyde's last battle was at Banki on 30 December 1858, where the last insurgents escaped across the Rapti into Nepal. On 7 January a group of chiefs who had been fighting against Clyde entered his camp to avail themselves of the terms offered by Queen Victoria's Proclamation, read out at Allahabad and across India on 1 November 1858. This had announced the transfer of all the East India Company's undertakings, contracts and servants to the British Crown in Parliament. The rights, honour and dignity of Indian princes were guaranteed and the religious beliefs and worship of all were expressly protected from interference. With the exception of individuals who had led the revolt or who had murdered British subjects (taken to mean Europeans) or knowingly sheltered murderers, all those who laid down their arms before 1 January 1859 would be granted amnesty.

At first many were suspicious of British good faith and there were indeed instances where special commissioners made little distinction between murderers and rebels. The government, however, had realized that the only way of bringing bloodshed to an end was to treat ordinary insurgents as the losing side in what the Queen herself, in discussions on the draft of her proclamation, called 'a bloody civil war'. Begam Hazrat Mahal issued a counter proclamation of her own, warning her people to place no faith in British promises, broken so often in the past, but gradually, as the policy of reconciliation came into force and the last insurgent leaders were captured or exiled, the ordinary fighters laid down such arms as they still had. Clyde himself set an example by treating the surrendered nobles with respect. They told him they had fought for their king, whose salt they had eaten long before the British took his country. He invited them to sit in his presence and told them that he had been a soldier for fifty years and seen enough of war to rejoice when it was at an end.

The war, however, was not quite at an end. Rao Sahib and Tatya Tope, after their defeat by Napier on 22 June 1858, marched to Tonk in Rajasthan. The Nawab of Tonk took refuge in his citadel but his troops defected to the Peshwa's army. From there they slipped between pursuing British columns and forded the Chambal (thought to be impassable in the monsoon floods) to reach Jhalwar, where the local raja's troops joined them and forced their master to pay a large ransom. From there they headed for Indore, with a view to repeating their coup at Gwalior, but Major General John Michel, an experienced British Army officer commanding the Malwa Field Force, defeated them at Biowra on 15 September. Exhaustion prevented the British from following and in Michel's two British infantry regiments (72nd and 92nd Highlanders) a third of the men became casualties from the heat. Tatya then marched against Chanderi while Rao Sahib went towards Jhansi, but neither move was successful and they were again defeated by Michel in an encounter battle at Mangrali on 10 October. From there they headed west and were joined by some of the Holkar's mutinied troops. Intercepted before they could enter Gujarat, they crossed the Narmada and went back into Rajasthan. There, in early December 1858, one of the pursuing British columns made contact with them at Pratapgarh, but again they escaped.

In December William Russell wrote to *The Times* that for six months Tatya Tope had kept Central India in a fever. 'He has sacked stations, plundered treasuries, emptied arsenals, collected armies, lost them, fought battles, lost them, taken guns from native princes, lost them, taken more, lost them … He has marched between our columns, behind them and before them … Up mountains, over rivers, through ravines and valleys, amid swamps, on he goes, backwards and forwards and sideways ... evasive as Proteus.'

The Rajputana Field Force left Gwalior on 6 June, marching 56 miles back through the monsoon to reach Shivpuri (Sipri) a month later. They were kept there by the rains for another month and then ordered to Pohri (Powrie), 18 miles to the north-west. The march, with the infantrymen's boots rotting on their feet, troop horses falling into hidden potholes and baggage camels lying down to die in the mud, took two days. More orders and counter-orders followed in attempts to find the elusive Tatya Tope. Fanny Duberley, still with the 8th Hussars, echoed the frustration of the troops when she wrote in her journal: 'I think that if I were in a subordinate command in India I should either throw the whole thing up and run away in the night or I should carry out my own plans in the teeth of everybody.' Brigadier General Smith, commanding her column, made her cross: 'Our brigadier, good-natured and unselfish as he is, is a *dreadful* old woman. He is afraid of the papers, afraid of public opinion, afraid to do anything but march, march, march, backwards and forwards and round and round anything and anywhere as long as the newspapers do not report him halting anywhere.' She had more respect for the various Indian ladies who had played their parts in the emergency, and told her sister: 'After all, one determined woman is worth more than six men.' Another lady, Mrs L. Paget, who in 1865 published her own memoirs of the campaign, *Camp and Cantonment*, was equally scathing of male inefficiency. In her view, each column commander wanted to catch Tatya Tope but 'as each wanted his own column to do it without interference from another, in addition to chasing the rebels, the columns were often running from one another.'

Smith, however, had another enemy to find, in the person of Man Singh, a Rajput nobleman who disputed his uncle's possession of Pohri, part of the dominions of Gwalior. When Sindhia's troops defected, he rose up against his overlord and seized the fort, but the British, acting in support of their ally, drove him out and he established a fortified camp in the jungle near Mangrol, 40 miles north-west of Kota. On 20 November, Smith made a dawn attack, taking Man Singh completely by surprise and opening a devastating artillery fire on the sleeping camp. Many of Man Singh's infantry, armed only with match-locks, were ridden down with their matches still unlit. Fanny

Duberley, armed only with a riding crop, a small revolver and an ornamental dagger, rode into the camp with the horse artillery. 'The rebels fled, leaving their very children behind them. We pursued at a gallop, the guns getting into action whenever opportunity offered but the execution was chiefly done by the hussars and lancers ... Maung Sing, aroused by the first gun, threw himself on his famous cream-coloured horse and galloped for his life.' She saw a man, shot in the head and bleeding badly, being tendered by his daughter, a girl of about twelve, who held up her hands to ask for mercy, and stopped to try and comfort her. A six-month-old baby with a small dog was found sitting up on a bed, laughing at the soldiers and horses as they passed. A woman among the British camp followers took the baby into her care, and Fanny Duberley found herself possessed of the dog. Less mercy was shown to the men, and she recorded in her journal: 'It seems to me that this Indian warfare is unsatisfactory work and ... there have been cases of ruthless slaughter of which the less said the better.'

Early in 1859 Tatya Tope joined Man Singh, who had rallied his men at Nahargarh, but soon left him and met Shahzada Firoz Shah at Indargarh, 20 miles north-west of Mangrol. After being driven from Rohilkhand, this prince had crossed the Ganges and headed south, only to be intercepted and defeated by Napier in an encounter battle at Ranod, 50 miles south-west of Jhansi. He retreated another hundred miles south to the jungle near Aron, but was driven out by a column coming from Guna. He turned north and after 120 miles met Tatya Tope at Indargarh, but by this time their combined forces amounted to under 2,000 men. The British were close behind and they retreated another 90 miles northward to Dausa, between Jaipur and Bharatpur. There, on 14 January 1859, a force under Brigadier Showers caught up with them and killed two hundred men. The rest escaped and camped at the desert capital of the Rao Raja of Sikar, 60 miles north-west of Jaipur. A force from Nasirabad, including 247 men of the 83rd Foot and 600 native cavalry, artillery and infantry marched rapidly northwards and surprised them on 21 January, after covering 90 miles in thirteen days.

This defeat marked the break-up of the Peshwa's army. If the continual marching through every extreme of climate and terrain had taken its toll of the British, it had affected the insurgents even more. As in the other bands still fighting, without arsenals and depots to replace worn-out weapons and uniforms, the distinctions of dress and equipment that play an essential part in the maintenance of unit discipline gradually lapsed. With all the treasure seized from Sindhia and the other princes long spent, there was no money to buy supplies at a fair rate (something that Rao Shaib had originally insisted on) and reliance was made on forced contributions. As an example to those who resisted, the town of Isangarh was sacked, with the men killed and the women humiliated. The insurgents, who at first moved through the people as fish swim in the sea, had changed from soldiers into bandits and could no longer rely on the co-operation of either chiefs or villagers.

Tatya Tope told his remaining men to save themselves while he sought refuge with Man Singh in the jungle near Kota. A few days later, 600 of them surrendered to the Maharaja of Bikanir, a British ally. Rao Sahib and Firoz Shah moved south-westwards and reached the Araoalli (Aravalli) Hills, with four British columns in pursuit. The British searched the jungle area into which the insurgents disappeared and found their deserted camp, but of the two leaders there was no sign. During February and March their last few hundred men took advantage of the amnesty and surrendered. Man Singh literally joined the British camp on 2 April and demonstrated his change of heart by delivering Tatya Tope to them a week later. After a brief show trial, in which he stoutly denied any responsibility for the massacres at Kanpur, Tatya was hanged as a rebel on 15 April. The British offered amnesty to Rao Sahib and Firoz Shah, subject to their having done no murder and agreeing to reside where they were directed, but neither accepted. Rao Sahib travelled in disguise through northern India until 1862 when he too was betrayed and hanged for his alleged involvement in the massacre of the women and children at Kanpur. Firoz Shah made his way through Sind to Afghanistan and thence to various courts in central Asia. He died in poverty at Mecca in 1877 and the Government of India granted a small personal pension to his widow.

With British arms triumphant everywhere, the war gradually petered out. By mid-February, the authorities had disarmed Awadh to the extent of collecting 378 cannon, 134,517 small arms and 444,074 swords, and demolishing 756 out of 1,100 forts. Of the insurgent leaders, Bakht Khan, still fat but no longer jovial, was killed in a skirmish on 13 May 1859. Khan Bahadur

Khan, sometime Nawab of Rohilkhand, was one of the several princes who fled to Nepal only to be arrested by Jang Bahadur and handed over for victors' justice. He was hanged at Bareilly in 1860. The Nawab of Farrukhabad, held responsible for the massacre of Europeans at Fatehgarh, was also sentenced to death, but the sentence was commuted to exile in Mecca. The Nawab of Banda, who surrendered in good time, was spared and given a modest pension. Bala Sahib was said to have died of fever in the Terai. The same was reported of Azimullah Khan, though by other accounts he made his way to Constantinople and was eventually murdered there. His master, Nana Sahib, was also reported to have died of fever, but as is often the case when a famous person disappears, conspiracy theories abounded and occasional sightings were said to have been made as late as 1895. After Begam Hazrat Mahal's starving and fever-ridden troops finally dispersed, Jang Bahadur allowed her and her son to remain in Nepal, where she refused all offers of conciliation from the British. Ordinary clansmen were allowed to go free. Convicted mutineers were granted their lives, but such a serious military offence could not go unpunished and they were exiled to a penal settlement in the Andaman Islands.

On 8 July 1859, two years and two months after the outbreak at Meerut, Canning, by this time Viceroy as well as Governor-General, proclaimed the restoration of peace throughout India.

Chapter 11

THE IMPACT ON THE BRITISH ARMY

These are the stories our Colours have to tell. Not mere gallantry in action – that is a small thing and one inherent to our race. They tell of privations uncomplainingly borne, of difficulties nobly surmounted, of steadfast loyalty to the Crown and of cheerful obedience to orders even when that obedience meant certain death.

C.B. *Norman* Battle Honours of the British Army

The war ended as it began, in a maze of conspiracy theories, some of which had such plausibility as to be periodically revived, for at least the next 150 years. The least plausible, though at times of Russo-phobia among the most popular, was that the Mutiny had been engineered or at least encouraged from St Petersburg in the aftermath of the Crimean War. This was widely believed despite the fact that Russian statesmen, pursuing their *mission civilatrice* in Muslim-ruled central Asia, proposed that the two great Christian empires should extend their territories to a common frontier, from which each could aid the other in the event of an Islamic jihad against either.

The idea that Shi'a-ruled Iran, recently at war with the British, fomented the rising is equally fanciful, though it was advanced against the King of Delhi when he was tried for rebellion and subsequently exiled to Rangoon. The ex-King of Awadh was certainly a Shi'a, and the King of Delhi was suspected by Sunni puritans of having Shi'ite tendencies, but neither had any political association with the Shah of Iran, the recognized leader of Shi'a Muslims. The decision of the Shah to make peace with the British just before the Mutiny and thereby release troops desperately needed in India, suggests that it came just as much of a surprise to him as to them.

Suggestions that the rising was a conspiracy of the Wahabis, much favoured at the time by Commissioner Taylor and his supporters, owed much to conjecture. The Reverend Midgeley Jennings, the leading missionary murdered with his daughter and other Europeans in the King's palace at Delhi, was suspicious of their influence there, but his views were inevitably influenced by his own zeal and Wahabi doctrines teach their followers to shun worldly affairs. There was a strong Wahabi community in Bareilly, of which Subadar Bakht Khan was a member, and also in the mountainous tribal territory bordering the Punjab, but the latter remained quiet during the Mutiny and their subsequent rising had no connection with its events. Some Wahabi leaders actively aided the government, and Sir Frederick Halliday, Lieutenant Governor of Bengal, later minuted that nothing was proved or even alleged against the Wahabis in his province.

The conspiracy theory most favoured at the time was that dissidents planned for every Bengal regiment to rise simultaneously, kill their officers and restore the Indian princes deposed by Dalhousie's expansionist policies. This was especially supported by Colonel Carmichael Smyth at Meerut. So far from accepting that it was his own ambition and stubbornness that started the war, he argued that by his firmness he anticipated the rising and led the mutineers to begin their operations at Delhi ahead of the planned date, supposedly set for two or three weeks later. There were, however, so many variations in the timings and conduct of each mutiny that the detection of any pattern in them depends upon imagination rather than hard Intelligence.

As with most Intelligence analysis, the simplest method of evaluating such conspiracy theories is a rigid application of Occam's Razor ('Entities are not to be multiplied'). On this principle, all unnecessary theories, no matter how attractive or ingenious, can be disregarded in favour of the obvious, no matter how simple or apparent. The plain tale of 1857 is that of a series of military revolts by soldiers fearful for their future, in this world or the next, and the exploitation of these by civil and religious leaders who wished to do away with the changes brought by British rule and return to what, for them, had been the good old days.

The campaigns of 1857–8 were the British Army's greatest, and last, major operations within India. Thereafter it fought on the borders of the subcontinent to extend or maintain British power, ending with the defence of the north-east frontier against the Japanese Imperial Forces in 1942–5. In 1947, with the achievement of independence by the successor states, India and Pakistan, it ended a presence that had lasted for nearly two centuries. Of all the dramatic events that occurred there during that period it was the Indian Mutiny that most affected the development of the British Army.

After various parliamentary wrangles, the India Act of August 1858 ended the rule of the East India Company and set up a new department, the India Office, in which the Secretary of State for India took the place of the President of the Board of Control. To provide the Indian expertise formerly offered by the Court of Directors and to protect Indian revenues from raids by the Treasury, a Council of India was established, with its members appointed by the government and given control over expenditure. One result of this was that British troops in India were funded by the perennially cash-strapped Government of India to standards different from, and usually even lower than, those applied by the War Office. Guns, for example, tended to be of obsolescent patterns, though there was far more space available for exercises, and it was said that the Royal Artillery in India could ride, but not shoot, whereas at home it could shoot but not ride.

The number of native troops was reduced from 226,000 to 190,000 but that of Europeans was increased from 24,000 to 80,000 with the Company's European units being transferred to the British Army. British cavalry in India was increased from the pre-war level of 4 regiments to 9, and infantry from 31 battalions to 50. All artillery, with the exception of a few mountain, light or garrison batteries, was placed in European hands, effectively doubling the size of the Royal Regiment.

With the introduction of the short-service system in 1870, many more men returned home with tales of Indian service and a smattering of Urdu that passed into common speech. One example out of many is the word 'padre', often believed to derive from the seven-years-long Peninsular War (fought at a time when no Protestant Englishman would call his priest 'father' in any language). It is the Urdu *padri*, a loan word taken from the Portuguese period in India, meaning a Christian priest of any kind, and thus applied by the British soldiers in India to their own military chaplains, both there and when they returned home. Other examples are 'chit' from *chitthi* (a letter) or 'dhobi' (for laundry) from the Urdu word for a washerman.

India, a land of many castes, fostered the British Army's perception of itself as a body marked out from its own community by its increasing professionalism, and from the subject populations of the British Empire by its race, religion and conquests. The pre-existing regimental spirit, a powerful element of the British military ethos, was intensified by the numinous atmosphere of India. After the events at Meerut, few British soldiers in India had doubts about the need to maintain their own exclusivity. Those who did had only to remember why, after Meerut, they always went on church parade with rifles in their hands and ball ammunition in their pouches.

For a whole generation, senior British officers remembered the Mutiny. Of the twenty-eight non-royal field marshals appointed between 1862 and 1908, fourteen (Campbell, Rose, Napier, Grant, Michel, Haines, Stewart, Wolseley, Roberts, Chamberlain, Norman, Wood, Brownlow and White) were present in India at the time. Many other future generals were there too and for them the army in India was an army of occupation, with its Indian component deliberately kept less well armed than the British. It was not until Kitchener (who had never served in India) became C-in-C India in 1902 that it was reconfigured as an army whose primary role was to conduct large-scale continental operations.

The same generation was affected even among the civil community. In the middle of the nineteenth century, most opinion-formers in the United Kingdom were confident in the strength of their society and its values. Their country was the richest and most powerful in the world – in modern terms, a superpower. Its values were taken as a model by progressives everywhere, and in 1848 it had remained at peace while Europe was swept by revolution. Its industries prospered, served by railways, steamships and other triumphs of British invention, science and technology. There were, indeed, anxieties, arising from the existence of poverty, religious disputes, even demands for women's rights, while the reverses suffered during the Crimean War led to some unease. British India, however, had been seen as a place where the benefits of Western civilization, as expressed through the introduction of British institutions, brought peace, progress and prosperity. When mutinous sepoys and insurgent princes rejected these benefits, they were demonized, with atrocity stories being echoed in literature and illustrations of every degree of artistic merit. Among the best known was Walter

Paton's painting *In Memoriam*, depicting a group of English-women and children crouching in terror at Kanpur, while brutal sepoys rush in through an opened doorway. Exhibited in the Royal Academy's Spring Exhibition of 1859, it was roundly condemned by the *Illustrated London News* as the art of the charnel house, and Paton eventually had to replace the ravening sepoys with rescuing Highlanders, implying that the episode was set at Lucknow. In print, Wilkie Collins's highly popular *The Moonstone* (1868) has a group of Indians invading an English country house in search of a misappropriated jewel, and, by implication, threatening the chastity of the heroine, Rachel, and the sanctity of the British home. Fear of Indian men laying violent hands on Western women became a standard element in English fiction set in India, even in works sympathetic to their Indian characters.

In fact, as the examples given in preceding chapters have demonstrated, Englishwomen of the time were by no means the fragile angels of Victorian male fantasy. Most of those caught up in the fighting seem to have behaved with all the resilience and fortitude that goes with being a soldier's wife. Indeed, the performance of Southern belles during the siege of Vicksburg five years later and Parisiennes during that of their own city in the Franco-Prussian War seven years after that, shows that it was not only Englishwomen who could endure bombardment and privations, even without the knowledge that capitulation meant certain death.

It was, however, the idea of chivalrous endeavour in defending, rescuing, or avenging helpless women and children that most influenced popular British perceptions of the Mutiny narrative. It was, indeed, the imperative to rescue the non-combatants besieged in Lucknow that initially distorted the strategy of the British commanders, by causing them to hurry forward their few available troops instead of waiting to assemble a large force. Orders issued by British generals to their soldiers in the field made much of the superiority of British courage and Christian beliefs. Havelock, the hero of the powerful Baptist lobby, was seen as the perfect Christian soldier, and his reported last words to his son were, 'See how a Christian can die.' Rose's farewell order to the Central India Field Force praised his men's Christian chivalry.

Battlefield despatches and memoirs invariably maximized enemy strengths and minimized British ones, if only by taking every Indian in the insurgent camp as hostile but counting only the regular soldiers in the British one. Nevertheless, it was certainly the case that, by any standards, the British were operating with tiny armies and doing so in the midst of an alien, though largely apathetic, population that greatly outnumbered them. Many, soldiers and civilians alike, drew the conclusion that their success was proof of the superiority of British manhood. Muscular Christians such as Thomas Hughes or Samuel Smiles saw the battlefield as a place where men could prove their masculinity by fighting the good fight. Such attitudes spread through all classes despite the influence of Quakers and pacifists, and an ingrained objection to military conscription among those likely to be affected by it. Public schools and Board schools alike taught a national history in which British achievements in battle played a major part. The Napoleonic Wars were too far away and those of the First World War were yet to come, so that it was to the Indian Mutiny that they turned for their examplars. Indeed, because many public schoolboys found careers in the Indian services, and many Board school boys went there as soldiers, the subject, if not the interpretation, was entirely appropriate.

While British defeats were presented as stemming from enemy treachery, itself evidence of moral degradation, British victories were taken as evidence of superior British racial qualities. The achievements of Indian troops fighting for the British, especially when no British officers were present, were taken to show that their own martial traditions approximated to British codes. The uncomfortable fact that Sikhs and Gurkhas also shared with their British comrades a fondness for strong drink and looting was glossed over. Among all classes of British society, the concept of going to war in a righteous cause and defending the defenceless, just as British soldiers had done in the Mutiny, became widely accepted as a way of proving a man's moral and physical worth. Many of the volunteers who flocked to the colours in 1914 were swayed by it. Fighting the mutineers, or the unspeakable Hun, was the same as fighting the devil.

To the soldiers who did the fighting came the honours sanctioned by government. Victoria Crosses were awarded to 183 recipients, fourteen of them in the 9th Royal Lancers. Some

290,000 men were issued with the Indian Mutiny campaign medal, given to anyone in the British or Company's service who had borne arms and (unusually for campaign medals) actually been present at an engagement. Battle honours were awarded to eight out of the British Army's twenty-eight regiments of cavalry (the 2nd and 6th Dragoon Guards, the 7th and 8th Hussars, 9th and 12th Lancers, 14th Light Dragoons and 17th Lancers), and to twenty-six out of its one hundred regiments of Foot (the 5th, 8th, 10th, 20th, 23rd, 32nd, 34th, 38th, 42nd, 52nd, 53rd, 60th, 61st, 64th, 71st, 72nd, 75th, 78th, 79th, 82nd, 83rd, 84th, 86th, 88th, 93rd and 95th) and the Rifle Brigade. All these regiments have changed their titles since then, some many times; all have been amalgamated with others and some among the infantry have been disbanded completely. Of their present-day (2007–08) successors, five of the eight regular cavalry regiments in the Royal Armoured Corps and eight of the twelve regular regiments of Infantry of the Line have Indian Mutiny battle honours among their distinctions and thus preserve the achievements of the soldiers who won them.

SELECT BIBLIOGRAPHY

Aitchison, Charles, *Lord Lawrence*, Clarendon Press, Oxford, 1897.

Allen, Charles, *God's Terrorists: The Wahabi Cult and the Hidden Roots of Modern Jihad*, Little, Brown, London, 2006.

Anglesey, Marquess of, *A History of the British Cavalry*, Vol. II, Leo Cooper, London 1972.

Askwith, W.H., *List of Officers of the Royal Regiment of Artillery*, RA Institute, Woolwich, 1900.

Atkinson, C.T., *The South Wales Borderers, 24th Foot, 1689–1937*, University Press, Cambridge, 1937.

Barrett, C.R.B., *The 7th (Queen's Own) Hussars*, RUSI, London, 1914.

Barter, Richard, *The Siege of Delhi: Mutiny Memoirs of an Old Officer*, The Folio Society, London, 1984.

Bayly, C.A., *The New Cambridge History of India: Indian Society and the Making of the British Empire*, CUP, Cambridge, 1988.

Belfield, Eversley, *The Queen's Dragoon Guards*, Leo Cooper, London, 1978.

Beveridge, *A Comprehensive History of India, Civil, Military and Social, from the first landing of the English to the suppression of the Sepoy Revolt*, 3 vols, Blackie and Son, London, Glasgow and Edinburgh, 1865.

Biddulph, John, *The Nineteenth and their times, being an account of the four cavalry regiments in the British Army that have borne the number Nineteen etc.*, John Murray, London, 1899.

Blake, Robert, *Disraeli*, Eyre and Spottiswoode, London, 1966.

Bloomfield, David, (ed.), *Lahore to Lucknow: The Indian Mutiny Journal of Arthur Moffatt Lang*, Leo Cooper (Pen & Sword), London and Barnsley, 1992.

Broeld, Wayne G., Jr., *Crisis of the Raj: The Revolt of 1857 through British Lieutenants' Eyes*, University Press of New England, Hanover, New Hampshire, and London, 1986.

Burne, Owen Tudor, *Clyde and Strathnairn. The Suppression of the Great Revolt*, Clarendon Press, Oxford, 1895.

Butler, F.W., *A Narrative of the Historical Events connected with the 69th Regiment*, W. Mitchell & Co., London, 1870.

Butler, Lewis, *The Annals of the King's Royal Rifle Corps*, Vol. III, John Murray, London, 1926.

Cadell, Patrick, *History of the Bombay Army*, Longmans, Green & Co., London, 1938.

Cardew, F.G., *Services of the Bengal Native Army*, Govt. of India, Calcutta, 1903.

Cary, A.D.L and McCance, S., *Regimental Records of the Royal Welch Fusiliers*, Forster, Groom & Co., London, 1923.

Cavendish, A.E.J., *An Reisimeid Chataich. The 93rd Sutherland Highlanders 1799–1927*, printed privately, 1928.

Chattopadhaya, Haraprasad, *The Sepoy Mutiny 1857*, Bookland Private Ltd, Calcutta, 1957.

Chaudhuri, Sashi Prasad, *Civil Rebellion in the Indian Mutinies*, World Press Private Ltd, Calcutta, 1957.

Collier, Richard, *The Sound of Fury: An Account of the Indian Mutiny*, Collins, London. 1963.

Cooper, Frederick, *The Crisis in the Punjab*, Smith, Elder & Co., London, 1858.

Cope, William, *History of the Rifle Brigade (The Prince Consort's Own)*, Chatto and Windrush, London, 1877.

Creagh, O., and Humhris, E.M., *The VC and DSO*, Standard Art Book Co., London, [c.1930].

Cunliffe, Marcus, *The Royal Irish Fusiliers 1793–1950*, Oxford UP, London, 1952.

Dalrymple, William, *The Last Mughal: The Fall of a Dynasty, Delhi, 1857*, Bloomsbury, London, 2006.

Daniell, David Scott, *Cap of Honour: The Story of the Gloucestershire Regiment (The 28th/61st Foot)*, George G. Harrap & Co., London, 1951.

Datta, K.K., *Biography of Kunwar Singh and Anwar Singh*, K.P. Jayaswal Research Institute, Patna, 1957.

Davidson, C.J. Lloyd, *The Royal Inniskilling Fusiliers 1688–1914*, Constable & Co., London, 1928.

Dawson, Lionel, *Squires and Sepoys* [memoirs of Lt. George Blake, 84th Foot], Hollis and Carter, London, 1960.

Duberly, Frances Isabella, *Campaigning Experiences in Central India and Rajputana during the suppression of the Mutiny*, Smith, Elder & Co., London, 1859.

Dunn-Pattison, R.P., *The History of the 91st Argyllshire Highlanders*, William Blackwood & Sons, Edinburgh, 1910.

Edwardes, H.B. and Merivale, H., *Life of Sir Henry Lawrence*, 2 vols, Smith, Elder & Co., London, 1872.

Edwardes, Michael, *Red Year: The Indian Rebellion of 1857*, Hamish Hamilton, London, 1973.

Fichett, W.H., *The Tale of The Great Mutiny* [incl journal of the siege of Lucknow by 'E.S.', the wife of an officer of irregular cavalry], Smith, Elder, & Co., London, 1908.

Forbes, Archibald, *The "Black Watch". The Record of an Historic Regiment*, Cassell and Co., London, 1896.

Forrest, George W., *Selections from the Letters, Despatches and other State Papers preserved in the Military Department of the Government of India 1857–58*, Military Department Press, Calcutta, 1893.

Forrest, George W., *The Life of Lord Roberts*, Cassell & Co., London, 1914.

Forrest, George W., *Life of Field Marshal Sir Neville Chamberlain*, William Blackwood & Sons, Edinburgh, 1909.

Fortescue, J.W., *A History of the British Army, Vol. XIII, 1852–1870*, Macmillan and Co., London, 1930.

Fortescue, J.W., *A History of the 17th Lancers (Duke of Cambridge's Own)*, Macmillan & Co., London, 1895.

Gardyne, C.G., *The Life of a Regiment. The History of the Gordon Highlanders*, David Douglas, Edinburgh, 1903.

Germon, Maria, *Journal of the Siege of Lucknow*, published privately, London, 1870

Gupta, Pratul Chandra, *Nana Sahib and the Rising at Cawnpore*, Clarendon, Oxford, 1963.

Hamilton, Henry-Blackburne, *Historical Record of the 14th (King's) Hussars 1715–1900*, Longman's, Green & Co., London, 1901.

Harris, Mrs J.A., *A Lady's Diary of the Siege of Lucknow*, John Murray, London, 1858.

Heathcote, T.A., *The British Field Marshals 1736–1997: A Biographical Dictionary*, Leo Cooper/Pen & Sword, Barnsley, 1999.

Heathcote, T.A., *The Military in British India: The Development of British Land Forces in South Asia 1600–1947*, Manchester University Press, Manchester and New York, 1995.

Hewitt, James (ed.), *Eye-witnesses to the Indian Mutiny*, Spey Publishing Ltd., London, 1972.

Hibbert, Christopher, *The Great Mutiny: India 1857*, Allen Lane, London, 1978.

Jocelyn, Julian R.J., *The History of the Royal and Indian Artillery in the mutiny of 1857*, John Murray, London, 1915.

Johnston, S.H.F., *The History of the Cameronians (Scottish Rifles) 1689–1910*, Gale & Polden, Aldershot, 1957.

Jones, James P., *A History of the South Staffordshire Regiment*, Whitehead Bros., Wolverhampton, 1923.

Jourdain, H.F.N. and Fraser, Edward, *The Connaught Rangers, 1st Battalion, formerly 88th Foot*, RUSI, London, 1924.

Kaye, J.W., *A History of the Sepoy War in India*, 4th edn., W.H. Allen & Co., London, 1877–78.

Laurie, George Benton, *History of the Royal Irish Rifles*, Gale & Polden, London, 1914.

Lawrence, John, *Lawrence of Lucknow*, Hodder & Stoughton, London, 1990.

Lebra-Chapman, Joyce, *The Rani of Jhansi: A Study in Female Heroism in India*, University of Hawaii Press, Honolulu, 1986.

Lee, Albert, *The History of the Tenth Foot (The Lincolnshire Regiment)*, Gale & Polden, Aldershot, 1911.

Levinge, Richard G.A., *Historical Records of the Forty-Third Regiment, Monmouthshire Light Infantry*, W. Clowes & Sons, London, 1868.

Low, Charles Rathbone, *Major-General Sir Frederick S. Roberts. A Memoir*, W.H. Allen & Co., London, 1883.

McCance, S., *History of the Royal Munster Fusiliers*, Aldershot, 1927.

Maclagan, Michael, *"Clemency" Canning, Charles John, 1st Earl Canning, Governor-General and Viceroy of India 1856–1862*, Macmillan & Co., London, 1962.

MacMunn, George, *The Indian Mutiny in Perspective*, G. Bell & Sons, London, 1931.

Malleson, W., *The Revolt in Central India*, Army HQ, India, Simla, 1908.

Mann, Michael, *The Regimental History of 1st The Queen's Dragoon Guards*, Michael Russell (Publishing), Norwich, 1991.

Martin, R. Montgomery, *The Indian Empire, with a full account of the mutiny of the Bengal Army, the insurrection in Western India and an exposition of the alleged causes*, 3 vols, London Printing and Publishing Co, Ltd, London, 1858–61.

Maude, Francis Cornwallis, *Memories of the Mutiny*, 2 vols, Remington & Co., London, 1894.

Mead, Henry, *The Sepoy Revolt. Its Causes and Consequences*, John Murray, London, 1857.

Moon, Penderel, *The British Conquest and Dominion of India*, Duckworth, London, 1989.

Moorsom, W.S., *Historical Record of the Fifty-Second Regiment (Oxfordshire Light Infantry) 1755–1858*, Richard Bentley, London, 1860.

Muter, Mrs D.D., *My Recollections of the Sepoy Revolt (1857–58)*, John Long Ltd, London, 1911.

Norman, H.W., *Delhi 1857. The Siege Assault and capture as given in the Diary and Correspondence of the late Colonel Keith Young*, W.R. Chambers, London, 1902. Reprinted Naval and Military Press, Uckfield, 2004.

Oates, L.B., *'I Serve'. Regimental History of the 3rd Carabiniers (Prince of Wales's Dragoon Guards)*, published privately, Norwich, 1966.

Oatts, L.B., *Proud Heritage: The Story of the Highland Light Infantry*, Thomas Nelson & Son, London, 1952.

Oatts, L.B., *The Emperor's Chambermaids: The Story of the 14th/20th King's Hussars*, Ward Lock, London, 1973.

Parry, D.H., *"The Death or Glory Boys": The Story of the 17th Lancers*, Cassell & Co., London, 1899.

Pearce, Hugh W., *History of the 31st Foot, Huntingdonshire Regiment, and 70th Foot, Surrey Regiment*, Spottiswoode, Ballantyne & Co., London, 1916.

Pearson, Hesketh, *The Hero of Delhi: A Life of John Nicholson, Saviour of India*, Collins, London, 1939.

Pollock, T.C., *Way to Glory. The Life of Havelock of Lucknow*, John Murray, London, 1957.

Purdon, H.G., *Memoirs of the services of the 64th Regiment*, W.H. Allen & Co., London [c.1882].

Rhe-Phillipe, George William de (ed.), *Soldiers of the Raj: Indian Monumental Inscriptions*, Vol. II, 1910, 1912, reprinted London Stamp Exchange, London, 1989.

Roberts, Frederick Sleigh (Lord Roberts), *Forty-One Years in India. From Subaltern to Commander-in-Chief*, 2 vols., Richard Bentley & Son, London, 1897.

Robertson, A. Cunningham, *Historical Records of the King's, Liverpool Regiment of Foot, 1685–1881*, Harrison & Sons, London, 1885.

Rotton, John E.W., *The Chaplain's Narrative of the Siege of Delhi*, Smith, Elder & Co., London, 1858.

Sandes, W.C., *The Military Engineer in India*, Institute of Royal Engineers, Chatham, 1933.

Saul, David, *The Indian Mutiny 1857*, Penguin, London, 2003.

Sen, Surendra Nath, *Eighteen Fifty-Seven*, Publications Division, Government of India, 1957.

Sheppard, E.W., *The Ninth Queen's Royal Lancers 1715–1936*, Gale & Polden, Aldershot, 1939.

Sherer, J.W., *Daily Life during the Indian Mutiny. Personal Experiences of 1857*, Swan Sonneschen & Co., London, 1898.

Smith, R. Bosworth, *Life of Lord Lawrence*, 2 vols, Smith, Elder & Co., London, 1883.

Smith, Vincent A., *The Oxford History of India*, 3rd edn, Clarendon Press, Oxford, 1958.

Spear, P., *The Twilight of the Moghuls*, C.U.P., Cambridge, 1951.

Sutherland, Douglas, *Tried and Valiant: The History of the Border Regiment (34th and 55th Foot)*, Leo Cooper, London, 1972.

Swiney, G.C., *Historical Records of the 32nd (Cornwall) Light Infantry*, Simpkin, Marshall, Hamilton, Kent & Co., London, 1893.

Sym, John (ed.), *Seaforth Highlanders*, Gale & Polden, Aldershot, 1962.

Taylor, P.T.O., *A Companion to the Sepoy Mutiny of 1857*, Oxford University Press, Delhi, 1996.

Temple, Richard, *Lord Lawrence*, Macmillan and Co., London, 1904.

Thakeray, Edward, *Reminiscences of the Indian Mutiny and Afghanistan*, Smith, Elder & Co., London, 1916.

Thompson, Edward, and Garratt, G.T., *Rise and Fulfilment of British Rule in India*, Macmillan & Co., London, 1934.

Thorn, William, *A Memoir of Major-General Sir R.R. Gillespie*, T. Egerton, London, 1816.

Threlfall, T.R., *The Story of the King's (Liverpool) Regiment*, Country Life, London, [1916].

Trinman, Richard, *An Historical Memoir of the 35th Royal Sussex Regiment of Foot*, Southampton Times, Southampton, 1873.

Trotter, Lionel J., *The Life of John Nicholson, Soldier and Administrator, based on private and hitherto unpublished documents*, John Murray, London, 1897.

Trotter, Lionel J., *'The Bayard of India', A Life of Sir James Outram*, William Blackwood & Sons, Edinburgh and London, 1903.

Verney, G.L., *The Devil's Wind: The Story of the Naval Brigade at Lucknow, from the letters of Edward Hope Verney*, Hutchinson, London, 1956.

Vibart, Edward, *The Sepoy Mutiny as seen by a subaltern from Delhi to Lucknow*, Smith, Elder & Co., London, 1898.

Wakeham, Eric, *The Bravest Soldier. Sir Rollo Gillespie, 1766–1814: A Historical Military Sketch*, William Blackwood & Sons, Ltd, Edinburgh and London, 1937.

Walker, H.M., *A History of the Northumberland Fusiliers 1674–1919*, John Murray, London, 1919.

Ward, Andrew, *Our Bones Are Scattered: The Cawnpore Massacres and the Indian Mutiny of 1857*, Henry Holt and Company, New York, 1996.

Weintraub, Stanley, *Disraeli: A Biography*, Hamish Hamilton, London, 1993.

Wilberforce, Reginald G., *An Unrecorded Chapter of the Indian Mutiny*, John Murray, London, 1894.

Wilson, W.J., *History of the Madras Army*, Government Press, Madras, 1883.

Whitehorne, A.C., *The History of the Welsh Regiment, Part I, 1719–1914*, Western Mail & Echo, Cardiff, 1932.

Wood, Evelyn, *From Midshipman to Field Marshal*, Methuen & Co., London, 1906.

Wylly, H.C., *The York and Lancaster Regiment*, pub. privately (Sheffield?), 1930.

INDEX